Charles Abel Heurtley

Justification

Eight Sermons Before the University of Oxford, in the Year MDCCCXLV

Charles Abel Heurtley

Justification

Eight Sermons Before the University of Oxford, in the Year MDCCCXLV

ISBN/EAN: 9783337115982

Printed in Europe, USA, Canada, Australia, Japan

Cover: Foto ©ninafisch / pixelio.de

More available books at **www.hansebooks.com**

EIGHT SERMONS

PREACHED BEFORE

THE UNIVERSITY OF OXFORD,

IN THE YEAR MDCCCXLV,

AT

THE LECTURE

FOUNDED BY

THE LATE CANON BAMPTON.

BY

CHARLES A. HEURTLEY, B.D.

RECTOR OF FENNY COMPTON, WARWICKSHIRE; AND LATE FELLOW OF CORPUS CHRISTI COLLEGE.

"I acknowledge one baptism for the remission of sins." *Nicene Creed.*

OXFORD,
JOHN HENRY PARKER;
F. AND J. RIVINGTON, LONDON.
1846.

TO THE

HEADS OF COLLEGES

IN THE

UNIVERSITY OF OXFORD,

THE

FOLLOWING SERMONS,

PREACHED BY THEIR APPOINTMENT,

ARE RESPECTFULLY INSCRIBED

BY

THE AUTHOR.

EXTRACT

FROM

THE LAST WILL AND TESTAMENT

OF THE LATE

REV. JOHN BAMPTON,

CANON OF SALISBURY.

———

—— " I give and bequeath my Lands and Estates to
" the Chancellor, Masters, and Scholars of the University
" of Oxford for ever, to have and to hold all and singular
" the said Lands or Estates upon trust, and to the intents
" and purposes hereinafter mentioned: that is to say,
" I will and appoint, that the Vice-Chancellor of the
" University of Oxford, for the time being, shall take and
" receive all the rents, issues, and profits thereof, and
" (after all taxes, reparations, and necessary deductions
" made) that he pay all the remainder to the endowment
" of eight Divinity Lecture Sermons, to be established for
" ever in the said University, and to be performed in the
" manner following:

" I direct and appoint, that, upon the first Tuesday
" in Easter Term, a Lecturer be yearly chosen by the
" Heads of Colleges only, and by no others, in the room
" adjoining to the Printing-House, between the hours of
" ten in the morning and two in the afternoon, to preach
" eight Divinity Lecture Sermons, the year following, at

"St. Mary's in Oxford, between the commencement of
"the last month in Lent Term, and the end of the third
"week in Act Term.

"Also I direct and appoint, that the eight Divinity
"Lecture Sermons shall be preached upon either of
"the following Subjects:—to confirm and establish the
"Christian Faith, and to confute all heretics and schis-
"matics—upon the divine authority of the holy Scrip-
"tures—upon the authority of the writings of the primitive
"Fathers, as to the faith and practice of the primitive
"Church—upon the Divinity of our Lord and Saviour
"Jesus Christ—upon the Divinity of the Holy Ghost—
"upon the Articles of the Christian Faith, as compre-
"hended in the Apostles' and Nicene Creeds.

"Also I direct, that thirty copies of the eight Divinity
"Lecture Sermons shall be always printed, within two
"months after they are preached, and one copy shall be
"given to the Chancellor of the University, and one copy
"to the Head of every College, and one copy to the
"Mayor of the City of Oxford, and one copy to be put
"into the Bodleian Library; and the expense of printing
"them shall be paid out of the revenue of the Land or
"Estates given for establishing the Divinity Lecture
"Sermons; and the Preacher shall not be paid, nor be
"entitled to the revenue, before they are printed.

"Also I direct and appoint, that no person shall be
"qualified to preach the Divinity Lecture Sermons, unless
"he hath taken the degree of Master of Arts at least, in
"one of the two Universities of Oxford or Cambridge;
"and that the same person shall never preach the Divinity
"Lecture Sermons twice."

PREFACE.

The present Volume may be regarded as a sequel to a series of Sermons, preached before the University of Oxford, and published a few years ago, on the Union between Christ and His people; being an application of the principles laid down in those Sermons, to the subject of Justification, which is a branch of the subject of which they treat.

Whatever blessings we either have or hope for, pertaining to life and godliness, are given us *in Christ*, and become ours, *through our union with Him*. Justification is one of these: and to be viewed rightly, it must be viewed in connection both with the root from which it springs, and also with the kindred blessings, which spring with it from the same root.

The present work then is an attempt to treat the subject of Justification professedly as a branch of a wider and more comprehensive subject, the Christian's union with his Lord. The connection of the one subject with the other is indeed the basis of *whatsoever* has been written to good purpose respecting Justification: only that which, in many instances, has been tacitly implied, is here professedly the central principle of the whole work. Hooker has pursued this course in treating of the Sacraments; and the Author believed that it was the surest method to be pursued in treating of Justification. If he has failed of his object, the fault is to be ascribed not to the principle which he has adopted, but to his unskilfulness in the application of it.

The design of the Founder of the Lecture, at which these Sermons were preached, was to provide for the counteraction of such errors, as, from time to time, might be most imminent. It is impossible to shut our eyes to the fact, that the danger of late chiefly to be apprehended, at least in certain quarters, lies on the side of Rome. This circumstance, as it contributed to determine the Author in the choice of his subject, so it influenced him especially in the direction in which he has suffered himself to be led by his subject. But yet his main aim has been to set forth those great, broad, and immutable principles of truth, which may serve to counteract error, from whatsoever quarter it may arise.

Such as his work is, the Author commends it to Him, whose glory and whose approbation he desires to seek, with the earnest prayer, that He will mercifully forgive whatever has been amiss in the execution of it, and that He will graciously bless it to the furtherance of the end which the Founder of the Lecture had in view—the setting forth of truth, the counteraction of error, and the advancement of God's glory.

SERMON I.
Page 1.
MAN FALLEN IN ADAM.

Rom. v. 19.

By one man's disobedience many were made sinners.

SERMON II.
Page 47.
MAN RESTORED IN CHRIST.

Rom. v. 15.

If through the offence of one many be dead, much more the grace of God, and the gift by grace, which is by one Man, Jesus Christ, hath abounded unto many.

SERMON III.
Page 81.
IMPUTED RIGHTEOUSNESS.

2 Cor. v. 21.

He hath made Him to be sin for us who knew no sin, that we might be made the righteousness of God in Him.

CONTENTS.

SERMON IV.
Page 123.
INHERENT RIGHTEOUSNESS.

2 Cor. v. 17.

If any man be in Christ, he is a new creature

SERMON V.
Page 161.
FAITH.

Hebrews xi. 1.

Faith is the substance of things hoped for, the evidence of things not seen.

SERMON VI.
Page 195.
THE CONNECTION BETWEEN FAITH AND JUSTIFICATION.

Rom. iv. 16.

It is of faith, that it might be by grace.

SERMON VII.
Page 243.
THE CONNECTION BETWEEN BAPTISM AND JUSTIFICATION.

Acts xxii. 16.

Arise, and be baptized, and wash away thy sins, calling on the name of the Lord.

SERMON VIII.
Page 291.
JUSTIFICATION IN CONTINUANCE.
Rev. iii. 11.

Behold, I come quickly; hold that fast which thou hast, that no man take thy crown.

SERMON I.

MAN FALLEN IN ADAM.

"Διὰ γὰρ τοῦτο καὶ τύπος ἐστὶν Ἰησοῦ Χριστοῦ ὁ Ἀδάμ. Πῶς τύπος, φησίν; Ὅτι, ὥσπερ ἐκεῖνος τοῖς ἐξ αὐτοῦ, καίτοιγε μὴ φαγοῦσιν ἀπὸ τοῦ ξύλου, γέγονεν αἴτιος θανάτου τοῦ διὰ τὴν βρῶσιν εἰσαχθέντος· οὕτω καὶ ὁ Χριστὸς τοῖς ἐξ αὐτοῦ, καίτοι γε οὐ δικαιοπραγήσασι, γέγονε πρόξενος δικαιοσύνης, ἣν διὰ τοῦ σταυροῦ πᾶσιν ἡμῖν ἐχαρίσατο. Διὰ τοῦτο ἄνω καὶ κάτω τοῦ ἑνὸς ἔχεται, καὶ συνεχῶς τοῦτο εἰς μέσον φέρει, λέγων· Ὥσπερ δι' ἑνὸς ἀνθρώπου ἡ ἁμαρτία εἰς τὸν κόσμον εἰσῆλθε· καὶ, Ἐν τῷ τοῦ ἑνὸς παραπτώματι οἱ πολλοὶ ἀπέθανον· καὶ, Οὐχ ὡς δι' ἑνὸς ἁμαρτήσαντος, τὸ δώρημα· καὶ, Τὸ κρίμα ἐξ ἑνὸς εἰς κατάκριμα· καὶ πάλιν, Εἰ γὰρ τῷ τοῦ ἑνὸς παραπτώματι ὁ θάνατος ἐβασίλευσε διὰ τοῦ ἑνός· καὶ, Ἄρα οὖν ὡς δι' ἑνὸς παραπτώματος· καὶ πάλιν, Ὥσπερ διὰ τῆς παρακοῆς τοῦ ἑνὸς ἀνθρώπου ἁμαρτωλοὶ κατεστάθησαν οἱ πολλοί. καὶ οὐκ ἀφίσταται τοῦ ἑνός, ἵν' ὅταν λέγῃ σοι ὁ Ἰουδαῖος, πῶς, ἑνὸς κατορθώσαντος τοῦ Χριστοῦ ἡ οἰκουμένη ἐσώθη; δυνηθῇς αὐτῷ λέγειν, πῶς, ἑνὸς παρακούσαντος τοῦ Ἀδὰμ, ἡ οἰκουμένη κατεκρίθη;" Chrysost. in Rom. v. 14. Hom. x. §. 1.

Romans v. 19.

By one man's disobedience many were made sinners.

How shall sinful man be justified before God? is the grand practical question, which serious and earnest persons, in proportion as they have had light sufficient to discern the misery of their natural condition, have anxiously asked in every generation since the fall—a question, to which it was reserved for the Gospel, as its peculiar glory, to give the true answer. And of that answer it so nearly concerns us to have a right understanding that we cannot misapprehend it, but we so far incur the risk of missing the way to heaven.

And yet it has too often been the lot of this, as of kindred subjects, to be handled as though it were a cold theory, or to be made matter of rude and unhallowed strife. And men have embraced a shadow, when they thought they held the substance, or they have lost their tempers and the truth together. Whereas, in reality, it is a subject to be studied almost upon our knees, and with a constant aim to bring it to bear upon our daily practice.

In this spirit I desire to bring before you and you to receive such considerations connected with the subject I have referred to, the subject of *Justification*, as God shall enable me. Certainly if ever there were a time when we had more than ordinary need to pursue our enquiries into divine truth with humility and devout reverence, with perpetual application to the throne of grace for spiritual guidance, and unceasing aspirations and endeavours after a holy life, it is the present. The way of truth indeed is the same now that it ever was—not hard to be found by those who love the truth, and seek it with single hearts, and earnest minds, and in the fear of God. But there is danger, if not of our being jostled out of it in the throng, at least of our losing the simplicity of aim and calmness of spirit, which are necessary to discern and keep it, and thereby mistaking other ways for it, which seem to be the ways of truth, but are not.

I said that the question, How shall sinful man be justified before God? has been asked with an anxiety proportioned to the sense which men have had of the misery of their natural condition. For the disease must be felt in order to our enquiring in good earnest for the remedy. We may study the subject as an interesting speculation, or engage in it as a matter of discussion, but we shall never enter into it with real, heartfelt earnestness, unless we are deeply sensible of the misery of being without justification.

There is therefore a previous question, practically at any rate, of great importance to the right understanding of the subject I have referred to:—What is the condition of man in his natural state? What is the condition of man, as he is, and has been since the fall and prior to the grace of Christ? In other words, What is the condition of man as he is apart from Christ?

Nothing can be more plain on the very surface of Scripture than that that condition is a most miserable one. Christ is the only ark in which we can be borne in safety above the waters, which overwhelm the world. And they who are without Christ, who have no part nor lot in His salvation, by whatever name they may be called, are lost hopelessly. "He that hath the Son, hath life; and he that hath not the Son of God, hath not life [a]."

One thing might reasonably have been concluded even if we had had no light from Revelation, that the condition of man was not originally what it is now. It is contrary to all our notions of the wisdom and goodness and power of God to believe that any of His works, much less the greatest which this lower world affords, should have been sent forth from His hands *imperfect*. It is contrary to all our notions to believe that God should have created, and not have endued the creature which He had made with ability to fulfil the laws of the nature with which He had framed him [b]. However it came to pass that the laws of that nature were transgressed, the transgression of them must have been contrary to the

---

[a] 1 John v. 12.

[b] "The ancients speak of deviating from nature as vice; and of following nature so much as a distinction, that according to them the perfection of virtue consists therein." Bp. Butler, Serm. ii. on Human Nature, p. 28.

purpose which God had in view in creation. He must have designed the keeping of those laws, and have endued the creature with power to keep them, though, as the event has proved, He must have left it to him to use that power or not as he would. God could not have made man with a heart such as naturally we find all men's hearts now, averse from Himself, and prone to sin, with lusts and passions ever ready to rise in rebellion against that higher power which He has set over them to control and regulate them. Reason therefore, if we had no other guide to follow, would lead us to the conclusion, that man's original condition was very different from what it is now.

We have, however, a surer guide than reason. We are told in Scripture that " God made man upright[c]," framed him, i. e. in accordance with the rule which He had given him for his governance, and in every way capable of observing that rule. He endued him with reason and conscience; caused these to revolve round Himself, the chief good, as their centre, and made them in turn a centre to the lower faculties.

We are told further, that our first father was made " in the *image of God*," " *after His likeness*." The other animals were created severally " after their kinds,"—with the properties and characteristics belonging to their respective classes, and man had a body framed of the dust of the earth, and an animal life in common with them. But man has a nobler

[c] Eccles. vii. 29.

part, spoken of in the New Testament as his *spirit*[d], and it was in having this, which the lower animals have not, and in having it made the habitation of the Holy Spirit, and by the Holy Spirit so dwelling in it conformed to God, as the Apostle's words imply, in knowledge, righteousness, and holiness, that his likeness to his Maker consisted[e]. He

---

[d] This threefold division is referred to by the Apostle, 1 Thess. v. 23. ὁλόκληρον ὑμῶν τὸ πνεῦμα, καὶ ἡ ψυχὴ, καὶ τὸ σῶμα. "Tria sunt quibus homo constat, spiritus, anima, et corpus: quæ rursus duo dicuntur, quia sæpe anima simul cum spiritu nominatur; pars enim quædam ejusdem rationalis, qua carent bestiæ, spiritus dicitur: principale nostrum spiritus est; deinde vita qua conjungimur corpori, anima dicitur; postremo ipsum corpus, quoniam visibile est, ultimum nostrum est. . . .Hic spiritus etiam vocatur mens, de quo dicit Apostolus, 'mente servio legi Dei:' qui item alio loco dicit, 'Testis est mihi Deus, cui servio in spiritu meo.' Anima vero cum carnalia bona adhuc appetit, caro nominatur. Pars enim ejus quædam resistit spiritui non natura sed consuetudine peccatorum. Unde dicitur 'mente servio legi Dei, carne autem legi peccati.' Quæ consuetudo in naturam versa est secundum generationem mortalem peccato primi hominis. Ideoque scriptum est, 'Et nos aliquando fuimus naturaliter filii iræ' id est vindictæ per quam factum est ut serviamus legi peccati." August. Liber de Fide et Symbolo. § x.

[e] Ephes. iv. 24. Coloss. iii. 10. Γέγονε μὲν συνδίαιτον ἀρχῆθεν τὸ Πνεῦμα τῇ ψυχῇ, τὸ δὲ Πνεῦμα ταύτην ἕπεσθαι μὴ βουλομένην αὐτῷ καταλέλοιπεν. Tatian. c. 13. p. 255. quoted by Bp. Bull, On the State of Man before the Fall, Works, vol. ii. p. 86. Restituitur homo Deo ad similitudinem ejus, qui retro ad imaginem Dei conditus fuerat, &c. *Recipit enim illum Dei Spiritum, quem tunc de afflatu ejus acceperat, sed post amiserat per delictum.* Tertull. de Baptismo, c. 5. ibid. p. 89. St. Basil compares the divine insufflation upon Adam, spoken of Gen. ii. 7. with our Lord's upon his Apostles, John xx. 22. and tells us that it was the same Son of God by whom God

knew God, whom to know is life eternal. He *loved* God, and love is the spring and safeguard of obedience. He had the *idem velle, idem nolle*—the entire conformity of his will to God's will, which was fitted to be the basis of a lasting union between himself and God, and of his own true happiness. And God beheld him when He surveyed the works which He had made, and pronounced him, in common with the rest, *very good*. How could he be otherwise than good when fresh from his Creator's hands? God could not have been the Author of evil under any form or in any measure.

And yet evil has found its way into the world. Man is no longer such as our first parents were at their creation. Adam fell, and in him his whole race.

With regard to the change produced by the fall upon Adam *personally*, he passed from a state of life to a state of death, of which transition his exclusion from the tree of life was a significant token; more indeed, it may be, than a token, if at least that tree, as it has been conjectured, was not only a pledge of immortality, but also, whether physically or sacramentally, a means of ensuring it^e. But death, in its

---

gave the insufflation; τότε μὲν, i. e. at the creation, μετὰ ψυχῆς, νῦν δὲ (i. e. at the time referred to by St. John,) εἰς ψυχήν. Many of the Fathers understand what is said in Gen. ii. 7, as Tertullian and St. Basil in the above passages, to refer not merely to the gift of *natural* life, but also to *the grace of the Holy Spirit* infused together with it, as the principle of *spiritual* life. See Bp. Bull as above quoted, p. 90, &c.

^f " Habebat enim, quantum existimo, et de lignorum fructibus

literal sense, was but a faint emblem of other and infinitely worse results. When it is said that our

refectionem contra defectionem, et de ligno vitæ stabilitatem contra vetustatem." August. de l'eccat. mer. et rem. l. 1. §. iii. see also De Genes. ad lit. l. 9. §. iii. and vi. St. Austin's belief, and, it may be added, that of the Fathers generally, was that Adam was created mortal, insomuch that his body, if left to the operation of natural causes, would, in the course of years, have decayed and died. And there was good reason for this belief. The whole analogy of the world around us points to the same conclusion. Perishableness and decay are written in plain characters on every thing earthly. It seems to be a law of the existence of all material beings which have life, in any sort, that when they have fulfilled severally the purposes for which they were created they should depart hence, and make room for another generation. And though it is not safe to reason from what man is now, to what he was before the fall, yet certainly the teaching of Scripture, as far as Scripture touches upon the subject, points in the same direction. When the way to the tree of life was barred against our first father, the reason assigned, " lest he put forth his hand and take also of the tree of life, and eat and live for ever," would seem to imply, that if left to the tendency of his natural constitution, he would not have been exempt from death. And in like manner when sentence of death was passed upon him for his sin, it was coupled with a declaration which seemed to signify, that God was now leaving him to the operation of those laws, to which his material frame was by its constitution subject. " *Dust thou art, and unto dust thou shalt return.*" And St. Paul accordingly distinguishes between the *natural* or *physical* body which Adam received at his creation, and the *spiritual* body which Christ has in heaven. And he adds presently, " Now this I say, brethren, *that flesh and blood cannot inherit the kingdom of God,* neither doth corruption inherit incorruption," and if *flesh and blood* cannot, then neither could Adam's body. Habits of vice had not enfeebled that body, as our own vices and those of our forefathers have

first parents after the commission of their sin, knew that they were naked, that they were afraid of God, enfeebled ours: but it was made of the same material as ours, it was flesh and blood, it was of the earth, earthy, and therefore it contained within itself the seeds of death: it could not, such as it was, inherit the kingdom of God.

While, however, it would seem that man was created mortal at the first, it is a certain truth that when death did enter the world, it was *sin* that brought it. But for sin man would not have died.

The Pelagians denied this truth: and they supported their denial of it by interpreting those passages of Scripture which speak of death as the penalty of sin, exclusively of *spiritual* death. (See August. de Peccat. Mer. et Rem. l. i. §. ii. &c.) But those passages cannot be so restricted. It was of death, in its *most literal* sense, and as the punishment of sin, that God spoke when He pronounced sentence upon Adam, " In the sweat of thy face shalt thou eat bread, till thou return unto the ground; for out of it wast thou taken; for dust thou art, and unto dust thou shalt return." Gen. iii. 19. And it was of the same death, and that likewise as the punishment of sin, that the Apostle wrote, " By one man sin entered into the world, and death by sin, and so death passed upon all men, for that all have sinned." Rom. v. 12. And this is his meaning, when he says elsewhere, (1 Cor. xv. 56.) that " the sting of death is sin;" i. e. it is sin which arms death with its sting, and gives it the power to kill. " Aculeus quippe mortis peccatum, id est aculeus cujus punctione fit mors, non aculeus quo pungit mors." August. contra duas Epist. Pelag. lib. iv. §. iv. And thus, mortal though the human body would seem to have been even in its original structure, still, if man had not sinned, death would not have had dominion over it; but that, as St. Augustine conjectures, would probably, without the intervention of death, have eventually taken place in all, which we know will take place in those of God's saints who shall be found alive at the last day: this corruptible would have put on incorruption, and this mortal would have put on immortality, and thus death would have

and hid themselves, as they vainly thought, from His sight; what does this but imply that the light of God's countenance was withdrawn from them, and that they had passed from a state of favour and acceptance, to a state of condemnation and wrath? They saw themselves stripped of the robe of innocence in which their Creator had arrayed them, and they were conscious that some fearful and merited judgment awaited them. By the same tokens it is plain that a change had passed upon their *nature*, that the image of God, in which they had been created, was effaced, and that the Spirit of God, by whose operation that image was at first formed within them, and by whose indwelling its integrity was preserved, was withdrawn. They had moreover by hearkening to the voice of the Tempter in opposition to the command of God, transferred their allegiance from their rightful Lord to Satan, who thenceforward became the prince, the god of this world.

But Adam stood as the representative of his whole

---

been swallowed up in victory, and mortality would have been swallowed up of life. 1 Cor. xv. 53, 54. 2 Cor. v. 4. Quamvis enim secundum corpus terra esset, et corpus in quo creatus est animale gestaret; tamen si non peccasset, in corpus fuerat spirituale mutandus, et in illam incorruptionem quæ fidelibus et sanctis promittitur, sine mortis periculo transiturus... Proinde si non peccasset Adam, non erat exspoliandus corpore, sed supervestiendus immortalitate et incorruptione, ut absorberetur mortale a vita, id est, ab animali in spirituale transiret." August. de Peccat. Mer. et Rem. l. i. §. ii. On this whole subject see Bp. Bull on the Condition of Man before the Fall.

race. We see, in every respect in which the comparison can be made, that our condition is such as his was *after* the fall. The world in which we dwell is no longer like the Paradise in which he was at first placed. Pain, sickness, sorrow, death, which are now the common lot of all, were unknown in Eden; and sin, which never found entrance into that happy land till the day our first parents were driven out, now abounds on all sides. These facts alone point very significantly to the conclusion that Adam stood as our representative. We have followed his fortunes most entirely; and the sentence pronounced upon him and Eve in the day they were driven forth from Paradise, is fulfilled in every individual of their descendants. But Scripture does not leave us to gather this truth from remote inferences. Adam is there spoken of expressly as our *Head*—the Head of the old creation, as Christ is of the new. As such he is called the *first* man in opposition to Christ, who is called the *second* man[g]. And we are told that *in Adam* we all die, as *in Christ* we shall all be made alive[h]; that as is the earthy, such are they also that are earthy, in like manner as, as is the heavenly, such are they also that are heavenly[i]; and that we now bear the image of the earthy, as hereafter we shall bear the image of the heavenly[k]. And elsewhere the like contrast is instituted between Adam and Christ, who are declared to be type and antitype

[g] 1 Cor. xv. 47. [h] 1 Cor. xv. 22. [i] 1 Cor. xv. 48.
[k] 1 Cor. xv. 49.

in this very respect, that each is to be regarded as the federal head of those descended from him[1]. From all which it is plain that Adam stood as the representative of our race; that *his* fortunes were, and were designed to be, *our* fortunes.

Nor is it to be thought, that the arrangement by which the fortunes of the whole human race were thus bound up with those of their first father, is inconsistent with the Divine justice and goodness. That indeed which is undeniably of God's appointment cannot but be just and good. And it is a sufficient answer to abstract objections which might be raised against the assertion that it is of God's appointment, to shew, as might easily be done, in the present instance, that there are analogous cases in God's ordinary way of dealing with his creatures. The world indeed is full of such analogies, and nothing is more common than for a father's conduct in the more important steps of life to affect, either for good or evil, the fortunes and even the characters of his children and his children's children to remote generations. It is true no instance can be produced except that of the second Adam where the consequences are at all comparable either in extent or importance, but yet the case referred to of a father's conduct affecting his children and his children's children, seems plainly to belong to the same great law, and to point therefore to the same lawgiver:

[1] Rom. v. 12—19.

and no objection can be urged against the one which does not lie equally against the other.

Scripture draws a fearful picture of the condition which we have inherited from our first father. Observe e. g. in the following passage, how many dark circumstances are crowded together within the compass of a few verses. " You hath he quickened who were dead in trespasses and sins, wherein in time past ye walked according to the course of this world, according to the prince of the power of the air, the spirit that now worketh in the children of disobedience;" and, lest any should think that his description belonged to the Gentiles only, the Apostle adds, " Among whom also *we all* had our conversation in times past, in the lusts of the flesh, fulfilling the desires of the flesh and of the mind, and were by nature the children of wrath, even as others[m]."

Here is *death—spiritual death—*" Ye were *dead* in *trespasses* and sins;"—*subjection under the power of Satan—*" Ye walked according to the course of this world, according to the prince of the power of the air, the spirit that now worketh in the children of disobedience;"—the *uncontrolled supremacy of the carnal part of our nature—*" We had our conversation in the lusts of the flesh, fulfilling the desires of the flesh and of the mind;" *exposure to condemnation,* and that *from our very birth—*" We were *by nature* the children of wrath."

[m] Ephes. ii. 1—3.

To the like purpose is the Baptist's declaration, " He that believeth not the Son shall not see life; but the wrath of God *abideth* on him ⁿ." It *abideth* on him *unremoved*. He was " by *nature a child of wrath*," and he *continues* such. To the same effect is the whole tenour of our Lord's discourse with Nicodemus. " Verily, verily, I say unto thee, Except a man be *born again*, he cannot see the kingdom of God." " That which is born of the flesh is flesh, and that which is born of the Spirit is Spirit°." No words can express more unequivocally our utterly lost and ruined state by nature. As we come into the world, we are not, and cannot be, the subjects of God's kingdom. We need a *second birth*, a *new creation*. Again, " He that believeth on the Son is not condemned, but he that believeth not *is condemned already* ᵖ." Not, he shall be—but, he is—the sentence has been already pronounced. Nothing can be stronger than these passages: and it is observable, if any should be disposed to question ᑫ, whether St. Paul's strong expressions, " dead in trespasses and sins" and the like, in the passage just now quoted, could be meant to apply to our race generally, Jews as well as Gentiles, that our Lord was in this instance addressing himself to a Jew, and one too, of whom there is every reason to think that what St. Paul says of himself might be said with equal truth,

ⁿ John iii. 36. ° John iii. 3, 6. ᵖ ἤδη κέκριται, John iii. 18.
ᑫ See Whitby on Ephes. ii. 3.

"touching the righteousness which is in the law" he was "blameless[r]."

In St. John v. we find our Lord again using similar language; "Verily, verily, I say unto you, He that heareth my word and believeth on Him that sent me, hath everlasting life, and shall not come into condemnation, but is *passed from death unto life*[s]." If he is *passed* from death unto life, then was he previously in a *state of death*. And to this agree St. Paul's reasoning, "If one died for all, then *were all dead*[t]," and St. John's declaration, "He that hath the Son hath life, and he that hath not the Son of God hath not life[u];" not "he *shall not* have," but *he hath not, even now*; he is yet in a state of death.

These passages afford a *general* view of the condition in which all are prior to the grace of Christ, and this condition is to be ascribed to the sin of our first father, *in whom* all die, both physically and spiritually, both temporally and eternally, even as *in Christ*; all who believe in Christ shall be made alive.

But a *general* view will not suffice in a matter of so great importance; to speak therefore more definitely, our condition, such as it is on our entrance into the world may be described as twofold:

[r] Phil. iii. 6.   [s] John v. 24.
[t] 2 Cor. v. 14. Ὡς πάντων ἀπολομένων, φησίν· Οὐ γὰρ ἂν, εἰ μὴ πάντες ἀπέθανον, ὑπὲρ πάντων ἀπέθανε. Chrysost. in loc.
[u] 1 John v. 12.

1. We are born *under condemnation*. 2. Our *nature is corrupted and debased*.

1. We are born under condemnation. For when it is said that the wrath of God *abideth* on him that doth not believe on the Son, and that he that believeth not is *condemned already*[x], it is implied that the state in which every man enters the world, is a *state of condemnation*, so that we need have no hesitation in receiving the Apostle's expression, "*by nature* the children of wrath," in its literal and obvious meaning. We are not only "truly" the children of wrath, as some would render the word φύσει[y], nor "altogether" such as the Pelagians did of old[z]; but we are such *naturally*—we are *children of wrath born*. The condemnation which Adam drew down upon himself cleaves to us and to all his posterity from the moment we come into the world[a].

---

[x] John iii. 36. 18.   [y] See Whitby in loc.

[z] "Prorsus." On which St. Augustine remarks, "Quod autem dicis ' Ubi ait Apostolus, *natura* filii iræ, posse intelligi, *prorsus* filii iræ,' nonne hinc admoneri debuisti, antiquam contra vos defendi catholicam fidem : quia non fere invenitur Latinus codex, si non a vobis nunc incipiat emendari, vel potius in mendum mutari, ubi non *natura* sit scriptum. Quod utique cavere debuit interpretum antiquitas, nisi etiam fidei hæc esset antiquitas, cui vestra cœpit resistere novitas." Contra Julianum Pelag. l. vi. §. x.

[a] John iii. 36. "' Ira Dei manet super eum:' non ait *veniet* sed *manet;* cum hac quippe omnis homo nascitur. Propter quod dicit Apostolus, ' Fuimus enim et nos natura filii iræ sicut et cæteri.' " August. Enchirid. §. xxxiii.

There is one passage bearing on this subject, which, as it has always been regarded as the principal seat of the doctrine, will require a fuller consideration. "By one man," says St. Paul, in his Epistle to the Romans[b], "sin entered into the world, and death by sin, and so *death passed upon all men, for that all have sinned:* for until the law sin was in the world, but sin is not imputed when there is no law; nevertheless death reigned from Adam to Moses, even over them that had not sinned after the similitude of Adam's transgression, who is the figure of him that was to come." And presently afterwards, "And not as it was by one that sinned, so is the gift; for the judgment was by one to condemnation, but the free-gift is of many offences unto justification." And once more; "Therefore as *by the offence of one judgment came upon all men to condemnation;* even so by the righteousness of one the free-gift came upon all men unto justification of life. For as *by one man's disobedience many were made sinners,* so by the obedience of one shall many be made righteous."

Now whatever other truths may be collected from this passage, this is plainly contained in it, that the sin of Adam in eating of the forbidden tree *has made all men sinners,* and *therefore brought all men under condemnation.*

The Pelagians attempted to evade the force of the Apostle's words, by explaining them to mean that

[b] Rom. v. 12. &c.

Adam brought sin into the world in that he first transgressed the law of God, and that men are sinners through him in that they have followed his evil example [c].

But St. Paul plainly teaches that all have sinned *in Adam;* for this is the force of the words ἐφ' ᾧ πάντες ἥμαρτον, whether we translate them "*in whom* all have sinned," which seems to have been anciently [d] the ordinary rendering, or, "*for that* all

[c] August. de Peccat. Mer. et Rem. l. i. §. ix. "Hoc autem Apostolicum testimonium in quo ait, 'Per unum hominem peccatum intravit in mundum, et per peccatum mors,' conari eos quidem in aliam novam detorquere opinionem, tuis literis intimasti; sed quidnam illud sit, quod in his verbis opinentur tacuisti. Quantum autem ex aliis comperi, hoc ibi sentiunt, quod et mors ista, quæ illic commemorata est, non sit corporis, quam nolunt Adam peccando meruisse, sed animæ, quæ in ipso peccato fit: et ipsum peccatum non propagatione in alios homines ex primo homine, sed imitatione transisse. Hinc enim etiam in parvulis nolunt credere per Baptismum solvi originale peccatum, quod in nascentibus nullum esse omnino contendunt."

[d] The old Latin version was "in quo," as it is repeatedly quoted by St. Augustine. With St. Augustine the point of criticism was not so much whether "in quo" is the right translation, as what is the antecedent to which "quo" refers. In the Treatise Contra duas Epist. Pelag. l. iv. c. iv. after assigning reasons why *quo* cannot be supposed to refer either to *death* or to *sin,* he proceeds, " Restat ut in illo primo homine peccâsse omnes intelligantur, quia *in illo fuerunt omnes quando ille peccavit*, unde peccatum nascendo trahitur, quod nisi renascendo non solvitur. Nam et sic sanctus Hilarius intellexit quod scriptum est " in quo omnes peccaverunt:" ait enim, " In quo, id est in Adam, omnes peccaverunt." Deinde addidit : " Manifestum in Adam

have sinned," according to our received version. For even in the latter case, the words which follow compel us to understand them thus. "For," the Apostle continues, explaining the assertion he had just made that "all have sinned," "until the law sin was in the world, but sin is not imputed when there is no law;" and if so, those who died before the law was given, died for some other cause than the breach of the law. "Nevertheless death reigned from Adam to Moses even over them that had not sinned after the similitude of Adam's transgression," and who had not therefore made themselves obnoxious in their own persons to the sentence, "In the day thou eatest thereof thou shalt surely die." It is true that many of these were guilty of actual sins against the law of nature written on their consciences, but the Apostle does not in the present instance appear to take account of such sins. "Sin was in the world," he says, but it was "not imputed." Not that it was not sin, and was not most hateful in God's sight,—yea, and did not, as in the instances of the antediluvian world, and the cities of Sodom and Gomorrha, draw down most severe judgments— but yet there was another and a higher cause of condemnation, and one which took in all, of whatsoever age or condition. *All sinned in Adam.* They

omnes peccasse, quasi in massa. Ipse enim per peccatum corruptus omnes quos genuit nati sunt sub peccato." St Augustine comments at considerable length upon the whole passage De Pecc. Mer. et Rem. lib. i. §. ix. &c.

were sinners not by imitation but *by birth;* they belonged to an *attainted family.* Their first father had violated the covenant, wherein he stood as the representative of his whole race, and they had violated it in him.

There were numbers between the time of Adam and that of Moses, as there have been numbers since, who could in no sense be said to have sinned in their own persons—those, namely, *who died in infancy,* who yet were subjected to death, the penalty of sin. The Apostle can scarcely be said to refer to these *exclusively* when he speaks of such as had not sinned *after the similitude of Adam's transgression;* but his words *include* them, and his reasoning applies to them in full force. And if death be the penalty of sin, as according to the Apostle's teaching it most surely is, then for whose sin but that of Adam— theirs as sprung from the loins of Adam—did these infants die? And why, as the defenders of the truth repeatedly urged in the Pelagian controversy, why are infants baptized, according to the universal practice of the Church from the earliest times, *for the remission of sins,* when they have never sinned in their own persons, but because they are bound by that ancient curse entailed upon them by their first father? They need to be born again the children of the second Adam, that they may be freed from the misery which they inherit as the children of the first Adam. They are the more readily to be admitted to the holy ordinance, as St. Cyprian says, explicitly recognising this doctrine, because the sins to be forgiven them are not their own, but another's[c].

And this is yet further evident as the Apostle's argument proceeds. For he says that Adam was a figure or type of Christ who was to come; and then goes on to institute a contrast between Adam and Christ, making the common ground on which the contrast is raised, the circumstance that each was the federal head of those whom he represented; and the points of contrast, that Adam derived death to all his descendants, Christ life to all His; Adam condemnation, Christ justification; Adam condemnation for one offence, the eating the forbidden fruit; Christ justification, not only from that one, but from what-

[c] " Si etiam gravissimis delictoribus, et in Deum multum ante peccantibus, cum postea crediderint, remissa peccatorum datur, et baptismo atque gratia nemo prohibetur; quanto magis prohiberi non debet infans, qui recens natus nihil peccavit, nisi quod secundum Adam carnaliter natus, contagium mortis antiquæ prima nativitate contraxit? qui ad remissam peccatorum accipiendam hoc ipso facilius accedit, quod illi remittuntur non propria sed aliena peccata." Cypr. Ep. 64. ad Fidum. St. Augustine, after quoting the above-cited passage from St. Cyprian in proof that the Church had all along held the doctrine of original sin, thus comments upon the words *aliena peccata*. " Nec sic dicuntur ista aliena peccata tanquam omnino ad parvulos non pertineant, siquidem *in Adam omnes tunc peccarerunt*, quando in ejus natura illa insita vi qua eos gignere poterat *adhuc omnes ille unus fuerunt:* sed dicuntur aliena quia nondum ipsi agebant vitas proprias, sed quidquid erat in futura propagine, vita unius hominis continebat." De Pecc. Mer. et Rem. l. iii. §. v. and vii. See also St. Jerome quoted by Wall on Infant Baptism, Part I. c. xix. §. 26.

soever other offences could be laid to their charge So that as by one man sin entered into the world, and death by sin, and so death passed upon all men, for that all have sinned in that one; so—to complete the antithesis—by one man righteousness entered into the world, and life by righteousness, and thus life was bestowed on all, all i. e. who belong to that one Man, for that all are righteous in Him. Thus that one offence which brought death upon our first father, cleaves to us in its guilt and condemnation from our birth '.

But it will be objected, perhaps, that thus to represent mankind as lying under condemnation for Adam's sin is at variance with the notions which God has taught us to form of His own character. Does not God Himself, it may be asked, reject the like imputation in Ezek. xviii. which the Jews blasphemously cast upon Him, when they complained that the fathers had eaten sour grapes, and the children's teeth were set on edge? And does he not say expressly that thenceforward they should no more have occasion to use that proverb—that " the

---

' " Aliena lavit aqua, quos culpa inquinaverat aliena Nec tamen sic alienam dixerim ut negem nostram, alioquin nec inquinaret. Sed aliena est quia in Adam omnes nescientes peccavimus; nostra, quia etsi in alio, nos tamen peccavimus et nobis justo Dei judicio imputabatur licet occulto. Veruntamen ut jam non sit quod causeris, O homo, contra inobedientiam Adæ datur tibi obedientia Christi, ut si gratis venundatus es, gratis etiam redimaris." Bern. Dominica 1. post octav. Epiph. Serm. 1.

soul that sinned it should die; the son should not bear the iniquity of the father, neither should the father bear the iniquity of the son—the righteousness of the righteous should be upon him, and the wickedness of the wicked should be upon him?"

To this I answer, that they who allege this passage from Ezekiel for the purpose of overthrowing the doctrine that the sin of Adam is become the condemnation of his whole race, are bound, before they allege it, to resolve with themselves how it is to be reconciled with another passage, wherein God is represented as describing his own character on the most solemn occasion and in the most explicit terms. " The Lord descended in the cloud and stood with Moses there, and proclaimed *the name of the Lord*... The Lord, the Lord God, merciful and gracious, long-suffering, and abundant in goodness and truth, keeping mercy for thousands, forgiving iniquity and transgression and sin, and that will by no means clear the guilty, *visiting the iniquity of the fathers upon the children, and upon the children's children unto the third and to the fourth generation*[e]. This is God's immutable character, immutable as His great Name. And the objection, if it lies at all against the doctrine that He has permitted Adam's sin to be the condemnation of the world, lies at least equally against the description of his character here drawn by his own hand.

But, in fact, the passage in Ezekiel so far from

[e] Exod. xxxiv. 5—7.

affording matter of objection to the doctrine rather confirms it. For when God declares that the Jews should *no more* have occasion to use the Proverb which they had adopted, he implies that till then they had had occasion, though not to make it the basis of the blasphemous complaint, which they had founded upon it. The Jews *were* suffering for the sins of their fathers, as well as their own. God Himself had declared as much, when he threatened the judgments which had now come upon them, and the penitent Jews are represented as expressing by the mouth of Jeremiah the very same sentiment as that contained in the Proverb, " Our fathers have sinned and are not, and we have borne their iniquities[h]," only with this difference, that the one was the language of humiliation, the other of insolence and rebellion.

Nor are we so to interpret the expression, " Ye shall *no more* have occasion to use this proverb," as though God intended thenceforward to abandon the principle on which till then he had acted. It is evident that the Jews continued and still continue under the same dispensation. " Our fathers have sinned and are not, and we have borne their iniquities," might be as justly the lament of the present generation of that people as it was of Jeremiah's. Nor indeed is the rule restricted to the Jews. There is enough apparent in the ways of Providence to

[h] Lam. v 7.

convince us, even if revelation had spoken less plainly, that it is of general application.

The truth is, that God was directing the minds of His people to another dispensation, wherein while the *temporal* consequences of national or ancestral sins would still in many respects be permitted to run their course, the *spiritual and eternal* evil should be cancelled, and every man should be dealt with according to his individual conduct. And in whatsoever measure God acted upon this principle in His dealings with His people before that dispensation was formally begun, His doing so was in anticipation of the Gospel Covenant. It was only by Christ's becoming a curse for us, that the law was counteracted which involved the children in the fathers' punishment[1].

[1] St. Augustine thus deals with the argument from Ezek. xviii. on which, as it seems, the Pelagians laid much stress: "Quod vero causae tuae postremum et quasi fortissimum firmamentum propheticum testimonium esse voluisti, ubi per Ezechielem dictum legimus, Quod non erit parabola, qua dicebam, parentes uvas acerbas edisse, et dentes obstupuisse filiorum; nec morietur filius in peccato patris, nec pater in peccato filii, sed anima quae peccat ipsa morietur: non intelligis hanc esse promissionem Testamenti novi et spiritualis haereditatis ad aeternum saeculum pertinentis. Id enim agit gratia Redemptoris, ut paternum chirographum deleat, et unusquisque pro se rationem reddat. Caeterum quam multa sint divinarum testimonia Litterarum, quae parentum peccatis obligant filios, numerare quis possit? Cur enim peccavit Cham et in ejus filium Chanaan vindicta prolata est? &c. . . . Sed carnalis generatio etiam populi Dei pertinens ad Testamentum vetus, quod in servitutem generat, parentum peccatis obligat filios; spiritualis autem generatio, sicut haereditatem, ita poenarum atque praemiorum

God's dealings indeed with Adam and his descendants have but one complete parallel in the whole history of his dealings with our race, namely, his dealings with Christ, and those who belong to Christ, the one being an instance of *sin* affecting the welfare of generations yet unborn, the other of *righteousness*. And he who objects to the principle acted on in the one case, is bound to object to the principle acted on in the other[k]. Adam stood as the representative of his posterity. God beheld in him

comminationes promissionesque mutavit. Quod Prophetæ in spiritu prævidentes ista dixerunt; sed apertius Ieremias: " In diebus illis" inquit " non dicent Patres manducaverunt" &c. nempe manifestum est ita hoc prophetice pronuntiari, sicut ipsum Testamentum novum, quod prius occultum fuit, et per Christum postea revelatum est. Denique, ne nos moverent ea quæ commemoravi, et cætera hujusmodi plurima de reddendis in filios peccatis parentum, quæ utique veraciter scripta sunt, et huic prophetiæ contraria putarentur, continuo solvit istam molestissimam quæstionem, conjungendo atque dicendo, " Ecce dies venient, dicit Dominus, et consummabo domui Israel et domui Juda *Testamentum novum,* non secundum Testamentum quod disposui patribus eorum." (Ierem. xxxi. 29—32.) In hoc igitur Testamento novo per sanguinem Testatoris deleto paterno chirographo, incipit homo paternis debitis non esse obnoxius renascendo quibus nascendo fueret obligatus." August. contra Julian. Pelag. lib. vi. c. xxv.

[k] " Διὰ τοῦτο ἄνω καὶ κάτω τοῦ ἑνὸς ἔχεται, καὶ συνεχῶς τοῦτο εἰς μέσον φέρει, λέγων "Ωσπερ δι' ἑνὸς ἀνθρώπου ἡ ἁμαρτία εἰς τὸν κόσμον εἰσῆλθε κ. τ. λ. . . . . καὶ οὐκ ἀφίσταται τοῦ ἑνὸς, ἵν' ὅταν λέγῃ σοι ὁ Ἰουδαῖος, Πῶς, ἑνὸς κατορθώσαντος τοῦ Χριστοῦ, ἡ οἰκουμένη ἐσώθη; δυνηθῇς αὐτῷ λέγειν, Πῶς ἑνὸς παρακούσαντος τοῦ Ἀδὰμ, ἡ οἰκουμένη κατεκρίθη;" Chrysost. in Rom. Hom. x. §. 1.

the whole race of mankind, and in dealing with him, dealt with them. It is vain for any man to find fault with this arrangement. We are in no sort judges what would have been the working of any other arrangement. Will any one say, that had we been dealt with *individually*, he would have stood where Adam fell? But indeed it is not a matter to admit of such reasoning. "Nay but, O man, who art thou that repliest against God?" This is the proper answer to make to those who would object to the *justice* of the arrangement, and if any should question its *goodness*, we must adopt St. Paul's words again on another occasion, "O the depth of the riches both of the wisdom and knowledge of God! How unsearchable are His judgments, and His ways past finding out!"

2. There is, however, another circumstance to be considered which places the matter in a different light, and enables us to see, though we might not have doubted, even if we could not have seen, that God's dealings with us in this respect are just and true. The *nature of man*, in consequence of the fall, is *corrupted and debased,* He is " very far gone from original righteousness." He has lost the divine image in which his first father was created. He has become the subject and slave of Satan. And in this evil case he continues, without power to deliver himself, till Christ makes him free, renewing him by His Spirit, and creating him again, after His own likeness, in righteousness and true holiness. So that,

even though we should hesitate to take the view of an entailed condemnation, we are still brought virtually to the same point; for all are born with a sinful nature, and this, as our article declares, deserves God's wrath and damnation[1].

It is not denied indeed that the natural man may possess many estimable qualities. We read of sundry instances among the ancient heathens of generosity, disinterestedness, patriotism, self-control, temperance, courage, veracity, filial and parental affection, and the like. And St. Paul speaks of the Gentiles, who had no revealed law to guide or restrain them, as yet doing by nature the things contained in the law, and as shewing the work of the law written in their hearts, their conscience also bearing witness, and their thoughts the meanwhile accusing or else excusing one another[m]. And he tells us of himself in his unconverted state, that, touching the righteousness which is in the law, he was blameless[n]. And St. Mark says of the young ruler, who asked our Lord what good thing he should do that he might inherit eternal life, and who, when our Lord referred him to the commandments, answered, how ignorant soever of their full extent, that he had kept them all from his youth up, that our Lord *beholding him loved him*[o]; which certainly implies, that there was that in him which was amiable and good. Some traces then of what man once was are still left amid the ruins of his original nature—such as may serve

[1] Art. ix. [m] Rom. ii. 14, 15. [n] Phil. iii. 6. [o] Mark x. 17—21.

to shew, in some measure, the goodly design of the Almighty Architect[p].

And yet with all these, even under the most favourable circumstances, there is not a greater and more real difference between a marble statue and a living man, than there is between man in his natural and in his renewed state. And the change which must pass upon him in his transition from one state to the other is so essential, that nothing short of such expressions as a *passing from darkness to light*[q], from *death to life*[r], a *new birth*[s], a *new creation*[t], can sufficiently describe it:—expressions which would fill us with amazement, were it not that long use has familiarized us with them, and they pass from our lips, or fall upon our ears, without exciting any idea corresponding to their astounding import.

The truth is, *God is dethroned in the heart of the natural man.* He is not supreme. Other lords beside him have the dominion. Man would be his own god, dependent on himself alone for happiness. Or he would make the world his god, or the flesh, or the devil, or all three. And so no place is found for the fear of God, and the love of God, which are the spring and centre of true religion, and in the absence of which, no amount of virtues, such as the world calls virtues, is in respect of religion of any account.

[p] See August. de Spir. et Lit. §. xxvii. xxviii.
[q] Ephes. v. 8. Acts xxvi. 18.   [r] 1 John iii. 14.
[s] John iii. 3. 1 Pet. i. 23.   [t] Gal. vi. 15. 2 Cor. v. 17.

St. Paul in the seventh and eighth chapters of his Epistle to the Romans draws a lamentable picture of man in his natural state; for whatever view we take of the question, whether the Apostle speaks in the former of these chapters in the person of a regenerate or an unregenerate man, the bearing of the passages I refer to is still the same. "When we were in the flesh," he says, "the motions of sins which were by the law, did work in our members to bring forth fruit unto death." "We know that the law is spiritual, but I (so far as I am in my natural state) am *carnal, sold under sin*, (its very slave;) for that which I do I allow not; for what I would that do I not, but what I hate that do I.... I know that in me, that is, in my flesh, (in my old nature) dwelleth no good thing; for to will is present with me, but how to perform that which is good I find not. For the good that I would I do not, but the evil which I would not that I do. . . . I find then a law, that when I would do good, evil is present with me; for I delight in the law of God after the inward man, (I heartily assent to and acquiesce in it,) but I see another law in my members warring against the law of my mind, and bringing me into captivity to the law of sin which is in my members. O wretched man that I am, who shall deliver me from the body of this death!" "They that are after the flesh do mind the things of the flesh." "To be carnally minded is death." "The carnal mind is *enmity against* God, for it is not subject to the law of God, neither indeed can be:" "they that are in the flesh, cannot please God."

Such is man in his natural state. Make all the allowance you will for the noble qualities which are to be found in this or the other individual, still this is the description given of him by the pen of inspiration. Carnal—sold under sin—its very slave—no good thing in him—enmity against God—not subject to the law of God, and incapable of being so—incapable of pleasing God. Is it possible to find stronger language in which to set forth the miserable corruption and debasement to which his nature has been subjected? Is this the being whom God made upright, whom He created in His own image, and after His own likeness?

We may notice before we leave this passage how the case stands with regard to the *freedom of the will*. God sets before us good and evil, life and death, and He leaves us free to choose as we list. In Paradise Adam had no corrupt bias inclining his will to evil. But it has been otherwise since the fall. Man is still as free to choose as before. But he has a bias now which he had not then. His will—free in itself—as free as Adam's was in Paradise—is become the slave of sin. And the corruption of his nature, even where he would have chosen good, draws him to evil in spite of his better choice. When he would do good, evil is present with him. The good that he would he does not, and the evil which he would not that he does".

But, in truth, in his natural state man is too

" Rom. vii. 21, 19.

ignorant, for the most part, to know good from evil in spiritual matters. One of the effects of the fall has been to blind his understanding, and to hide from him the things which belong unto his peace. Thus St. Paul tells his converts, that in their heathen state they had had " their understanding darkened, being alienated from the life of God, through the ignorance that was in them, because of the blindness of their heart^x;" and again, that they had been darkness, though now they were light in the Lord^y; and on another occasion, " that the natural man receiveth not the things of the Spirit of God, neither can he know them, because they are spiritually discerned^z. And it is in accordance with this view, and as the proper remedy for man's natural ignorance, that we find so much stress every where laid on knowledge in the New Testament, as, e. g. where our Lord says, "This is life eternal, that they might *know* Thee the only true God, and Jesus Christ Whom Thou hast sent^a;" and where He calls Himself " the Truth^b" and " the Light^c;" and where St. Paul makes it one of the principal characteristics of the new man that he is " *renewed in knowledge* after the image of Him that created him^d."

^x Ephes. iv. 18.   ^y Ephes. v. 8.   ^z 1 Cor. ii. 14.
^a John xvii. 3.   ^b John xiv. 6.   ^c John ix. 5.
^d Col. iii. 10. Οὐδὲ γὰρ ἄσημα τὰ γεγραμμένα, ὡς Θεὸς ἀπ' ἀρχῆς ξύλον ζωῆς ἐν μέσῳ παραδείσου ἐφύτευσε, διὰ γνώσεως ζωὴν ἐπιδεικνύς· ᾗ μὴ καθαρῶς χρησάμενοι οἱ ἀπ' ἀρχῆς, πλάνῃ τοῦ ὄφεως γεγύμνωνται·

And thus though our will is free, and we may choose good or evil as we list, yet we know too little wherein our happiness consists to choose aright. We call evil good and good evil. "What have I to do with Thee, Jesus, thou Son of God?" is the natural language of our hearts to Him, who is our peace and our life. And thus through very ignorance we make a wrong choice, and our will takes a wrong bias.

But to say that man is naturally *ignorant* of the things which make for his peace, is but a partial account of his case. The corrupt bias which he has received, inclines him to *prefer* ignorance to knowledge. He *loves* darkness rather than light. The things of the Spirit of God are *foolishness* to him; he scorns and derides them. And St. Paul is describing the conduct and character not of any particular class, but of all who are not under the influence of Divine grace, when he speaks of the *deceivableness of unrighteousness* in them that perish, because they *received not the love of the truth* that they might be saved. No man loves the truth who is not of the truth—whose heart has not been taught to love it by Him who is the Truth. It was a just judgment upon our first parents, that as they sinned through the desire of knowledge, which God had

---

οὐδὲ γὰρ ζωὴ ἄνευ γνώσεως, οὐδὲ γνῶσις ἀσφαλὴς ἄνευ ζωῆς ἀληθοῦς· διὸ πλησίον ἑκάτερον πεφύτευται. Justin. M. Epist. ad Diogn. c. ult. p. 240. quoted by Bp. Bull on the State of Man before the Fall. Works, vol. ii. p. 83.

seen fit to withhold from them, so their punishment should be not merely ignorance, but the love of ignorance^e.

The natural freedom of the will on the one hand, and its actual subjection under the power of ignorance and sin on the other, afford the true solution to the apparent inconsistency between the invitations and exhortations, which are addressed to us in Scripture, and the uniform declaration, in every part of the sacred volume, that the work of our conversion is a supernatural work, that we have no power of ourselves to turn to God. God addresses us in His Word as free agents; He bids us repent and be-

---

^e "Non enim laborat intellectus humanus nuda carentia scientiæ debitæ; sed propensus est ad veritatem sugillandum, odio habendam, atque ad errores et stultas ac vanas opiniones avide amplexandas. Dixit ergo Apostolus, Hominem animalem non modo 'non percipere quæ sunt Dei,' sed addidit 'sunt enim ei stultitia;' hoc est, deridet et exibilat veritatem divinam, tanquam rem ludicram et solis stultis dignam. Nec deridet solummodo homo animalis salutiferam veritatem, sed odit et illam et prædicatores ejusdem: 'Ego dedi iis sermonem tuum, et mundus eos odio habuit;' 'Dilexerunt homines magis tenebras quam lucem.' Jam quod attinet ad errores et vanam scientiam, cupide et utrisque (quod aiunt) ulnis intellectus humanus ea amplexatur. Notavit Apostolus hoc vitium in sapientissimis philosophorum; Ἐματαιώθησαν ἐν τοῖς διαλογισμοῖς αὐτῶν· Omnibus enim hoc insitum est hominibus non-renatis, ut quemadmodum amorem veritatis non recipiunt, ita mendaciis facilem fidem adhibent. Atque hæc omnia pullulant ex illa originali contagione, quæ intellectum humanum occupavit." Bp. Davenant de Justitia habituali, c. xiv. See Miller's Sermons, Serm. ii. p. 33—36.

lieve the Gospel that we may be saved[f]. He invites us to come unto Him, as many as are weary and heavy laden, that we may have rest[g]. He warns us to work out our own salvation with fear and trembling[h]; and yet, at the same time, he teaches us that both repentance[i] and faith[k] are His gifts; that no man can come unto the Son except the Father, which hath sent Him, draw him[l]; and that it is God which worketh in us both to will and to do of his good pleasure[m].

But to return to the account which Scripture gives us of the corruption of our nature. The language of the Old Testament entirely harmonizes with that of the New. Thus God testifies of the antediluvian race, that "the wickedness of man was great in the earth, and that every imagination of the thoughts of his heart was only evil continually[n]." And lest any should think that the waters of the flood had left no traces remaining of such extreme wickedness, we have the very same description repeated immediately after the flood, when as yet the whole human race was comprised in that favoured family which had been so signally distinguished. "The Lord said in His heart, I will not again any more curse the ground for man's sake, for (or, though) the imagination of man's heart is evil from his youth[o]." As though God's desolating judgments

---

[f] Mark i. 15.   [g] Matt. xi. 28.   [h] Phil. ii. 12.
[i] Acts v. 31.   [k] Eph. ii. 8. Phil. i. 29.   [l] John vi. 44.
[m] Phil. ii. 13.   [n] Gen. vi. 5.   [o] Gen. viii. 21.

must never cease, if he should always deal with man as he had dealt with him, seeing that man's nature remained the same. This is a dark picture indeed,—the imagination of man's heart, every imagination—evil—only evil—continually—even from his youth. And yet how remarkably in keeping with the Apostle's language, "I know that in me, that is in my flesh, dwelleth no good thing p." "They that are in the flesh cannot please God q." How remarkably in keeping with the Prophet's declaration, "The heart is deceitful above all things and desperately wicked: who can know it r?"

And to this passage from the book of Genesis may be added what David says in the fifty-first Psalm, "Behold I was shapen in iniquity, and in sin did my mother conceive me:" a truth which the ceremonial law not obscurely intimated in the ordinances for the purification of women after childbirth s. To the like purpose is Job's question, with his despairing answer, "Who can bring a clean thing out of an unclean? not one t." And Eliphaz's exclamation in the following chapter, "What is man that he should be clean? and he which is born of a woman that he should be righteous u?" Passages, which imply that we are corrupt from our very birth—that it is not imitation and the following of evil example, which has made us what we are, but that

---

p Rom. vii. 18.   q Rom. viii. 8.   r Jerem. xvii. 9.
s Lev. xii.   t Job xiv. 4.   u Job xv. 14.

the evil is innate—inbred—in our *very grain;* that apart from the condemnation which rests on us inherited from our first father, we are each of us guilty in our own persons,—sinners in *habit* even before we have committed a single sin *in act.* The tree is corrupt, and it only lacks time and opportunity to bear fruit of the same description. The fountain is polluted, and the waters which issue from it cannot but be polluted too.

And this corruption of nature is to be traced to the sin of our first father. Adam was not created thus. Very remarkable is the change of language, in the summary account given of our earliest ancestors in the book of Genesis, from the description of Adam's original to that of Seth's. Of Adam it is said, " In the day that God created man, in the likeness of God made he him[x]." Of Seth, " Adam begat a son in his own likeness, after his image[y]." We hear no more of *God's* likeness, which Adam had lost. Seth is the sinful child of a sinful father. How indeed should it be otherwise? " That which is born of the flesh is flesh." " Who can bring a clean thing out of an unclean?"

But there is another circumstance to be taken into the account, if we would fully understand the extent of the corruption of our nature and of our alienation from God, to which the sin of our first father has subjected us. We are born *the subjects of Satan's kingdom.*

[x] Gen. v. 1. [y] Gen. v. 3.

It is wonderful how little, practically, this fact is recognised among us: how little, in spite of what is implied by our solemn renunciation of Satan in our baptism, the power of the evil one is realized, and his sway over the unregenerate believed. Yet Scripture speaks of his agency, in the most express terms, describing him as the prince of this world[f], the god of this world, the ruler of the darkness of this world[b], the prince of the power of the air, the spirit that worketh or energizeth in the children of disobedience[c], possessing and actuating them and moulding them according to his will. His subjects and servants we are all till Christ sets us free, and turns us from darkness to light, and from the power of Satan unto God[d]. And even after we have been set free, he is ever striving to win us back again under his yoke[e].

---

[f] John xiv. 30.   [a] 2 Cor. iv. 4.   [b] Ephes. vi. 12.
[c] Ephes. ii. 2.   [d] Acts xxvi. 18.

[e] "Pervicacissimus hostis ille numquam malitiæ suæ otium facit. Atquin tunc maxime sævit, cum hominem plene sentit liberatum: tunc plurimum accenditur, dum extinguitur. Doleat et ingemiscat necesse est, venia peccatorum permissa, tot in homine mortis opera diruta, tot titulos damnationis retro suæ erasos. Dolet quod ipsum et angelos ejus Christi servus ille peccator judicaturus est. Itaque observat, oppugnat, obsidet: si qua possit aut oculos concupiscentia carnali ferire, aut animum illecebris sæcularibus irretire, aut fidem terrenæ potestatis formidine evertere, aut a via certa perversis traditionibus detorquere: non scandalis, non tentationibus deficit." Tertull. de Pœnitent. §. vii.

It is mainly through his agency that the ignorance which has been already referred to, as one of the principal features in our fallen nature, is fostered. And by this ignorance he retains his sway. Thus he is said to " blind the eyes of them that believe not, lest the light of the glorious Gospel of Christ, who is the image of God, should shine unto them[f]." He is described as catching away the seed of God's word sown in men's hearts, lest they should believe and be saved[g]. He is represented as deceiving the nations[h]. And the coming of the man of sin is spoken of as being after the working of Satan, with all power and signs and lying wonders, with all deceivableness of unrighteousness in them that perish[i]. And it was by his instrumentality that the whole system of idolatry was framed, by which the heathen world were held in bondage. He was the god whom they ignorantly worshipped. He furnished their oracles with responses; he taught them the impure and cruel rites of their idolatrous service; he ministered the power of bewitching them with sorceries, and lying miracles, and other deceitful arts. And though his dominion in these respects has been in part broken in Christian lands, yet he still exercises his ancient sway in full force in heathen countries. Little do we think how much it is owing to his influence that the course of the Gospel has been hindered, and the kingdoms of this world still

[f] 2 Cor. iv. 4.   [g] Luke viii. 12.   [h] Rev. xx. 3.
[i] 2 Thess. ii. 9, 10.

withheld from their allegiance to their rightful sovereign.

We have now seen what man's nature is in itself—how fallen and debased—how perverted from its high original! The image of God lost; God no longer supreme; reason and conscience dethroned; the will, however free in itself, enslaved by sinful lusts; Satan ruling and bearing sway in the soul as though he were its rightful lord.

And the actual working of this evil nature is no other than was to have been looked for. The fruit corresponds to the stock on which it grows.

In his Epistle to the Romans, St. Paul sets forth, at considerable length, the actual condition of both Jews and Gentiles in their natural state. He begins with the latter, and shews into what gross ignorance and extreme depravity they had fallen through their wilful perverseness. Some knowledge of the true God they might have had from tradition, and some they might have gained from His works in nature and the course of His providence; but they heeded neither the one nor the other. They glorified Him not as God, neither were thankful, but became vain in their imaginations, and their foolish heart was darkened; professing themselves to be wise they became fools, and changed the glory of the incorruptible God into an image made like unto corruptible man, and to birds, and fourfooted beasts, and creeping things. And then, in just judgment for their sinful course, God gave them over to a reprobate mind. He took off the restraint which, in mercy, He had still held upon the corrupt principle, and suffered it to have its course unchecked, till they were borne along by it to the most extreme length of wickedness[k]. Such is the Apostle's account of the Gentile world. If among the Jews there was more profession of religion, there was in reality no less aversion from God and His laws. Insomuch that he does not scruple to apply to them the Psalmist's words, "There is none righteous, no not one: there is none that understandeth; there is none that seeketh after God; they are all gone out of the way, they are together become unprofitable, there is none that doeth good, no not one[l]."

It may be asked, indeed, Were there no exceptions? Had all run to these extreme lengths of sin? Doubtless all are not equally far gone in *actual* wickedness. Natural temperament and various external circumstances have their influence in fostering or restraining the innate principle of evil. But that principle *lives* and *reigns* in the heart of every unregenerate person, and manifests its presence and vindicates its sovereignty in his life and conversation wherever time and opportunity are given. And there is no one, who has attained to years of discretion, who has not superadded to his original guilt the guilt of manifold actual transgressions. Accordingly the Apostle, in the dark picture which he draws,

[k] Rom. i. [l] Rom. iii. 10—12.

makes no exceptions: he speaks of *all as guilty;* he shuts up *all under sin.* He himself indeed, if any, might have seemed worthy to be exempted from so sweeping a charge, for he says of himself in one place, referring to his manner of life before he became a Christian, that touching the righteousness which is in the law he was *blameless*[m]*;* and yet we find him on another occasion, when he had been describing the actual condition of the Gentiles, in the darkest colours, as dead in trespasses and sins, as walking according to the course of this world, according to the prince of the power of the air, the spirit which now worketh in the children of disobedience, seizing, as it were, the opportunity of acknowledging that his own case and that of the rest of his nation was in no wise more favourable: " Among whom," he says, " *we* all had our conversation in times past, in the lusts of our flesh, fulfilling the desires of the flesh and of the mind, and were by nature the children of wrath *even as others*[n]."

And here we may close the subject we have been considering. Whether we look at the condemnation entailed upon us as the descendants of an *attainted* ancestor, or at the corrupt nature derived from him by propagation, or at the actual transgressions, the fruit of that corrupt nature, which, wherever there have been time and opportunity, have been superadded to our original guilt, nothing can be more deplorably

[m] Phil. iii. 6.   [n] Eph. ii. 1—3.

miserable than our condition. We are all guilty before God. We have all sinned and come short of the glory of God. That one offence of our first father has made all men sinners, and has brought indignation and wrath upon the whole world.

But blessed for ever be His Name who has not left us to perish in this our wretchedness. The coats of skins with which He clothed our first parents, as they were a token that in judgment He remembered mercy, so were they also an earnest of a better covering, with which He should for ever hide the shame of His people. What that covering is, and how to be put on, and how to be preserved in its purity and integrity, are among the most deeply important subjects which it is possible for us to have brought under our consideration. To these I purpose, if God permit and enable me, on some future occasions to draw your attention. In the mean time, may the consideration of the misery and wretchedness of our natural condition lead us, on the one hand, to walk humbly with our God, as remembering the rock whence we were hewn, and the hole of the pit whence we were digged, on the other, stir us up to earnest and heart-searching enquiries as to whether we are indeed availing ourselves of that deliverance, which God, in His abundant mercy, hath provided for the sons of men. In spite of our Christian name and Christian profession, if we are not true and living members of Christ's body, quickened by His Spirit, renewed after His image, the curse entailed upon his race by our first father, rests on us in its full weight: and with this aggravation of our wretchedness, that we might have been blessed, and would not.

SERMON II.

MAN RESTORED IN CHRIST.

" Illud unum peccatum, quod tam magnum in loco et habitu tantæ felicitatis admissum est, ut in uno homine originaliter, atque, ut ita dixerim, radicaliter, totum genus humanum damnaretur, non solvitur ac diluitur, nisi per unum Mediatorem Dei et hominum, hominem Christum Jesum, qui solus potuit ita nasci, ut ei opus non esset renasci." August. Enchirid. xlviii.

ROMANS v. 15.

If through the offence of one many be dead, much more the grace of God, and the gift by grace, which is by one Man, Jesus Christ, hath abounded unto many.

In the preceding Sermon, I endeavoured to set forth the miserable condition in which we all are by nature. By one man sin entered into the world, and death by sin—death in both its senses, death temporal, and death spiritual—the death of the body, and the death of the soul; and so death passed upon all men, for that all have sinned in that one man, in Adam. We are born under condemnation; we bring into the world with us a sinful nature; and from the moment we are able to distinguish good from evil, we are daily adding to our condemnation by our own personal transgressions, and strengthening our sinful habit by acts of sin. Had we been left to ourselves—as we might have been most justly—we should have gone on increasing in wickedness, till the world, defiled with our iniquities, like Canaan of old, would have vomited out its guilty inhabitants[a].

But we have not been left to ourselves. It has pleased God, in His unsearchable wisdom and

[a] See Lev. xviii. 25.

abounding love, to devise a plan for our recovery corresponding to our fall, that as we derive all our misery from *one man*, the first father of our race, so we should derive all our happiness from *one man*, our progenitor in respect of another and better existence; that " as by one man's disobedience many were made sinners, so by the obedience of one should many be made righteous[b]."

To this end the eternal Son took man's nature in the womb of the blessed Virgin, purifying and ennobling that nature by its union with the divine. He came to be the counterpart of Adam, the second head of a second race, the fountain and source of life to as many as should be engrafted into Him. He came to reconcile God and man; yea more, to knit together in one God and man, being Himself both God and man; that as the Father dwelleth in Him, and He in the Father, so He might dwell in His people, and His people in Him. In Him all must dwell, and He in all who would partake of the benefits which He hath procured for the sons of men. Into Him all must be engrafted, as living branches into a living stock, who would bring forth fruit answerable to those benefits. " As we are really partakers of the body of sin and death received from Adam, so except we be truly partakers of Christ, and as really possessed of His Spirit, all we speak of eternal life is but a dream[c]."

[b] Rom. v. 19. See Chrysost. in Rom. v. 14.
[c] Hooker, E. P. book v. §. 56.

And if so, it is obvious how much it concerns us, in order to our having a right understanding of those high blessings towards which all our better hopes are directed, that we regard them in connexion with this great and central truth, *that they are bestowed upon us in Christ, and flow to us through our union with Him.* From no other point can they be seen adequately and in their just bearings. And very much of the confusion of thought and variance of opinion, which have prevailed respecting them, is to be traced to no other cause than that they have been viewed without sufficient reference to it. Thus subjects, which though inseparably connected are yet essentially distinct, have been, on the one hand, confounded with each other, on the other, treated as though they were isolated and detached. Nor have any suffered more in this way than Justification and those akin to it.

It shall be the object therefore of the present Sermon, to consider in what sense Christ may be said to be in His people, and His people in Him, and to point out, how, through the union implied in that mutual indwelling, God has graciously provided a remedy for the miseries which our first father entailed upon his race. There is doubtless much that is mysterious and beyond our utmost reach of thought in this high subject, but it is one on which Scripture has spoken so frequently and so explicitly, that, if we will be content with what Scripture teaches, we cannot be greatly at a loss.

I. I would observe then, that when we are said to be *in Christ*, this is meant partly in a sense corresponding to that in which we are said to have been *in Adam*, partly in an infinitely higher sense.

We may be said to have been *in Adam*, inasmuch as every effect is *in* the original cause which gives it being. When God created Adam he created us in him. And, on the other hand, Adam may be said to be *in us*, inasmuch as every original cause is, after a sort, in the effects which spring from it[d]. From Adam, considered in this respect, we derive both our natural life, and also that corrupt nature—the likeness of his—which is transmitted by propagation, through successive generations, to his whole race.

Again, we may be said to be *in Adam*, inasmuch as we were represented by him in the covenant which God made with him, and, in him, with all who should be descended from him. He was the federal head of that covenant, and we were included under him. What he did and contracted, in regard to it, is set down to our account. And in this respect, we derive from him condemnation and death. Thus by one man sin entered into the world, and death by sin, and so death passed upon all men, for that all have sinned in him; thus, by one man's disobedience many were made sinners; thus by the offence of one judgment came upon all men to condemnation.

Now in both these senses, our being *in Christ* in part corresponds to our being *in Adam*, in part

[d] See Hooker, E. P. ch. vi. §. 56.

transcends it infinitely. Christ is in us as the source of our spiritual life, and we in Him as the stream in the source. And as from Adam we derive corruption of nature, so from Christ we derive incorruption. The Apostle's words, which were spoken with reference to bodily, apply with equal truth to spiritual, resemblance. "The first man is of the earth, earthy; the second man is the Lord from heaven. As is the earthy, such are they also that are earthy: and as is the heavenly, such are they also that are heavenly. And as we have borne the image of the earthy, we shall also bear the image of the heavenly[e]." Again, we are in Christ, inasmuch as He is the federal Head of the new covenant. God's covenant was with Christ, and, in Christ, with all His people, as it had before[f] been with Adam, and, in Adam, with his whole race. And as Adam, by violating his covenant, brought death and condemnation upon all descended from him, so Christ in that He stood to His, brought justification and life. And thus, since by man came death, by man came also the resurrection of the dead; as in Adam all die, even so in Christ shall all be made alive[g]; as by the one[h]

[e] 1 Cor. xv. 47—49.

[f] *Before*, if we regard the times at which the two covenants were respectively *revealed;* but *afterwards* in reality, seeing that God's covenant with Christ, and, in Christ, with those who are Christ's, was *from everlasting.* See Heb. xiii. 20. 1 Pet i. 20. Eph. iii. 11. 2 Tim. i. 9, 10. Tit. i. 2, 3. Rev. xiii. 8. &c.

[g] 1 Cor. xv. 21, 22.

[h] Rom. v. 19. τοῦ ἑνός. Where εἷς in this passage refers to Adam

man's disobedience many were made sinners, so by the obedience of the One Man shall many be made righteous; as by the offence of one, or rather by one offence, the one sin of Adam, judgment came upon all men to condemnation, so by the righteousness of One, or rather by one righteousness, the perfect, complete, unbroken righteousness of Christ, the free gift came upon all men to justification of life.

But then it is to be borne in mind that Christ is God as well as man. And this consideration gives a depth and force of meaning to our words, when we speak of *Christ's being in us,* and *our being in Christ,* which otherwise they could not have had. Had Christ been only man, none of the blessed effects just referred to could have resulted to us from any connexion we could have had with Him. It would no longer have been true, that as by man came death, by man came also the resurrection from the dead; that as in Adam all die, even so in Christ shall all be made alive. His obedience, however complete, could have been of no avail towards making us righteous, His righteousness, however perfect, could have brought to us neither justification nor life.

or to Christ it usually has the article; see v. 15, 17, 19. Δι' ἑνὸς παραπτώματος in v. 18. is obviously, as our Translators have rendered it in the margin, " by one offence," not, " by the offence of one," as in the text: by one offence—that one offence by which Adam violated his covenant. Δι' ἑνὸς δικαιώματος, in the corresponding clause, is by one righteousness—that one unbroken course of perfect sinless obedience, which Christ rendered. Its equivalent phrase in the next verse is διὰ τῆς ὑπακοῆς τοῦ ἑνὸς—by the obedience of that one man.

In respect of our *natural* life, God, who is the *highest* cause, and *first original* of that life, is in us in an infinitely higher sense than any *subordinate* cause can be, and that not merely as its Author, but as its Preserver and Conservator. We not only have life *from* Him, but He is *our life*, and we *live in Him*. Life would cease the instant He should withdraw His presence. So it is likewise with regard to our *spiritual* life, the life which we derive from the second Adam. Christ, in that He is God as well as man, is not only the Author but also the Preserver and Conservator of that life. And thus St. Paul's words to the Colossians[h] hold most strictly, whether we take them as referring to the *natural* creation or to the *spiritual*. Not only were all things created by Him that are in heaven and that are in earth, but also, by Him, or *in* Him, all things *consist*. He gave them their existence at the first, and He preserves it and will preserve it unto the end. And what the same Apostle said of himself may be truly spoken by every Christian. "I live, yet not I, but *Christ liveth in me*[i]." Christ is our life; He lives in us and we live in Him. And thus our life *is hid with Christ* in God; and when Christ *who is our life* shall appear, then shall we also appear with Him in glory[k].

And yet, on the other hand, we must not look so exclusively to our Lord's *divine* nature, as to forget that it is by His *human* nature that He *takes hold* of us, (so to speak,) and unites Himself to us and us to Himself. Christ, *as God*, indeed, would have been

[h] Col. i. 16, 17.   [i] Gal. ii. 20.   [k] Col. iii. 3, 4.

in us, and we in Him, (for God is in all things, and His being in them is the cause of their existence,) whether He had assumed our nature or not. But it is His *manhood* which is the basis of that indwelling, whereby He dwells in His Church as He dwells in none other of His creatures. " There is one God," saith the Apostle, " and one Mediator between God and men, the *man* Christ Jesus¹." His *manhood* fitted Him for His office, in respect of the one party, as His *Godhead* did in respect of the other.

But we shall better understand the nature of our indwelling in Christ, and Christ's in us, or, in other words, of the union which subsists between Christ and His people, as well as the importance which the word of God attaches to the subject, if we consider in what terms it is spoken of in Scripture.

1. At times we have it referred to in express words. Thus Christ is said to be *in His people.* " Know ye not your own selves how that Jesus Christ is *in you* except ye be reprobates ᵐ?" " If Christ be *in you*, the body is dead because of sin, but the Spirit is life because of righteousness ⁿ." And as Christ is represented as being *in His people*, so, on the other hand, they are represented as being *in Him.* " There is no condemnation to them which are *in Christ Jesus*°." " Andronicus and Junia, who were *in Christ* before me ᵖ." " If any man be *in Christ*, he is a new creature ᑫ." Elsewhere we have

¹ 1 Tim. ii 5.   ᵐ 2 Cor. xiii. 5.   ⁿ Rom. viii. 10.
° Rom. viii. 1.   ᵖ Rom. xvi. 7.   ᑫ 2 Cor. v. 17.

Christ's indwelling in His people and theirs in Him spoken of together. "At that day ye shall know that I am in My Father, and *ye in Me*, and *I in you*ʳ."

2. Not the least remarkable way in which this union is set forth is by the variety of images which are employed to illustrate it. Thus Christians are spoken of as the members of that body, whereof Christ is the Head, "from which all the body by joints and bands having nourishment ministered and knit together increaseth with the increase of Godˢ:" elsewhere, as the stones of that building whereof "Christ Himself is the chief corner-stone, in whom all the building fitly framed together groweth unto a holy temple in the Lordᵗ." Once more, Christians are spoken of as branches, Christ as the Vine out of which they grow, and from which they derive both their life and fruitfulnessᵘ. And, lastly, Christians are spoken of as the children of that mother whose husband is Christ, who loved the Church, and gave Himself for it, that He might sanctify and cleanse it with the washing of water by the word, that He might present it to Himself a glorious Church, not having spot or wrinkle or any such thing, but that it should be holy and without blemishˣ." Various as these images are, one cannot but observe how strikingly they agree in setting forth the common subject which they are brought to illustrate—the dependence which Christians have upon their Lord,

ʳ John xiv. 20.   ˢ Col. ii. 19.   ᵗ Eph. ii. 20—22.
ᵘ John xv. 1, &c.   ˣ Eph. v. 25—27.

and the close and intimate union in which they are united to Him.

In such terms does Scripture speak of this high subject. Mysterious, however, as the union is which is referred to, it is a real, substantial, and living union. Christians are as truly one with Christ as the members of the natural body are with the head—" members of His body, of His flesh, and of His bones[y]." Nay, even this, which is St. Paul's comparison, falls short of one to which our Lord likens the union between Himself and His people, when He speaks of it as corresponding to that between His Father and Himself. " At that day ye shall know that I am in my Father, and ye in Me, and I in you[z]." And in His prayer to His Father, the night before He suffered, " Neither pray I for these alone, but for them also which shall believe on Me through their word, that they all may be one, as Thou, Father, art in Me and I in Thee, that they also may be one in Us.....I in them, and thou in Me, that

---

[y] Eph. v. 30. " The questions concerning our union are in general, Whether this union come nearer to the nature of the union between bodies civil, natural, or artificial. And to this we answer, that each of these unions in part resembles it, all of them do not fully express it, because it is more real, more firm, more solid, than any union can be betwixt the parts of bodies civil, artificial, or natural. For this Church is a true and living body, consisting of parts, all really, though mystically and spiritually, united unto one Head; and, by their real union with one Head, all are truly and really united among themselves." Jackson's Works, vol. iii. p. 817.   [z] John xiv. 20.

they may be made perfect in one^a." And as our Lord, in these passages, speaks of His union with His people, as corresponding to the union of His Father with Himself, so elsewhere He compares the consequences of the one union with the consequences of the other. " As the living Father hath sent Me, and I live by the Father, so he that eateth Me even he shall live by Me^b."

And it is by the Holy Spirit's agency that this mysterious union is both formed and preserved. Christ dwells in us by His Spirit: " If any man have not the Spirit of Christ, he is none of His^c." " Hereby know we that we dwell in him and he in us, because He hath given us of His Spirit^d." " It is the Spirit that quickeneth^e"—the Spirit proceeding in the first instance from the Father, and poured forth without measure upon the Son, and flowing forth from the Son, as from the Head to the body, into His Church generally, and into the several members of His Church individually, as each from time to time is incorporated, breathing into them the breath of life, and uniting them all to Him, and in Him first to the Father and then to one another. And thus, to follow out the images with which Scripture has already furnished us—if Christ be the head, and His Church the body, the Holy Spirit is the soul which animates the body; if Christ be the vine, and His people the branches, the Holy Spirit is the vital

[a] John xvii. 20—23.   [b] John vi. 57.   [c] Rom. viii. 9.
[d] 1 John iv. 13.   [e] John vi. 63.

principle, which, through the juices of the tree, communicates life to the branches; if Christ be the chief corner-stone, and His Church the temple which that chief corner-stone supports and holds together, the Holy Spirit is the Shekinah, by which God manifests His presence in the temple. And lastly, as Christ, when He became incarnate, was conceived by the Holy Ghost, so likewise His people, when they are born again into that new life which they live in Him, are born of the Spirit.

It is obvious then, from the view here given, that while the sense in which we are *in Christ* in part corresponds to that in which we may be said to have been in Adam, in part it transcends it infinitely.

II. But we shall obtain a further insight into the matter, as well as be enabled more clearly to understand how God has, *in Christ*, provided a remedy for the evils which our first father entailed upon his race, if we proceed to enquire what Christ, *as God*, has received *from* us, and what, *as man*, He has received *for* us.

i. The first thing of ours which He has received, and which indeed is the basis on which His union with us rests, is our *nature*. He took not on Him the *person* of a man, already in being, for then, as Hooker says, should *that one* have been exalted[f],

---

[f] "It pleased not the Word or Wisdom of God to take to itself some one person amongst men, for then should that one have been advanced which was assumed and no more, but Wisdom

and no more; but He took on Him *our nature*. The *Word*, the second Person in the Sacred Trinity, *was made flesh;* and thus laid the foundation of a union with *every individual* of the human family, who should be willing to accept His salvation. And, as the Apostle to the Hebrews reasons, seeing that both He that sanctifieth—(Christ)—and they who are sanctified—(His people)—are all of one—(sprung from one common original)—therefore He is not ashamed to call them brethren[g]. He became bone of *our* bone and flesh of *our* flesh, that having sanctified and ennobled our nature, by its union with the Divine, He might in turn make us bone of *His* bone and flesh of *His* flesh.

For while He thus became man for our sakes, that Divine nature which He had originally, and of whose very essence it is to be eternal and immutable, still remained unchanged. He was as truly God, after His incarnation as before, but with this addition, that He was man also—God and man, in one person, and by consequence capable of meaner offices than otherwise He could have been: " the only gain he thereby purchased for Himself, being to be capable of loss and detriment for the good of others[h]." " Ye know the grace of our Lord Jesus Christ, (says the Apostle,) that though He was rich, yet for your

---

to the end she might save many, built her house of that *nature* which is common unto all; she made not *this or that man* her habitation, but dwelt *in us.*" Hooker, E. P. v. §. 52.

[g] Heb. ii. 11.   [h] Hooker, E. P. v. §. 54.

sakes He became poor, that ye through His poverty might be rich[1]." The Son of God became the Son of man, that He might make the sons of men sons of God.

It is deeply important that we should habituate ourselves to realize both the entire oneness of our Lord's human nature with our own, and also the intimacy of His union with us of which that oneness of nature is the basis. Whatever we may hold theoretically, it is perhaps not easy in practice to avoid one or the other of two extremes; either the looking so exclusively to His Godhead as to forget that He is very man, or the looking so exclusively to His manhood, as to forget that He is very God. Yet is He as truly one as the other. So far forth as He is God, one from all eternity with the Father; so far forth as He is man, in all respects one of ourselves, though exalted by reason of the union of Godhead with manhood in His person, infinitely above all other men. Nor yet does His union with us consist merely in the identity of His human nature with our own. "For what man in the world is there," as Hooker justly asks, "who hath not so far forth communion with Jesus Christ?" Though his human nature is the basis of His union with us, yet He with whom we are united is both God and man. And we, by being united to Him, become, to use St. Peter's expression,

---

[1] 2 Cor. viii. 9.

"partakers of the Divine nature." We are new creatures in Christ. The life we live is a divine life. Yea it is not we that live, but Christ liveth in us.

But while our Lord's infinite love to us led Him to humble Himself so as to become *flesh*, His infinite purity could not endure that He should defile Himself with *sinful* flesh[k]. The nature which He took was a *sinless* nature. It had all the *essential* properties of manhood, but it was without sin. Our Lord was made in the *likeness*[l] of sinful flesh, not *in* sinful flesh. His birth of the Virgin Mary gave Him thus much in common with us, that He was *as truly man* as we are; His conception by the Holy Ghost distinguished Him from all other men, in that He was wholly free from whatsoever of sin and guilt we have inherited from our first father. And therefore, even before He was conceived in the womb, He was spoken of as that *holy* thing which should be born[m]. He alone of all the sons of men, since the fall, was so born that He needed not to be born again. That which we become at our regeneration, He was, though in an infinitely higher and more perfect sense, at His natural birth. And His being such at His natural birth, is the cause of our becoming such at our second birth.

[k] See Bp. Pearson on the Creed, Art. iii. vol. i. p. 265.

[l] Vides in Domino carnem mortalem: non est caro peccati; *similitudo* est carnis peccati. August. Serm. 134. (alias 48.)

[m] Luke i. 35.

And this *original* holiness, which our Lord brought into the world with Him, He preserved, unsullied by the slightest taint, from His birth to His death. With a nature in every other respect such as ours,—as keenly sensible of pleasure and pain, joy and sorrow, applause and shame, ease and weariness,—He was tempted in all points like as we are, yet without sin. The tempter came[n], but he had nothing in Him. His heart never swerved, for an instant, from that law of love to God, which enthroned God supremely in His affections, and of charity to man, which first led Him to be born, and then to lay down His life for us. It was His *meat* to do the will of Him that sent Him, and to finish His work[o]: insomuch that he could appeal to His Father, when on the eve of leaving the world, that He had glorified Him on the earth, He had finished the work which He had given Him to do[p]. Thus, as He was wholly free from *original* sin, so was He from *actual* also. In the language of one sacred writer, " In Him is no sin[q]." In the language of another, " He knew no sin[r]." Whatsoever other unhappiness our nature is susceptible of, He knew full well. Hunger and thirst, fatigue and weariness, shame and reproach, sorrowfulness and dejection, cruel mockings and scourgings, torture and death— of these and the like, He had large experience; but of *sin* He knew nothing, save by what He saw

[n] John xiv. 30. [o] John iv. 34. [p] John xvii. 4.
[q] 1 John iii. 5. [r] 2 Cor. v. 21.

of it and encountered, in the world around Him. And truly it was not the least part of the suffering which He underwent for our sakes, that He was for so long a season constrained to dwell among sinners, and to have His habitation in a world lying in wickedness.

As our Lord's human nature was the basis on which His union with us rests, so was it also the stage, so to speak, on which He did and suffered whatsoever He came to do and to suffer on our behalf.

Our first father sinned by disobedience to God's law; and He who should redeem us must render a perfect obedience, and fulfil all righteousness both in doing and suffering the will of God. But he must do it in the nature in which the transgression was committed[¹]. *Man* had broken the law, and *man* must keep it. A body therefore was prepared for Him, that in that He might do and suffer the will of God; and He who was "*equal* with the Father," became the *servant* of the Father, and though He

---

[¹] Χριστὸς γὰρ ἡμᾶς ἐξηγόρασεν ἐκ τῆς κατάρας τοῦ νόμου· τὴν πλήρωσιν τοῦ νόμου, τὴν διὰ τῆς ἀπαρχῆς γενομένην ὅλῳ λογιζέσθαι τῷ φυράματι· γινώσκειν τὸ πρεπὸν καὶ τὸ ἀκόλουθον· ὅτι, Θεοῦ γυμνοῦ τὸν νόμον πληρώσαντος, ὕπερ οὐ καὶ λέγειν ἁρμόδιον, οὐκ ἦν ἄλλην οὐσίαν μετέχειν τοῦ κατορθώματος, σαρκὸς δὲ τῆς ἐξ ἡμῶν ἐν τῷ πληρώσαντι τὸν νόμον γνωριζομένης, ἀναφαίνεται τοῦ γένους· τὸ καύχημα, ὡς καταπατεῖν ἀδεῶς τοῦ θανάτου τὸ κέντρον, οἷα μηκέτι χώραν ἔχον κατὰ τῆς φύσεως, ἧς ἡ ἀπαρχὴ προλαβοῦσα κατεπάτησε καὶ ἤμβλυνε, καὶ πᾶσι δέδωκε τοῖς πιστεύουσι λέγειν· Ποῦ σου, θάνατε, τὸ κέντρον; ποῦ σου, ᾅδη, τὸ νῖκος; Athanas. in Faber on Justification, p. 125.

were a Son, yet learned He obedience by the things which He suffered. He laid aside His glory, the glory which He had with the Father before the world was, and took upon Him the form of a servant, and was made in the likeness of men. This was the first step in His humiliation, and that on which the rest followed. And being found in fashion as a man, He humbled Himself still more, and became obedient unto death, even the death of the Cross[l].

For, further, Adam, by his disobedience, had brought death into the world, with its mournful train of suffering and sorrow here, and of interminable woe hereafter—and therefore it was not enough for our surety to fulfil the law, and to render a perfect obedience, both active and passive, to the will of God. He must also, that we might benefit by His obedience, bear our iniquities, and sustain the penalty of our sins, by submitting to death on our behalf. But *as God*, He could not suffer; *as God*, He could not die. "Forasmuch therefore as the children are partakers of flesh and blood, He also Himself likewise took part of the same, that, through death, He might destroy him that had the power of death, that is, the devil, and deliver them, who, through fear of death, were all their lifetime subject to bondage[m]."

And thus our Lord's assumption of our nature

---

[l] Phil. ii. 6—8.   [m] Heb. ii. 14, 15.

was subsidiary to His susception of our guilt and of our punishment.

The writer of the Epistle to the Hebrews delights to dwell upon the types under which the Jewish law had shadowed forth the promised Saviour, both as the *sacrifice* which was to be offered for the sin of the world, and as the *High Priest* who was to offer it. And in both respects he speaks of Him as necessarily partaking of our nature. That He might be the *sacrifice*, a body was prepared for Him, and we are sanctified through the offering of that body once for all[v]. And in like manner, that He might be the High Priest, " in all things it behoved Him to be made like unto His brethren, that He might be a merciful and faithful High Priest in things pertaining unto God, to make reconciliation for the sins of the people"—*merciful* and *faithful*, as being touched with the feeling of their infirmities[x].

And yet again; it was necessary that as Adam, by yielding to the Tempter, had brought himself and his whole race under the yoke of Satan, He who should deliver us from that yoke, should Himself encounter the evil one, and overcome him. And for this cause also it behoved Him to take upon Him our nature, that as *man* had been subdued, so *man* also should subdue. It was the seed of the woman which must bruise the serpent's head. Accordingly it was in His human nature that our Lord engaged in that fearful conflict,

[v] Heb. x. 5—14.   [x] Heb. ii. 17.

struggling with the powers of darkness, as through His whole life, so more especially both at that season when it is expressly recorded that He was led by the Spirit into the wilderness to be tempted of the devil, and also in His mysterious agony in the garden, and during His hours of suffering upon the Cross, when all the waves and storms of His Father's wrath went over Him. He partook of flesh and blood, that He might be tempted in all points like as we are, and that through death He might destroy him that had the power of death, that is, the devil.

In all these respects, it is obvious how our Lord's assumption of our nature was necessary, in order to His doing and suffering whatsoever He came to do and to suffer in our behalf. But it was the *perfect sinlessness* of that nature in His Person, coupled with the circumstance that it was united to the Divine, which fitted Him to become a second Adam, the Progenitor of a second race, the Head and Representative of a second Covenant, and thus enabled Him to counteract the evils which the first Adam had entailed upon his descendants. Was it necessary that as by one man's disobedience many were made sinners, so by the obedience of one many should be made righteous[r]? Here was one both capable of rendering, and who actually did render, perfect obedience, and that obedience, as the obedience of Him who was God as well as man, of infinite merit. Was it necessary that one should be found,

[r] Rom. v. 19.

who might, in His own person, bear the sins of the whole world? Here was one, who being without sin Himself, both original and actual, and having the strength of Godhead bound up indissolubly with His human nature, was able to sustain the enormous load. Was it necessary, after God had provided a victim of sufficient price to make atonement, that a high priest should be found worthy to enter within the inmost recesses of the heavenly temple, and sprinkle its blood before the mercy-seat? Here was one, who needed not daily, as the priests under the law, to offer up sacrifice first for his own sins, and then for the people's, seeing that he was holy, harmless, undefiled, separate from sinners, and made higher than the heavens [a]. Was it necessary, that He who should rescue us from the yoke of Satan, under which our first father, through disobedience to the command of God, had brought himself and his posterity, should Himself encounter and overcome the evil one? Here was one, in whom the prince of this world, when He came, had nothing which He could challenge as His own [b]; who, though He was tempted in all points like as we are, was yet without sin [c]; and who, joining to this perfect sinlessness of His human nature the Almighty strength of Deity, was able to bind the strong man, and to lead captivity captive, and thus to spoil principalities and powers, and to make a show of them openly, triumphing over them in His Cross [d].

[a] Heb. vii. 26, 27. [b] John xiv. 30. [c] Heb. iv. 15. [d] Col. ii. 15.

ii. But we must pass on to consider what Christ, as man, has received *for us*. Hitherto, the subject we have had before us has been the wondrous humiliation of the eternal Word, who, for His great love wherewith He loved us, stooped so low as to become man, and, as man, submitted to a life of sorrow and a death of shame. We are now to consider the grace, which God hath given to that Man, who hath been so highly favoured as to be eternally joined in one Person with Deity.

Doubtless God hath many ways exalted Him infinitely beyond our conception, and possibly in many respects in which we are but remotely concerned. But thus much we know, that " God hath given unto Him a name, which is above every name, that at the name of Jesus (even *that name which belongs to Him as man*) every knee should bow, of things in heaven, and things in earth, and things under the earth, and that every tongue should confess that Jesus Christ is Lord, to the glory of God the Father*." And thus far we are concerned in His exaltation, that the object for which our nature was both assumed by Him, at His incarnation, and was glorified in His Person, on His ascension, was, that He might be the Head over all things to His Church, according to the good pleasure of the Father, which He purposed in Himself, " that in the dispensation of the fulness of times, He might gather together in one all things in Christ,

* Phil. ii. 9—11.

both which are in heaven, and which are on earth‘."

If then, it be asked, what hath Christ in His human nature received for us? we may answer generally, that as God hath exalted Him to be the Head of His Church, so hath He bestowed upon Him whatsoever blessings are requisite either for His Church collectively, or the members of His Church individually, to be derived from Him to all, as they severally have need. When He ascended up on high, He led captivity captive, and *received* gifts *for*[g] men, as we have it in the Psalmist[h], *gave* gifts *unto* men, as we have it in the Apostle[i]. He received that He might give. Yea, so intimately is He united to His Church, that as He became man for her sake, so, whatsoever He hath received as her Head, He hath received not for Himself alone,

[f] Eph. i. 9, 10.

[g] *In the man*, marg. As though, *In His human nature*. St. Augustine, who read, as the Vulgate still does, ' *In hominibus*,' understands the Psalmist to have an eye to Christ's oneness *with His Church*, the Apostle, to his oneness *with His Father*. As one with His Father, He *gave* the Holy Spirit, as one with His Church, He *received* the Holy Spirit in her members. " Secundum hoc (quod Deus cum Patre) ' *dedit dona hominibus*,' mittens eis Spiritum Sanctum, qui Spiritus est Patris et Filii. Secundum illud vero, quod idem ipse Christus in corpore suo intelligitur, quod est Ecclesia, propter quod et membra ejus sunt sancti et fideles ejus, (unde eis dicitur, ' Vos autem estis corpus Christi et membra') procul dubio et ipse ' *accepit dona in hominibus*.'" August. in Ps. lxvii.

[h] Ps. lxviii. 18. [i] Eph. iv. 8.

but for her with Himself; for Himself as the Head, for His Church as the body, for His people individually as the members of the body; and this, by the way, may throw light upon St. John's expression, when after declaring that "the Word was made flesh, and dwelt among us,....full of grace and truth," he adds, "and of His fulness have all we received, and grace for grace[j]," grace received by us answering to the grace bestowed in the first instance upon Him, grace in the members derived from and corresponding to the grace poured forth upon the Head.

Christ is represented in Scripture as the fountain of spiritual blessings of every description to His people. Whatever we have or hope for in respect of the divine life, is spoken of *as given us in Him*. *In him* we first became the objects of God's love[k]. *In Him* we were chosen before the foundation of the world[l]. God hath called us to His eternal glory *in Christ Jesus*[m]. God hath given to us eternal life, and this life is *in His Son*[n]. We become new creatures *in Christ*[o]. And we are created *in Christ Jesus* unto good works[p]. *In Christ* we have redemption through His blood, even the forgiveness of sins[q]; and God hath forgiven us *in Christ*[r], and *in Christ* hath reconciled the world unto Himself[s]; and hath justified us *in Him*[t], and He hath made us accepted

[j] John i. 14. 16. [k] Rom. viii. 39. 1 Cor. i. 4. [l] Eph. i. 4.
[m] 1 Pet. v. 10. [n] 1 John v. 11. 2 Tim. i. 1. [o] 2 Cor. v. 17.
[p] Eph. ii. 10. [q] Col. i. 14. [r] Ephes. iv. 32. [s] 2 Cor. v. 19.
[t] 1 Cor. i. 30. 2 Cor. v. 21. Gal. ii. 17.

in the Belovedⁿ. *In Christ* are hid all the treasures of wisdom and knowledge^x. He pours forth His Spirit upon His people, and they are sanctified *in Him*^y; and *in Him* have strength to serve God, and overcome the enemies of their salvation^z. The blessing of Abraham has come upon the Gentiles in *Christ Jesus*^a. *In Christ* we have fellowship with our fellow Christians, being with them joint members of that Church in which all are one, "where there is neither Jew nor Greek, circumcision nor uncircumcision, barbarian, Scythian, bond nor free, but Christ is all and in all^b."

Thus there is in truth no spiritual blessing which is bestowed upon Christians, but they receive it *from Christ;* and as they receive it from Christ, so He in the first instance received it *for them.* If Christians are anointed with the Holy Spirit^c, it is because the gift was first bestowed upon Christ, that from Him, the Anointed of the Father, it might flow forth to His people. If Christians are endued with spiritual life, it is because, as the Father hath life in Himself, so hath He given to the Son also to have life in Himself^d, and His life is the cause of theirs^e. If Christians are raised from the death of sin here, and if they shall be raised from the death of the body hereafter, and being so raised shall be exalted into heaven, it is because God exerts in them the same mighty power

---

ⁿ Eph. i. 6.   ^x Col. ii. 3.   ^y 1 Cor. i. 2.   ^z Eph. vi. 10.
^a Gal. iii. 14.   ^b Col. iii. 11.   ^c 1 John ii. 20, 27.
^d John v. 26.   ^e John xiv. 19.

which He wrought in Christ, when He raised Him from the dead, and set Him at His own right hand in the heavenly places, quickening them together with Christ, and raising them up together, and making them sit together in the heavenly places in Christ Jesus[f]. And in like manner we might follow out the connexion through a variety of particulars, in which, very observably and surely not without design, the very same words are applied by the sacred writers both to Christians and to Christ. Are Christians, e. g. spoken of as *God's elect people*[g]? It is because Christ is the *elect of the Father*[h], and they are elect in Him[i]. Are Christians called to be *Saints*[k]? Christ is *the Holy One*[l], and they are sanctified in Him. Are Christians, *sons of God*, and, if sons, *heirs, heirs of God, and joint-heirs with Christ*[m]? It is because Christ is *the Son of God and Heir of all things*[n], and they are sons and heirs in Him. Are Christians *Abraham's seed*[o]? It is because Christ is *the seed of Abraham*, and they are accounted such in Him[p]. Are Christians *the light of the world*[q]? It is because Christ is *the Light of the world*[r], and they are light in Him, they shine by His light and reflect His light by which they shine, to the eyes of men. Are Christians made *kings and priests unto God*[s]? It is because Christ is *the King*

---

[f] Eph. i. 19, 20. and ii. 5, 6.   [g] 2 Tim. ii. 10.
[h] Isaiah xlii. 1.   [i] Eph. i. 4.   [k] 1 Cor. i. 2.   [l] Mark i. 24.
[m] Rom. viii. 16, 17.   [n] Heb. i. 2.   [o] Gal. iii. 29.   [p] Gal. iii. 16.
[q] Mat. v. 14.   [r] John ix. 5.   [s] Rev. v. 10.

of kings, and the great High Priest of the Father[t], and they are kings and priests in Him.

In these respects then and the like has Christ, as man, received gifts for men. God hath anointed Him with the oil of gladness above His fellows[u]. Yet in such wise that they also are anointed with Him. The precious ointment which was poured upon the head, hath run down unto the beard and gone down even unto the skirts of His clothing, and the whole world is filled with its odour[x].

And thus, in the very exaltation of our Lord's human nature, we are reminded of the wondrous condescension of His divine. For even to be *capable of exaltation*, is what the eternal Son, *as God only*, could not have stooped to; and to be *capable of receiving*—otherwise than, as the Only-begotten of the Father, He hath received from all eternity from the Father, to be God of God, Light of Light, very God of very God—would but for His manhood have been impossible. But such was His marvellous love, that He, who, as God, is the fountain and source of grace, as man, received grace, that on us He might bestow grace. He, from whom the Holy Spirit proceeds, received the Spirit, that He might make us partakers of the Spirit. He, who dwelt in the bosom of the Father from all eternity, was exalted to the Father's right hand in the heavenly places, that He might exalt us with Himself, and make us partakers

---

[t] Rev. xix. 16. Heb. iv. 14.   [u] Ps. xlv. 7.   [x] Psalm cxxxiii.

of the glory which He had with the Father before the world was.

We have now seen what Christ hath received *from* us, and what He hath received *for* us. He hath received *from us our nature,* that, *as man,* He might render a perfect obedience to His Father's will and fulfil all righteousness; that, *as man,* He might bear our sins in His own body upon the tree; that, *as man,* He might both die for us, and, through death, destroy him that had the power of death, that is, the devil: and in the same nature having been exalted to His Father's right hand in heaven, He hath been made Head over all things to His Church, that receiving from the Father whatsoever blessings are needful whether for His Church collectively, or the members of His Church individually, He may be the fountain of life and grace to His people, quickening them by His Spirit, conforming them to His own divine image, in which man was originally created, and preparing them for that day when He shall complete what He has begun, when He shall raise them from the dead, and exalt them to heaven, and grant them to sit with Him on His throne, even as He is set down with His Father on His throne[y].

Thus Christ is become to us a second Adam; only with these infinite advantages over the first: that whereas the first Adam was made a *living soul,* the second Adam was made a *quickening spirit*[z]; whereas the first man was *of the earth, earthy,* the *second*

[y] Rev. iii. 21. [z] 1 Cor. xv. 45

man is the *Lord from heaven*[a]; whereas the first after fulfilling his appointed term of days, returned to the dust from which He was taken, the second abideth for ever, the perpetual and inexhaustible well-spring of life and immortality to His people. And hence the union which we have with Christ, while in part it corresponds with the connexion which we have with Adam, in part transcends it infinitely. We are *in both*, respectively, as every effect may be said to be in the cause, from which it derives its being: we are *in both*, respectively, inasmuch as we are represented by them in the covenants, in which each stands as the Head and Surety of all belonging to him. But Christ being *the great first cause* and *highest original*, and not only the Author, but also the *Preserver and Conservator*, as well of our spiritual as of our natural life, and having taken man's nature upon Him for the express purpose that of Himself, now both God and man, He might frame His Church, we are *in Him*, as it is impossible we should be in any *subordinate* cause. We dwell in Him, and He in us, we are one with Him, and He with us. We are members of that body of which He is the Head, united to Him by His Spirit, by which He quickens us and abides within us, in a true and living union. And what the Apostle says in reference to the inferior members is strictly applicable in reference to Him, who, as the Head, is the chief member. Whether one member suffer, all the members suffer

[a] 1 Cor. xv. 47.

with it, or one member be honoured, all the members rejoice with it[b]. Christ's sufferings are His Church's sufferings, Christ's exaltation is His Church's exaltation.

And this union is the true basis of the covenant relationship which He bears towards us[c]. As the Husband of His Church, He represents His Church; as the Father of His people, He represents His people; as the first-born among many brethren, He represents His brethren; as the Head of His body, whatsoever He hath done or suffered is accounted as the deed or suffering of His body, and whatsoever of grace or glory He hath received, is given Him for the ornament and exaltation of His body: God's covenant therefore is with Christ, and, in Christ, with His Church, and the individual members of His Church; and thus "all the promises of God in Him are yea, and in Him amen, to the glory of God by us[d]." They are made to Him, and, in Him, to His people. And seeing it is alike impossible that either the Son, to whom they are made, should fail of the conditions, or the Father, by whom they are made, of His word, they are established on an immovable and imperishable basis. O blessed security of our hope, which rests not upon the weakness or fickleness of man, but upon the Almighty strength of Christ, and the unchangeable truth of God!

[b] 1 Cor. xii. 26.   [c] see Gal. iii. 16.   [d] 2 Cor. i. 20.

Thus under whichsoever aspect we regard Him, whether as united to His Church as the Head to the body, in a true and living union; or as the Representative of His Church in the everlasting covenant which His Father made with Him before the world was, Christ is the remedy which the abounding love of God hath provided for the misery of our fallen and ruined race.

1. Did Adam bring death into the world,—the death of the body? Christ is the resurrection and the life: and because He lives, we, if we believe in Him, shall live also? "If the Spirit of Him that raised up Jesus from the dead dwell in you, He that raised up Christ from the dead shall also quicken your mortal bodies by His Spirit that dwelleth in you[d]." "Our corruptible bodies could never live the life they shall live, were it not that here they are joined with His body which is incorruptible, and that His is in ours as a cause of immortality, a cause by removing through the death and merit of His own flesh, that which hindered the life of ours[e]."

2. Again; Did Adam bring condemnation upon his whole race? Christ hath borne the penalty of the broken law, and we have borne it in Him. Christ hath rendered a perfect obedience to His Father's will, and His obedience is ours. God looks upon us no longer as we are in ourselves the guilty children of the first Adam, but as we are in Christ, His Son in whom He is well pleased. "Such we are, (to use

[d] Rom. viii. 11.   [e] Hooker, E. P. v. §. 56.

Hooker's well-known words,) in the sight of God the Father, as is the very Son of God Himself. Let it be counted folly or frenzy or fury whatsoever; it is our comfort and our wisdom. We care for no knowledge in the world but this, that man hath sinned and God hath suffered; that God hath made Himself the Son of man, and that men are made the righteousness of God[f]."

Lastly; Do we derive from Adam a corrupt nature? Is that glorious image of God in which our first father was created, marred and defaced? For this also we have a remedy *in Christ*. For our union with Christ involves necessarily the presence of the Spirit of Christ, insomuch that if any man have not the Spirit of Christ, he is none of His: and where that Spirit dwells, there must be holiness.

Thus, every way, Christ is the remedy for Adam's sin. As in Adam all die, in every sense of which the word death is capable, even so in Christ, and with the like extent of meaning, are all made alive. Our guilt is washed away in His blood; our corruption is cleansed by His Spirit; our death is swallowed up in His victory. In one word, Christ "is made unto us of God wisdom, and righteousness, and sanctification, and redemption, that according as it is written, He that glorieth, let him glory in the Lord[g]."

[f] Hooker on Justification, §. 6.   [g] 1 Cor. i. 30, 31.

SERMON III.

IMPUTED RIGHTEOUSNESS.

"Ipse ergo peccatum, ut nos justitia; nec nostra, sed Dei; nec in nobis sed in ipso: sicut ipse peccatum, non suum, sed nostrum; nec in se sed in nobis constitutum, similitudine carnis peccati, in qua crucifixus est, demonstravit." Augustin. Enchirid. xli.

"Adæ peccatum imputabitur mihi, et Christi justitia non pertinebit ad me?" Bernard. apud Davenant de Justitia habituali. c. xxviii.

"I must take heed what I say: but the Apostle saith, 'God made Him to be sin for us, who knew no sin, that we might be made the righteousness of God in Him.' Such we are in the sight of God the Father, as is the very Son of God Himself. Let it be counted folly, or frenzy, or fury, whatsoever; it is our comfort, and our wisdom; we care for no knowledge in the world but this, That man hath sinned and God hath suffered; that God hath made Himself the Son of Man, and that men are made the righteousness of God." Hooker on Justification, §. 6.

2 Cor. v. 21.

He hath made Him to be sin for us who knew no sin, that we might be made the righteousness of God in Him.

Our blessed Lord, in joining Himself to His Church, was both a giver and a receiver in various respects. The language which He addressed to His Father, He might fitly have spoken to her also—" All Mine are Thine, and Thine are Mine[a]." Thus, He took our nature, and made us partakers of the Divine. He became the Son of man, that we, in Him, might become sons of God. And if it be possible to find a more stupendous instance even than these, of the mutual participation which His people and He have in each other, it is that with which the text furnishes us. God hath made Him to be sin for us, who knew no sin, that we might be made the righteousness of God in Him. Christ received from us that which He had not and could not have of Himself. And we receive in Him that which we have not and cannot have of ourselves. He was made sin for us, we become the righteousness of God in Him.

[a] John xvii. 10.

We have here then an illustration, in the particular instance of the transfer of our sins to Christ, and of our being made the righteousness of God in Him, of the general principle of which I spoke at large in my last Sermon. Christ, whether we regard Him as united to His Church, as the head to the body, in a true and living union, or as the representative of His Church in the everlasting covenant which His Father made with Him before the world was, is the remedy which the abounding love of God hath provided for the evils entailed upon us by the offence of our first father.

These evils, we have seen, consist mainly in an entailed condemnation and a corrupt nature; and the actual transgressions proceeding from the latter, as well as its own inherent sinfulness, have added to the weight of the former. *In Christ* we have deliverance from both; deliverance from the *guilt* of sin, for He has been made sin for us, and we are made the righteousness of God in Him; deliverance from the *power* of sin, for we are made partakers of His Spirit, which flowing from Him to His people, as from the head to the body, assimilates them to Himself, and conforms them to the image of God. And the one deliverance is inseparably connected with the other. He who " once suffered for sins, the just for the unjust, that He might bring us to God[b]," is the same, who, " His own self, bare our

[b] 1 Pet. iii. 18.

sins in His own body on the tree, that we, being dead to sin, should live unto righteousness[c]."

Yet while these two deliverances are inseparably connected, it may be a question, whether they are so *co-ordinately, in that they spring together from one common source,* or *subordinately, in that one is derived from the other.* Is our deliverance from the power of sin the cause of our deliverance from its guilt and condemnation? or are both deliverances to be traced up simply and distinctly, like two separate streams issuing from the same fountain, to their common original?

This might seem, at first sight, a question of little moment. And yet it is the point on which one of the chief controversies with regard to our justification turns. That God is the *efficient cause* of our justification, and Christ the *meritorious and procuring cause,* there is no dispute. That we must have a principle of righteousness within us, and that principle so pregnant with life, that, wherever time and opportunity are given, it will shew itself in the fruits of a holy and religious conversation, is agreed by all parties who have any real earnestness in the matter of their salvation, however men, in the heat of controversy, may have charged their adversaries with denying it: but the question is, Is this the righteousness, which justifies us before God? True though it is, and wrought in us by the operation of Christ's Spirit, is it sufficient to bear the severity of

[c] 1 Pet. ii. 24.

God's righteous judgment? Or must not we rather rest simply and at once and without the interposition of any such medium *upon Christ*, accounting that the ground of our acceptance in the sight of God is not our own inherent but imperfect righteousness, but the perfect righteousness of Christ, ours because of our union with Christ?

This then is the subject which, with God's help, I would to-day bring before you. It shall be my endeavour to shew, that our justification consists, not, as the Church of Rome teaches, in our being *made* righteous, though this also we must be if ever we would reach heaven, but, as our own Church teaches[d], in our being *accounted* righteous, God dealing with us in Christ as though we had perfectly fulfilled the whole law, not because we have done so or can do so, but because our guilt in transgressing the law has been laid upon Christ, whose members we are.

If, in pursuing this plan, I shall make the passage which was read at the outset the basis of such considerations as I shall bring before you, there will be this advantage, in such a method, over what might be thought a more independent course, that I shall be enabled to commit myself more simply and unreservedly to the guidance of the divine word. I pray that both on the present and on such future occasions as I may be permitted to speak from this place, I may have grace to follow that guidance with

[d] Article xi.

all godly sincerity, and that so large a measure of God's Spirit may accompany what shall be spoken, that both our hearts and lives may bear witness to its sanctifying influence. Such subjects, of all others, have need to be studied with a continual view to practice. And indeed this is the only spirit in which we may safely approach any controverted subjects, especially in a time of such unnatural and harassing excitement as the present. "The secret of the Lord is *with them that fear Him*, and He will shew them His Covenant." "The meek will He guide in judgment, and the meek will He teach His way[e]." May He give us "the spirit of knowledge and of the fear of the Lord[f]," and endue us with "meekness of wisdom[g]."

That the righteousness of which the text speaks is the righteousness which forms the ground of our acceptance in the sight of God, is plain from the scope of the Apostle's argument, which is to shew, that the obstacle which formerly stood in the way of our reconciliation with God has been removed, and that we may now draw nigh to Him with confidence as to a most loving Father. "Now then," he says, after declaring that "God was in Christ reconciling the world unto Himself, not imputing their trespasses unto them," and that He had committed to him with others the word of reconciliation,—"now then we are ambassadors for Christ, as though God did beseech you by us, we

[e] Ps. xxv. 14. 9.   [f] Isaiah xi. 2.   [g] James iii. 13.

pray you, in Christ's stead, be ye reconciled to God. For He hath made Him to be sin for us who knew no sin, that we might be made the righteousness of God in Him. We therefore as workers together with Him beseech you also that ye receive not the grace of God in vain." As though he had said, Be ye reconciled to God; for, whereas our iniquities did separate between us and Him, he hath graciously removed the barrier, and provided us with a righteousness, in which we may approach Him acceptably.

The text has two obvious divisions, which mutually throw light upon each other. I. " God hath made Him to be sin for us who knew no sin." This is what Christ hath received from us. II. " That we might be made the righteousness of God in Him." This is what we receive in Him.

I. With regard to the former: It has already been sufficiently shewn in what sense Christ knew no sin; and I need not dwell upon this point now. He took our nature, but not its sinfulness, and He preserved what He took unsullied by the slightest stain from His birth to His death.

And yet God " made Him to be sin for us."

There are two ways in which this may be taken, though they both amount to the same thing in the end. Either, God dealt with our blessed Lord as a sinner, as altogether sinful, nay the word is stronger still, as though He were sin itself, the very personification of sin; or, God made Him a sin-offering, an offering for the sins of the whole world, according to the Prophet's description, " The Lord hath laid on Him the iniquity of us all[h];" and the Baptist's declaration, " Behold the Lamb of God, which taketh away the sin of the world[i]." For the former, we have the structure of the sentence, which, it should seem, designedly contrasts the *sin* which Christ was made for us, with the *righteousness* which we are made in Him[j]. For the latter, we have the fact that the word *sin* (ἁμαρτία) is frequently used for *sin-offering*[k]. Thus, for example, in the fourth chapter of Leviticus we have the following directions given for the sin-offering of the congregation of Israel. " If the whole congregation of Israel sin through ignorance....

[h] Isaiah liii. 6.   [i] John i. 29.   [j] See Chrysost. in loc.

[k] " Nulla igitur voluptate carnalis concupiscentiæ seminatus sive conceptus, et ideo nullum peccatum originaliter trahens; Dei quoque gratia Verbo Patris unigenito, non gratia filio sed natura, in unitate personæ modo mirabili et ineffabili adjunctus atque concretus, et ideo nullum peccatum et ipse committens; tamen propter similitudinem carnis peccati in qua venerat, dictus est et ipse peccatum, sacrificandus ad diluenda peccata. In vetere quippe Lege peccata vocabantur sacrificia pro peccatis: quod vere iste factus est cujus umbræ erant illæ. Hinc Apostolus cum dixisset 'obsecramus pro Christo reconciliari Deo,' continuo subjunxit atque ait, ' Eum qui non noverat peccatum, pro nobis peccatum fecit, ut nos simus justitia Dei in ipso'... id est, Christum pro nobis peccatum fecit Deus cui reconciliandi sumus, hoc est, sacrificium pro peccatis, per quod reconciliari valeremus." August. Enchirid. xli.

when their sin is known, then the congregation shall offer a young bullock *for the sin,* (or *for the sin-offering,* περὶ τῆς ἁμαρτίας,) and bring him before the tabernacle of the congregation, and the elders of the congregation shall lay their hands upon the head of the bullock before the Lord: and the bullock shall be killed before the Lord. And the priest that is anointed shall bring of the bullock's blood to the tabernacle of the congregation, and the priest shall dip his finger in some of the blood, and sprinkle it seven times before the Lord, even before the vail, and he shall put some of the blood upon the horns of the altar, which is before the Lord, that is in the tabernacle of the congregation, (the altar of incense,) and shall pour out all the blood at the bottom of the altar of the burnt-offering, which is at the door of the tabernacle of the congregation..... And he shall carry forth the bullock without the camp, and burn him as he burned the first bullock: *it is the sin of the congregation,*" (ἁμαρτία συναγωγῆς ἐστιν,) where sin is evidently used for *sin-offering,* and so accordingly our tranlators have rendered it, " it is a *sin-offering* for the congregation[1]."

Moreover our blessed Lord is frequently expressly spoken of or referred to in Scripture under the figure of a sin-offering. Thus, " That which the law could not do in that it was weak through the flesh, God sending His own Son, in the likeness of sinful flesh,

---

[1] Lev. iv. 13—21. Compare also Lev. iv. 25. and v. 9.

and *for sin,* (περὶ ἁμαρτίας, the usual term in the Septuagint for a *sin-offering,*) condemned sin in the flesh[m]." And the writer to the Hebrews, referring to the passage from Leviticus just quoted, and other like passages, speaks of Christ as the antitype which the Jewish sin-offering typified. "We have an altar, whereof they have no right to eat, which serve the tabernacle. For the bodies of those beasts, whose blood is brought into the sanctuary by the high priest, for sin, (that is, as sin-offerings, περὶ ἁμαρτίας) are burnt without the camp, (as in the instance above quoted.) Wherefore Jesus also, that He might sanctify the people with His own blood, suffered without the gate:" that is, He was the great and true sin-offering, of which the sin-offerings appointed by the law were but types and shadows[n].

These passages shew, that as the Apostle's term "*sin*" will bear the interpretation *sin-offering,* so there are instances enough elsewhere of Christ's being spoken of as a sin-offering to warrant the interpretation here.

And here we may observe the peculiar suitableness, in connection with the word he had just used, in the Apostle's mention of our blessed Lord's freedom from sin, forasmuch as it was invariably required in the victims to be offered in sacrifice, that they should be without spot or blemish. That which was re-

---

[m] Rom. viii. 3.   [n] Heb. xiii. 10—12. See also ix. 24—28.

quired in the type was pre-eminently fulfilled in the antitype. *He* was " a lamb without blemish and without spot°." " He was manifested to take away our sins, and in Him is no sin ᵖ."

The reason why the *sin-offering* was sometimes called sin, as in the passage in Leviticus above referred to, where the *sin-offering* of the congregation is called the *sin* of the congregation, was, it should seem, that the sin of the offerer was transferred to the victim offered, which was significantly intimated in the prescribed ceremonies. Thus the victim which was to be sacrificed, and which must be free from blemish of every sort, was to be placed before the tabernacle, before the Lord; and the elders of the congregation, as the representatives of those in whose behalf it was to be offered, were *to lay their hands upon its head,* as it were to connect themselves with it, and in token that their guilt was to be transferred from themselves to it. Then it was to be killed, the guiltless and unoffending animal for their sin, and some of its blood sprinkled before the Lord, before the vail of the tabernacle, some put upon the horns of the altar of incense, which was within the holy place, and the rest poured out at the bottom of the altar of burnt-offering at the door of the tabernacle. So many different ways were there in which the blood was to be presented before God, for a memorial. And last of all, the whole carcase was

° 1 Pet. i. 19. ᵖ 1 John iii. 5.

to be carried forth without the camp and there burnt, as though unclean and defiled, and not fit to be retained longer on holy ground.

The transfer of the sins of the offerer to the victim offered, which was intimated by the laying of the offerer's hands upon the victim's head, was indicated with still greater distinctness in the type of the scape-goat, on whose head the high priest was commanded to lay both his hands, and *confess over him all the iniquities of the children of Israel and all their transgressions in all their sins, putting them upon the head of the goat*, and then to send him away, by the hand of a fit man into the wilderness, " and the goat," it is added, " *shall bear upon him all their iniquities into a land not inhabited*[q]."

With these ceremonies the Jews were familiar from their childhood, and in them, though numbers possibly saw nothing but the outward rite, little dreaming of the depth of spiritual meaning hidden under them, the Gospel was virtually taught. As indeed the time of the promise drew nigh, other and clearer intimations were afforded in the more explicit declarations of prophecy, the whole heavens, as it were, being irradiated with the beams of the approaching Sun of righteousness; but yet when Isaiah spoke so explicitly in his fifty-third chapter of the sufferings and atonement of Christ, he, in

[q] Lev. xvi. 21, 22.

effect, declared little more, than the law had already intimated, though less openly, in its types and shadows. He used the same language in reference to the *true*, which it had used in reference to the *typical* sin-offering.

For it was not possible that the blood of bulls and of goats should take away sins[a]. The types of the law and the more express declarations of the prophets all pointed to a higher and better sacrifice, on whose head our iniquities should be laid, and to whose person our guilt should be transferred. And thus, as I observed at the outset, it comes to the same thing, whichever of the two meanings we put upon the word "*sin*" in the passage we are considering, "God hath made Him to be sin for us, who knew no sin," He hath transferred our guilt to Christ, He hath dealt with Him as though He were not merely a sinner, but sin, the very personification of sin, as though all the sins of all the world were concentrated in Him.

And it is very much to be remarked, how the whole history of our Lord's passion corresponds to this. It was surely not without design that the death by which He died was a public and judicial one, and that while on the one hand, there were so many (and these independent) testimonies to His innocence, on the other, all the principal circum-

[a] Heb. x. 4.

stances connected with His death tended to represent Him as a malefactor.

Thus, His judge, even while he gave sentence upon Him, acquitted Him: "I am innocent," he said, "of the blood of this just person," and vainly washed his hands in token that he disowned all participation in the guilt of His death[t]. And Pilate's wife's message was to the same effect: "Have thou nothing to do with that just man[u]." Herod's conviction agreed with Pilate's: "I having examined Him," said Pilate, "have found no fault in Him ... no, nor yet Herod[x]." We have besides the testimony of one of His fellow-sufferers: "We indeed justly,....but this man hath done nothing amiss[y];" and of the centurion who watched Him while He hung upon the cross: "Certainly this was a righteous man[z]." Nay, the very people who stood by beholding the crucifixion, many of whom, no doubt, had joined in the murderous cry, Crucify Him, Crucify Him, went away smiting their breasts, as though acknowledging His innocence and their own and their nation's guilt[a].

Here then were so many independent testimonies to His innocence. Not less remarkable are the multiplied instances of His being dealt with as a malefactor. Thus, when He was first apprehended, He was apprehended as a malefactor. And His

[t] Matt. xxvii. 24. [u] ib. v. 19. [x] Luke xxiii. 14, 15. [y] ib. v. 41. [z] ib. v. 47. [a] ib. v. 48.

words spoken to those who apprehended Him shew how keenly He felt the indignity. "Are ye come out *as against a thief*, with swords and staves for to take Me[b]?" When He was condemned by the Jews, He was condemned as a malefactor[c]. When He was delivered up to Pilate, He was delivered up as a malefactor: "If He were not a malefactor, we would not have delivered Him up unto thee[d]." When He was given over to be put to death, a malefactor was released, and He retained for punishment[e]. And the death by which He died was the death of a malefactor,—the death of the cross, a death accounted infamous by the Gentiles and accursed by the Jews. Nay, as though this were not enough to stamp His character with the brand of infamy, He must have two companions in His death, and they likewise malefactors[f]. And to complete all, when man had done his worst, to blacken and traduce His good name, and there seemed nothing left but that hidden stay of innocence in the midst of outward trials, the calm sunshine of God's presence felt within, even this was denied Him. For our sins, now become His, had hid His Father's face from Him, and He gave utterance to that cry which indicates perhaps the deepest and the most

---

[b] Matt. xxvi. 55. See Barrow's Sermon "Upon the Passion of our Blessed Saviour." Serm. xxxii.

[c] ib. v. 65, 66. [d] John xviii. 30. [e] Luke xxiii. 25.
[f] ib. v. 32, 33.

mysterious of His sufferings, " My God, my God, why hast Thou forsaken Me[g]?"

Thus was that innocent and most holy Person " numbered with the transgressors[h]," thus was He " wounded for our transgressions," thus was He " bruised for our iniquities," thus was " the chastisement of our peace upon Him[i]," thus, in one word, did God make " Him to be sin for us who knew no sin."

There are two passages which I shall notice separately as harmonizing very remarkably with the one under our consideration, and conveying most strikingly the same idea of the transfer of our sins to Christ.

1. That David, in the fortieth Psalm, speaks in the person of Christ, is put beyond a doubt by the author of the Epistle to the Hebrews, who quotes verses 6, 7, and 8, expressly as the words of Christ, declaring that He had come to be the true sin-offering for the sins of the world[k]. Now observe, in what perfect consistency with the figure of the sin-offering, though now the reference to that figure is dropped, Christ, whose words they are, is represented as speaking in the twelfth verse. " Innumerable evils," He says, " have compassed Me about; *mine iniquities* have taken hold upon Me so that I am not able to look up; they are more than the hairs of my head: therefore my heart faileth Me." And yet of

[g] Matt. xxvii. 46. [h] Isaiah liii. 12. [i] ib. v. 5.
[k] Heb. x. 5. &c.

H

Himself He knew no sin. But they were our iniquities transferred to Him, and made His by reason of His union with us, which pressed thus heavily upon His soul, and made it exceeding sorrowful even unto death. The Lord laid on Him the iniquity of us all. He took it off from us and charged it on Him. And it was not less in testimony of His meekness and patience, than in acknowledgment of the justice of the punishment under which He suffered, that He was so silent under His sufferings. And, as it has been truly remarked, "though His enemies dealt most unjustly with Him, yet He stood as convicted before the judgment-seat of His Father, under the imputed guilt of all our sins, and so eyeing Him, and accounting His business to be chiefly with Him, He did patiently bear the due punishment of all our sins at His Father's hands; according to that of the Psalmist, ' I was dumb, I opened not my mouth, because Thou didst it.' For which reason also, the prophet immediately subjoins the description of His silent carriage, to that which He had spoken of, the confluence of our iniquities upon Him: ' As a sheep before her shearers is dumb, so He openeth not His mouth[1].' "

2. We have the same truth taught us under another image in the Epistle to the Galatians: " Christ," saith the Apostle, " hath redeemed us from the curse of the law, being made a curse for us[m]." Both Jews and Gentiles (and St. Paul, as is evident

---

[1] Leighton on 1 Pet. ii. 24.   [m] Gal. iii. 13.

from the following verse, contemplates both) were under the curse. The Gentiles, as obnoxious to the ancient curse entailed by Adam on all His descendants; the Jews, over and above, as having come short of the requirements of the law, which pronounced a curse on every one that continued not in all things that were written in the book of the law to do them. How then shall any find deliverance? Christ hath redeemed us from the curse of the law, being made a curse for us. He who, on His own account, was obnoxious to no curse; He in whose favour is life, and the light of whose countenance is the everlasting joy of His people; He in whom men shall be blessed, and whom all the generations of the redeemed throughout eternal ages shall call blessed, became a curse for us. The curse was taken from our heads, and laid on His[a].

In this sense did God make His most holy Son to be sin for us, transferring our sins to Him, and dealing with Him as though He were laden with the iniquities of the whole world.

Here then we have an unquestionable instance,

[a] Ἐπεὶ οὖν καὶ ὁ κρεμάμενος ἐπὶ ξύλου ἐπικατάρατος, καὶ ὁ τὸν νόμον παραβαίνων ἐπικατάρατος, μέλλοντα δὲ ἐκείνην λύειν τὴν κατάραν ὑπεύθυνον οὐκ ἔδει γενέσθαι αὐτῆς, δεῖ δὲ δέξασθαι κατάραν ἀντ' ἐκείνης, τοιαύτην ἐδέξατο, καὶ δι' αὐτῆς ἐκείνην ἔλυσε. Καὶ καθάπερ τινὸς καταδικασθέντος ἀποθανεῖν, ἕτερος ἀνεύθυνος ἑλόμενος θανεῖν ὑπὲρ ἐκείνου, ἐξαρπάζει τῆς τιμωρίας αὐτόν· οὕτω καὶ ὁ Χριστὸς ἐποίησεν. Ἐπειδὴ γὰρ οὐχ ὑπέκειτο κατάρᾳ τῇ τῆς παραβάσεως, ἀνεδέξατο ὁ Χριστὸς ἀντ' ἐκείνης ταύτην, ἵνα λύσῃ τὴν ἐκείνων. Ἁμαρτίαν γὰρ οὐκ ἐποίησεν, οὐδὲ δόλος εὑρέθη ἐν τῷ στόματι αὐτοῦ. Chrysost. in Gal. iii. 13.

and that in the very point in hand, of *imputed guilt:* and shall we hesitate to admit, what rightly understood, is its inseparable correlative, *imputed righteousness?* If our sins have been transferred to Christ, then can they no longer be reckoned to our account. God's justice forbids Him to inflict on us the punishment which Christ hath already borne and He hath accepted on our behalf. And that eternal attribute of His which was before against us, is now on our side. And " if God be for us," as the Apostle triumphantly asks in language which conveys throughout the idea of *forensic* proceedings, " who can be against us? He that spared not His own Son, but delivered Him up for us all, how shall He not with Him also freely give us all things? Who shall lay any thing to the charge of God's elect? It is God that justifieth. Who is He that condemneth? It is Christ that died; yea rather that is risen again, who is even at the right hand of God, who also maketh intercession for us°."

And this view may prepare us for the more particular consideration of the righteousness which we become in Christ, so far forth as it is the ground of our acceptance with a righteous God.

II. The Scriptures, both in the Old and New Testament, speak of a twofold righteousness; *a righteousness imputed,* as when it is said that Abraham " believed in the Lord, and He counted it to him for righte-

° Rom. viii. 31—34.

ousness^p;" and *a righteousness inherent*, as in those words of St. John, " Little children, let no man deceive you; he that doeth righteousness is righteous^q." And in like manner the verb " to justify" is used both of *accounting* or *pronouncing righteous*, and of *making righteous*, though in the former sense, much more frequently than in the latter.

If however we look to those places, where the ground of our acceptance in the sight of God is spoken of, we shall find that the words are both used in a *forensic* sense,—righteousness, of *a righteousness accounted*, not *inherent*, to justify, of *accounting* or *pronouncing*, not *making righteous*. This has been often proved in detail^r; and I shall content myself with referring to two passages, one in which the sinner's justification is distinctly introduced, the other in which it is the subject which the sacred writer is treating expressly and of set purpose.

1. The first occurs in St. Paul's speech to the Jews at Antioch in Pisidia: " Be it known unto you, men and brethren, that through this Man is preached unto you the forgiveness of sins; and by Him all that believe *are justified* from all things from which ye could not be justified by the law of Moses^s:" where to be justified is plainly the same as to have forgive-

---

^{p} Gen. xv. 6. $\qquad$ ^{q} 1 John iii. 7.

^{r} See Bp. Andrewes' Sermon on Justification in Christ's name; Barrow's Sermons on the Creed, Serm. 5. Of Justification by faith; Bp. Bull, Harmon. Apostol. Diss. Prior. c. 1; Whitby's Preface to the Epistle to the Galatians; Waterland on Justification.

^{s} Acts xiii. 38, 39.

ness of sins. And it is all one as though the Apostle had said, By Him all that believe receive forgiveness of those sins, for which the law of Moses offered no forgiveness. For many sins the law had its prescribed sacrifices; the offerer laid his hands upon the head of the victim, his guilt was transferred to it, and he was thenceforward dealt with as an innocent person, both ceremonially, and also, through the virtue of the true sacrifice, the great sin-offering, really. There were other sins of a graver kind for which no sacrifice was appointed. But for these also, the Apostle says, provision is now made in Christ, and if we would express in other words what that provision is, we could not find any so fit to our purpose, as those with which he has himself furnished us in our text: " God was in Christ reconciling the world unto Himself, not imputing their trespasses unto them;" for which purpose, " He hath made Him to be sin for us who knew no sin, that we might be made the righteousness of God in Him[t]."

2. The other passage to which I refer, and which extends over part of the third and throughout the fourth chapter of the Epistle to the Romans, will require a fuller consideration, inasmuch as Justification is not here touched upon incidentally and by the way, but is treated of expressly and of set purpose. St. Paul enters upon the subject immediately on opening his Epistle, declaring that to reveal the righteousness of God, or, in other words, that righteousness, which God both requires and

[t] See Bp. Bull, Harmon. Apostol. Diss. Prior. c. 1. §. 4.

gives in order to our salvation, was one of the characteristic glories of the Gospel. Then, after shewing at considerable length the misery of all mankind, both Jews and Gentiles, in their natural state, and their utter inability to stand before God in a righteousness of their own, seeing that there is none righteous, no not one, so that every mouth must be stopped, and all the world brought in guilty before God, (observe how in the very approach to the subject we are prepared for a forensic righteousness,) he proceeds, towards the end of the third and throughout the fourth chapter, to describe the righteousness which the Gospel has brought to light, which yet had been intimated, though not clearly revealed, by both the Law and the Prophets.

Now I would remark, in the first place, that he speaks of this righteousness, *as God's righteousness,*—God's righteousness bestowed upon those, who, in themselves, were altogether void of righteousness. "For all have sinned," he says, repeating what he had elaborately proved in the former part of his argument, "and come short of the glory of God." And if it be God's righteousness, bestowed upon those, who, being in themselves altogether void of righteousness, are represented as standing at God's bar, without one word to plead in arrest of judgment, every mouth stopped, all the world guilty before God, the very law to which some at least were disposed to look, as though it would plead in their favour, only raising its voice to condemn them,—I say, if it be God's righteousness bestowed upon persons so circumstanced, this alone is a strong presumption that it is a *righteousness accounted*, not a *righteousness infused*.

It has been urged indeed that the righteousness which God works in His servants by the operation of His Spirit, may well be termed *God's righteousness* as distinct from any righteousness wrought in our natural strength and the fruit of our unassisted efforts. Let us see then, whether a further consideration of the passage we have in hand, does not exclude the one sense as well as the other, and constrain us to accept the Apostle's words as referring to an *extrinsic righteousness*.

Now St. Paul proceeds to describe it as a righteousness "which is by faith of Jesus Christ unto all and upon all them that believe." And on this ground he declares that *it shuts out boasting*. "For," says he, instancing the case of Abraham, "if Abraham were justified by works, he hath whereof to glory, though even so, not before God;" because his works, whatsoever they were, so far as they were good, must be traced up to God, as their true author. "For what saith the Scripture? Abraham believed God, *and it was counted unto him for righteousness. Now to him that worketh is the reward not counted of grace but of debt*"—it is not imputed as a matter of favour, freely bestowed, where no claim could be preferred,—it is a *debt due*. "But to him that worketh not, *but believeth on Him that justifieth the ungodly*, his faith is *counted for righteousness*." Here then plainly is an extrinsic righteousness, a righteousness not inherent but imputed; a righteousness bestowed as a matter of grace and favour, not a righteousness which can claim a reward.

I may add with regard to the description here given of God's character, "He that justifieth the ungodly," that though the expression, taken by itself, might possibly signify, as they who contend for justification by an inherent righteousness would maintain, *to make righteous* those who before were unrighteous, yet, taken with its context, " to him that worketh not, but believeth on Him that justifieth the ungodly, *his faith is counted to him for righteousness,*" there can be no doubt but that it is to be understood in the forensic sense, of *accounting righteous, pronouncing righteous.* Nor is it to be passed over, that the expression is the very same as that in the Prophet, " Woe unto them which justify the wicked for reward, (οἱ δικαιοῦντες τὸν ἀσεβῆ is the Septuagint Version,) and take away the righteousness of the righteous from him[u]," where the forensic sense is unquestionable. It might indeed be objected, that according to the sense of justification we have been contending for, God is represented as dealing with us in the very manner which he here reprobates in those inferior magistrates, who are, in some sort, his representatives to men. But this very objection confirms the view which has been taken, for it is precisely the objection which St. Paul felt that his doctrine was liable to, as is apparent from his adding, after he had been explaining the steps which God

---

[u] Isaiah v. 23.

had taken towards the justification of the ungodly, "that he may be just, and the justifier of him that believeth in Jesus." No doubt the justification of the ungodly could not but seem incompatible, at first sight, with our ideas of God's justice, and must remain so, but for the wondrous scheme, which he first devised for *our* justification, and then revealed for *his own*ʷ. But where would have been the difficulty, or apparent inconsistency, if the Apostle had used the word "justify" in the sense of *making righteous?* That God should *make righteous* those who before were unrighteous, is what all can understand; but that the just Judge of all the earth should forgive, freely forgive, those who had trampled upon His righteous laws, this was indeed a marvel, which could not be explained, till it was revealed how "God was in Christ reconciling the world unto Himself, not imputing their trespasses unto them," and this by making "Him to be sin for us who knew no sin, that we might be made the righteousness of God in Himˣ."

The Apostle had referred to the case of Abraham: still further to prevent mistake, and to shew that

---

ʷ "Sed quæ, inquis, justitia est ut innocens moriatur pro impio? Non est justitia, sed misericordia... At vero si justitia non est, non tamen contra justitiam est: Alioquin et justus et misericors simul esse non posset." Bernard. Exhort. ad mil. Templi, c. xi.

ˣ See a similar instance of the forensic sense of δικαιόω, Gal. ii. 17. Εἰ δὲ ζητοῦντες δικαιωθῆναι ἐν Χριστῷ, εὑρέθημεν καὶ αὐτοὶ ἁμαρτωλοί, ἆρα Χριστὸς ἁμαρτίας διάκονος; Such a supposition could not have been put where to be justified meant to be *made righteous*.

the righteousness he spoke of consists *not in the infusion of righteousness,* but *in the forgiveness of unrighteousness,* he adduces David as a witness, quoting, from the thirty-second Psalm, his description of the righteousness in which we must stand, if we would find acceptance before God: " Even as David also describeth the blessedness of the man to whom God imputeth righteousness without works." And in what doth this righteousness consist? "Blessed are they *whose iniquities are forgiven, and whose sins are covered; blessed is the man to whom the Lord will not impute sin.*" The Psalmist adds, "and in whose spirit there is no guile." But the Apostle, it is worthy of remark, omits this clause, as though, while it describes the state of heart which inseparably accompanies justification, it was yet beside his immediate object, which was to set forth the righteousness, which God imputes to us, not, works in us.

But we have not yet exhausted St. Paul's account of the righteousness we are considering. Not only does he speak of it as God's righteousness, thereby excluding our own righteousness, not only does he speak of it as a righteousness bestowed upon faith, thereby excluding works, shutting out boasting, making it a matter of grace and favour, and not of debt; not only does he expressly call it a righteousness *accounted,* but he proceeds to describe it particularly, and, in describing it, represents it as consisting not in an inherent righteousness, but *in the forgiveness of unrighteousness.* "All have sinned," he says, "and come short of the glory of God, being *justified freely* by His grace, through the redemption that is in Christ Jesus, whom God hath set forth to be a propitiation through faith in His blood, to declare His righteousness, for the remission of sins that are past, through the forbearance of God." Every word here points to a righteousness accounted, not inherent. The persons justified *sinners;* the justification bestowed upon them bestowed *freely, by God's grace;* the procuring cause of their justification, *the redemption that is in Christ Jesus*, with regard to which expression if we consult the Apostle for his own sense of his own words, we have it twice repeated in the self-same terms, once in the Epistle to the Ephesians, once in that to the Colossians. "In whom we have redemption through His blood, *even the forgiveness of sins*[r];" or, as he proceeds to explain himself here, "to declare His righteousness *for the remission of sins that are past* through the forbearance of God."

I have dwelt the longer on this passage, because it is one in which the sinner's justification before God is treated of expressly and of set purpose. And the clear testimony of one such passage is a sufficient answer to arguments drawn from the interpretation of other passages which are either less explicit, or which do not professedly treat of the subject in question. Bellarmine[s] attempts to force upon the Apostle's words the sense of an inherent righteousness, by urging that in the expression, "being

[r] Eph. i. 7. Col. i. 14.   [s] De Justificatione, lib. ii. c. 3.

justified freely by His grace," "*by His grace*" must mean *grace infused*. But even if the words were ambiguous, they would be of no avail against the overwhelming current of testimony running throughout the whole passage in the opposite direction. So far however from being ambiguous, they occur again a few verses further on in a sense which cannot be mistaken: "To him that worketh the reward is not reckoned *of grace*, but of debt," where *grace* is opposed to *debt*, and can only signify *that which is given freely and without claim*. With regard to the other passages[a], which Bellarmine adduces in proof that the righteousness by which we are justified is an inherent righteousness, they either come under the description above referred to, or else they plainly do not touch the subject at all. The utmost they prove is, that every justified person has an inherent righteousness, which is no matter of dispute. But it is one thing to prove that the Christian must have an inherent righteousness, another, that that inherent righteousness is the ground of his acceptance with a righteous God[b].

[a] Rom. v. 17, 18, 19. (on which, with reference to Bellarmine's remarks, see Barrow's Sermon on Justification by Faith.) 1 Cor. vi. 11. Tit. iii. 7. Heb. xi. 4, 7. Rom. viii. 29. 1 Cor. xv. 49. Rom. vi. 7. Rom. viii. 10. See Bp. Davenant on each of these passages, De Justitia habituali, c. xxiii.

[b] The same may be said of much that is alleged from the Fathers, who often use the words *Justification* and *Justify* indifferently of an inherent and an imputed righteousness. Controversy had not yet led men to weigh their expressions with

We have seen then in what sense the word *righteousness* is to be taken, when we speak of our justi-scrupulous accuracy. But yet the *things* themselves are distinguished plainly enough. " Illud præmittendum, quod Vasques observavit," says Bishop Davenant, " hanc controversiam de formali causa justificationis, a Patribus non tam exacte discussam, quam alteram de necessitate gratiæ ad operandum, quam contra Pelagii hæresin egregie illustrarunt. Si itaque aliquis patrum, propter arctam illam cognationem et individuam concatenationem gratiæ infusæ sive inhærentis cum gratia remissionis ac imputatione justitiæ Christi, hæc inter se commiscere videatur, non debemus nos idcirco illa confundere, quæ Spiritus Dei in Sacris Scripturis accurate solet distinguere. Illud etiam in memoriam revocandum est, nos contra inhærentem justitiam non pugnare : talem siquidem qualitatem infundi agnoscimus in actu justificandi ; sed asserimus tamen, remissionem peccatorum nostrorum, receptionem in favorem divinum, acceptationem ad æternam vitam, non ab hac qualitate dimanare, aut ea niti; sed gratuita Dei misericordia propter Christum, Christique obedientiam nos a peccatis absolventis, et ad æternam vitam acceptantis. Neque huic sententiæ nostræ reclamare patres illico judicandi sunt, si *justificandi* vocabulum ad justitiæ infusionem aliquando referant : nam idem vocabulum diverso sensu, non modo a patribus, sed etiam ab ipsis Scripturis quandoque usurpatur. Non itaque jam quærimus de diversis hujus vocabuli *justificationis* apud patres significationibus, sed, (quod theologicæ disquisitionis proprium est) de ipso dogmate justificationis quid illi senserint indagamus....
............Non negandum est, Augustinum uti *justificationis* vocabulo sub duplici sensu. Aliquando enim ex mente Apostoli, per *justificationem* intelligit gratuitam absolutionem a peccato, et acceptationem ad vitam æternam, per et propter obedientiam Mediatoris fide apprehensam : ut in Psalmum tricesimum primum, ' Si justificatur impius, ex impio fit justus. Sed quomodo ? Nihil boni fecisti, et datur tibi remissio peccatorum.' Multo planius, ' Quantælibet fuisse virtutis antiquos prædices justos, non eos

fication in God's sight. How aptly this sense is suited to the passage which we set out by considering will be apparent, whether we look at the structure of the sentence in which it occurs, or to the scope of the context. As Christ was made sin for us, in that our sins were laid on Him, so we become the righteousness of God in Him, in that God, beholding us in Him, deals with us as righteous persons, as persons in whom no spot of sin is to be found, and against whom no charge can be preferred; just as beholding Christ standing in our stead, He dealt with Him as a sinner, yea as charged with the sins of the whole world.

And that this is the true sense of the word *righteousness* in the passage before us, that it signifies an *imputed* not an *inherent* righteousness, a righteousness *accounted to us* not *wrought in us*, is further evident from the context. For the subject on which the Apostle is engaged, and on which, to the second verse of the following chapter, he continues to dwell,

salvos fecit, nisi fides mediatoris, qui in remissionem peccatorum sanguinem fudit.' (*Contra Duas Epist. Pelag.* lib. i. c. 21.) Sed aliquando, ex Latinæ vocis structura, per justificationem intelligit actionem Dei infundentem et imprimentem nobis gratiam habitualem sive justitiam inhærentem. Hoc igitur sensu dicit Pelagianos oppugnare illam gratiam qua justificamur, hoc est rejicere sanctificantem gratiam qua justitia perfundimur: sed interim non dicit hanc gratiam in nobis ad tantam perfectionem pervenisse, ut justificationis priore sensu acceptæ causa formalis habeatur." *Davenant de Justit. habituali*, c. xxv.

is the gracious message which had been given him to deliver—that " God was in Christ reconciling the world unto Himself, *not imputing their trespasses unto them.*" Where the implied ground of their reconciliation is not a righteousness which God found in them, or infused into them, but simply *the forgiveness of their unrighteousness*[d]. And it is to be observed, that the reconciliation of the sinner to God was the proper end of the legal sin-offerings, and they attained their end, so far as they did attain it, by the removal of the cause of enmity—by the transfer of the sins of the offerer to the victim offered. The victim was dealt with as though polluted with sin, the offerer, as though he were free from guilt. When therefore the Apostle proceeds to intreat the Corinthians, " We pray you, in Christ's stead, be ye reconciled to God," and follows up his intreaty by adding, " For He hath made Him to be sin for us who knew no sin, that we might be made the righteousness of God in Him," he is evidently declaring *how* God in Christ did reconcile the world unto Himself, and in order to this how He took away the sins of the world, namely, that, as under the law, in the case of such sins as had sacrifices prescribed for them, the sins of the offerer were transferred to the victim, so, under the Gospel, our sins are transferred to Christ, and we stand before God as righteous persons in Him not on the ground of an inherent

[d] " Ubi reconciliatio ibi remissio peccatorum; et quid ipsa nisi justificatio?" Bernard.

righteousness which we have in ourselves, though this also, whatsoever it be, is from Him, but of the forgiveness of our unrighteousness which we have in Christ. It is true, and a most deeply important truth it is, that under the law certain dispositions were required in the offerer: the sacrifice of the wicked was an abomination to God[e]; men must wash their hands in innocency who would come to God's altar with acceptance[f], that is, they must come with a sincere hatred of sin, and full purpose of forsaking it, and with a sure trust in God's mercy. And, in like manner, under the Gospel, whoever would be a partaker of the benefits of Christ's sacrifice, must draw nigh in true penitence, and with a lively faith, and with the sincere purpose of a holy life. These are indispensable, as dispositions or conditions required on our parts—though these also are from God. But the real ground of acceptance is in the one case, as it was in the other, not an inherent righteousness, but the forgiveness of unrighteousness. "God was in Christ reconciling the world unto Himself, not imputing their trespasses unto them." Their trespasses were the grand barrier, which separated between them and their God, and the least trespass as effectually as the greatest. God reconciled the world unto Himself by taking away the barrier. And He did so by laying those trespasses upon Christ, so making Him to be sin for us

[d] Prov. xv. 8.   [f] Ps. xxvi. 6.

who knew no sin, that we might be made the righteousness of God in Him.

"God made a righteous person to be a sinner," says St. Chrysostom, commenting upon this passage, "that he might make sinners righteous. Or rather, the Apostle saith not this, but what is much more—for the word he uses designates not the habit, but the quality. He saith not, God made him to be *a sinner;* but, God made him to be *Sin;* and not merely, Him who never sinned, but, who did not even know sin. And all this, that we might be made, not *righteous,* but more, *righteousness,* yea, *the righteousness of God.* For truly this is the righteousness of God, when we are justified not of works, for then no stain or spot of sin must be found, but of grace, where all sin is wholly taken away[k]." A passage most distinctly recognising the doctrine, that we are justified not by an inherent, but by an

---

[k] Τὸν μὴ γνόντα ἁμαρτίαν, φησὶ, τὸν αὐτοδικαιοσύνην ὄντα, ἁμαρτίαν ἐποίησε· τουτέστιν, ὡς ἁμαρτωλὸν κατακριθῆναι ἀφῆκεν, ὡς ἐπικατάρατον ἀποθανεῖν . . . . . . Τὸν γὰρ δίκαιον, φησὶν, ἐποίησεν ἁμαρτωλὸν, ἵνα τοὺς ἁμαρτωλοὺς ποιήσῃ δικαίους. Μᾶλλον δὲ οὐδὲ οὕτως εἶπεν, ἀλλ' ὃ πολλῷ μεῖζον ἦν· οὐ γὰρ ἕξιν ἔθηκεν, ἀλλ' αὐτὴν τὴν ποιότητα· οὐ γὰρ εἶπεν ἐποίησεν ἁμαρτωλὸν, ἀλλ' 'Αμαρτίαν· οὐχὶ τὸν μὴ ἁμαρτόντα μόνον, ἀλλὰ τὸν μηδὲ γνόντα ἁμαρτίαν· ἵνα καὶ ἡμεῖς γενώμεθα, οὐκ εἶπε, δίκαιοι, ἀλλὰ Δικαιοσύνη, καὶ Θεοῦ Δικαιοσύνη. Θεοῦ γάρ ἐστιν αὕτη, ὅταν μὴ ἐξ ἔργων, ὅταν καὶ κηλίδα ἀνάγκη τινὰ μὴ εὑρεθῆναι, ἀλλ' ἀπὸ χάριτος δικαιωθῶμεν, ἔνθα πᾶσα ἁμαρτία ἠφάνισται. Τοῦτο δὲ ὁμοῦ οὔτε ἐπαρθῆναι ἀφίησιν, ἅτε τοῦ Θεοῦ τὸ πᾶν χαρισαμένου, καὶ διδάσκει τοῦ δοθέντος τὸ μέγεθος. Ἐκείνη γὰρ ἡ προτέρα νόμου καὶ ἔργων δικαιοσύνη, αὕτη δὲ Θεοῦ δικαιοσύνη. Chrysost. in 2 Cor. v. 21.

imputed righteousness, a righteousness so perfect that it admits of no blemish.

It will be observed, that in the enquiry into the nature of Justification, which has now been made, I have proceeded altogether irrespectively of the *rationale*, if I may so speak, which was alluded to at the outset, and to establish which was the object of the preceding discourse, depending upon the mutual participation which Christ and His people have in each other. I was anxious to establish the doctrine by simply following out the teaching of Scripture in such passages as expressly refer to it. And thus much I trust has been shewn: that our guilt has been transferred to Christ, and that God deals with us as righteous persons, not because of an inherent righteousness, but because He mercifully passes by our unrighteousness.

But when the Apostle adds that we are made "the righteousness of God *in Christ*," our thoughts are carried forward of necessity to that wondrous union which subsists between Christ and His people, and the doctrine, though, to all intents and purposes, the same, is seen under another aspect, or rather from another point of view. If we are Christ's true servants, He is one with us and we with Him; our sins He bore, as though they had been His own, and His perfect obedience is put down to our account. When He suffered, God beheld in Him, as it were, the whole family of His redeemed people, whose representative He was, and who, being in Him, suffered in Him. And when He was released from the bonds of death, for that it was not possible He should be held by them, and dealt with by the Father, as though all the demands of Divine justice were now satisfied, we were released in Him, and justified in Him. God first justified the Head, that in Him He might justify the members. Our Lord's death, especially under the circumstances of shame and ignominy and desertion with which it was accompanied, might well have seemed in the sight of both men and angels—at least of evil angels—a visible demonstration of His guilt. But the resurrection, followed, as it was, first by the ascension, and afterwards by the outpouring of the Holy Spirit upon His disciples, wiped away every aspersion from His character. It was now plain beyond all question, that God had made that same Jesus, whom the Jews had crucified, both Lord and Christ. He, whom Satan had once bidden, as though he doubted his pretensions, "*If* Thou be the Son of God, command that these stones be made bread[h];" He whom the Jews had once bidden, as though they were confident of His imposture, "*If* Thou be the Son of God, come down from the Cross[i]," was now "declared to be the Son of God with power according to the Spirit of holiness, by the resurrection from the dead[k];" and His ascension into heaven, and His session at His Father's right hand, together with the outpouring of the Spirit on

---

[h] Matt. iv. 3.   [i] Matt. xxvii. 40.   [k] Rom. i. 4.

those who believed on Him and were willing to accept His offered grace, completed in all its parts the great mystery of godliness. "God was manifest in the flesh, *justified* in the Spirit, seen of Angels, preached unto the Gentiles, believed on in the world, received up into glory[l]." And we are only following out the Apostle's principle, who hath taught us that God exercises the same power " to usward who believe, according to the working of His mighty power which He wrought in Christ," in that He hath quickened us together with Him and raised us up together, and made us sit together in heavenly places in Christ Jesus[m], in saying that when God "*justified*" His Son, He did so, not for His Son's sake alone, but for theirs also who should believe in Him, that they might be *justified together with Him*. And thus Christ is " the Lord our righteousness"," "the Lord in whom all the seed of Israel,—the true Israel of God, His believing people,—shall be justified and shall glory[o]." And He " is made unto us of God wisdom and righteousness and sanctification and redemption, that according as it is written, He that glorieth, let him glory in the Lord[p]."

Nor is this view of the mutual interchange between Christ and His people, which is founded upon the intimate union which subsists between them, a modern invention. St. Augustine, in his Commen-

---

[l] 1 Tim. iii. 16.   [m] Ephes. i. 19,—ii. 6.   [o] Jer. xxiii. 6. Isaiah xlv. 25.   [p] 1 Cor. i. 30, 31.

tary on Psalm xxii, has some remarks on the first and second verses, which shew how fully he recognised the principle, in its application to the particular case of the transfer of our sins to Christ, and Christ's righteousness to us. " Why," he asks, " when God the Word was made flesh and did hang upon the Cross, and cried, ' My God, my God, look upon me, why hast Thou forsaken me?' why are these words spoken, but because *we* were there present, because the Church is Christ's body?" . . . . " Far from my salvation are the words of my sins," the Psalm continues, according to the old Latin version; on which he remarks, " What sins, when the Scripture saith of Him, ' Who did no sin, neither was guile found in His mouth?' How then doth He say Of my sins, but because it is for our sins He prays, and because He made our sins His sins, that He might make His righteousness our righteousness[q]?

[q] August. in Ps. xxi. §. 3. " Et cum Verbum Deus factum esset caro, pendebat in cruce, et dicebat ' Deus meus, Deus meus, respice me: quare me dereliquisti?' Quare dicitur, nisi quia nos ibi eramus, nisi quia Corpus Christi Ecclesia? Utquid dixit, ' Deus meus, Deus meus, respice me: quare me dereliquisti?' nisi quodammodo intentos nos faciens et dicens, Psalmus iste de me scriptus est? ' Longe a salute mea verba delictorum meorum.' Quorum delictorum, de quo dictum est. ' Qui peccatum non fecit, nec inventus est dolus in ore ejus?' Quomodo ergo dicit ' Delictorum meorum,' nisi quia *pro delictis nostris ipse precatur, et delicta nostra sua delicta fecit, ut justitiam suam nostram justitiam faceret?*" On the same principle of interpretation he continues, " ' Deus meus, clamabo ad te per diem, et non exaudies; et nocte, et non ad insipientiam mihi?' dixit

This may serve to shew that the *doctrine* which has been insisted upon is no modern invention. Let the following passage from St. Bernard exemplify the *practical application* which was made of it in earlier times. " I have sinned grievously," he says, " my conscience is distressed, but it shall not be overwhelmed in its distress. For I will remember His wounds who was wounded for our iniquities. And what so deadly which the death of Christ cannot undo?.........And therefore he erred who said, My sin is too great for me to merit pardon, unless it were that he was not of Christ's members, and had therefore no right in Christ's merit, so as to call that his own which belonged to Christ—the member to call that its own which belonged to the head. For my own part what I have not in myself, I draw confidently from the mercies of my Lord..........As for my merit, it is the Lord's mercy. I cannot lack merit, so long as He did not lack mercies. And if the mercies of the Lord be manifold, my merits also, in

---

utique de me, de te, de illo; corpus enim suum gerebat, id est, Ecclesiam. Nisi forte putatis, fratres, quia quando dixit Dominus, ' Pater, si fieri potest, transeat a me calix iste,' mori timebat. Non est fortior miles quam imperator. Sufficit servo ut sit sicut Dominus ejus. Paulus dicit, miles regis Christi, ' Compellor et duobus, concupiscentiam habens dissolvi et esse cum Christo;' Ille optat mortem ut sit cum Christo, et ipse Christus timet mortem? Sed quid nisi infirmitatem nostram portabat, et pro his qui adhuc timent mortem in corpore suo constitutis, ista dicebat? Inde erat illa vox, membrorum ipsius vox erat, non capitis; sic et hic, ' Per diem et noctem clamavi, et non exaudies.'"

spite of my sins, are manifold. What though I am conscious of manifold sins! Where sin abounded, grace did much more abound. And if the mercies of the Lord are from everlasting to everlasting, I also will sing of the mercies of the Lord for ever. What! shall I sing of my own righteousnesses? No, Lord, I will make mention of thy righteousness only; for that is mine too. Thou art made unto me of God righteousness. Should I fear lest that one righteousness which Thou art made should not serve us both? It is no short cloak, that it should not, to use the Prophet's words, cover twain. Thy righteousness is an everlasting righteousness, and what is longer than everlasting? Behold thy ample and everlasting righteousness will amply cover both Thee and me at once. In me it covereth a multitude of sins: in Thee, Lord, what doth it cover, but the treasures of goodness, the riches of bounty¹!"

¹ "Revera ubi tuta firmaque infirmis securitas et requies nisi in vulneribus salvatoris? Tanto illic securior habito, quanto ille potentior est ad salvandum. Fremit mundus, premit corpus, diabolus insidiatur, non cado, fundatus enim sum supra firmam petram. Peccavi peccatum grande, turbabitur conscientia, sed non perturbabitur, quoniam vulnerum Domini recordabor. Nempe 'vulneratus est propter iniquitates nostras.' Quid tam ad mortem, quod non Christi morte solvatur? Si ergo in mentem venerit tam potens tamque efficax medicamentum, nulla jam possum morbi malignitate terreri. Et ideo liquet errasse illum qui ait 'major est iniquitas mea quam ut veniam merear.' Nisi quod non erat de membris Christi, nec pertinebat ad eum de Christi merito, ut suum praesumeret, suum diceret, quod illius esset, tanquam rem capitis

membrum. Ego vero fidenter quod ex me mihi deest usurpo mihi ex visceribus Domini, quoniam misericordia affluunt............... Meum proinde meritum miseratio Domini. Non plane sum meriti inops, quandiu ille miserationum non fuerit. Quod si misericordiæ Domini multæ, multus nihilominus ego in meritis sum. Quid enim si multorum sim mihi conscius delictorum? Nempe, ' ubi abundavit delictum, superabundavit et gratia.' Et si ' misericordiæ Domini ab æterno et usque in æternum,' ego quoque ' misericordias Domini in æternum cantabo.' Nunquid justitias meas? Domine memorabor justitiæ tuæ solius? Ipsa est enim et mea: nempe factus es mihi tu justitia a Deo. Nunquid mihi verendum, ne non una ambobus sufficiat? Non est pallium breve, quod secundum Prophetam, non possit operire duos. ' Justitia tua justitia in æternum.' Quid longius æternitate? Et te pariter et me operiet largiter larga et æterna justitia. Et in me quidem operit multitudinem peccatorum; in te, autem, Domine, quid nisi pietatis thesauros, divitias bonitatis?" Bernard. Serm. lxi. in Cant. §. 3, 4, 5. Elsewhere he writes: " Quid enim? unus peccavit, et omnes tenentur rei, et unius innocentia soli reputabitur uni? Unius peccatum omnibus operatum est mortem, et unius justitia uni vitam restituet? Itane Dei justitia magis ad condemnandum quam ad restaurandum valuit? Aut plus potuit Adam in malo, quam Christus in bono? Adæ peccatum imputabitur mihi, et Christi justitia non pertinebit ad me? Illius me inobedientia perdidit, et hujus obedientia non proderit mihi? Sed Adæ, inquis, delictum merito omnes contrahimus, in quo quippe omnes peccavimus: quoniam cum peccavit, in ipso eramus, et ex ejus carne, per carnis concupiscentiam, geniti sumus. Atqui ex Deo multo germanius secundum Spiritum nascimur quam secundum carnem ex Adam; secundum quem etiam spiritum longe ante fuimus in Christo quam secundum carnem in Adam; si tamen et nos inter illos numerari confidimus, de quibus Apostolus: ' Qui elegit nos,' inquit, ' in ipso' (haud dubium quin Pater in Filio) ' ante mundi constitutionem.'" Bern. Exhortat. ad milites Templi, c. xi.

SERMON IV.

INHERENT RIGHTEOUSNESS.

"Sic itaque omnes, quicunque in hac vita divinarum Scripturarum testimoniis in bona voluntate atque actibus justitiæ prædicati sunt, et quicunque tales vel post eos fuerunt, quamvis non eisdem testimoniis prædicati atque laudati, vel nunc usque etiam sunt, vel postea quoque futuri sunt; omnes magni, omnes justi, omnes veraciter laudabiles sunt, sed sine peccato aliquo non sunt: quoniam Scripturarum testimoniis, quibus de illorum laudibus credimus, hoc etiam credimus, non justificari in conspectu Dei omnem viventem; ideo rogari, ne intret in judicium cum servis suis; et non tantum universaliter fidelibus omnibus, verum etiam singulis esse orationem dominicam necessariam, quam tradidit discipulis suis." Augustin. de Peccat. Mer. et Rem. lib. ii. §. xiv.

"Sed audi quid etiam hinc te admoneat beatus Hilarius. Cum enim exponeret Psalmum quinquagesimum primum, 'Spes,' inquit, 'in misericordia Dei in sæculum et in 'sæculum sæculi est. Non enim ipsa illa justitiæ opera 'sufficient ad perfectæ beatitudinis meritum, nisi miseri-'cordia Dei etiam in hac justitiæ voluntate, humanarum 'demutationum et motuum non reputet vitia. Hinc illud 'prophetæ dictum est: Melior misericordia tua super vitas.' Videsne hominem Dei ex illo numero esse beatorum, de quibus prædictum est, 'Beatus vir cui non imputavit Dominus peccatum, neque est in ore ejus dolus?' Confitetur enim etiam peccata justorum, magis eos asserens in Dei misericordia spem ponere quam de justitia sua fidere." Augustin. contra Julianum Pelagianum, lib. ii. §. viii.

2 Cor. v. 17.

If any man be in Christ, he is a new creature.

"WHAT shall we say then?" asks the Apostle, after he had been setting forth at large the doctrine of Justification by faith in Christ, and, as though anticipating an objection which both in his own and in subsequent times, would be urged against it— "What shall we say? Shall we continue in sin, that grace may abound? God forbid. How shall we that are *dead* to sin, *live* any longer therein[a]?" The same mercy which has provided a remedy for the *condemnation* entailed upon us by our first father, has provided a remedy also for the *corruption of nature* which we have derived from the same source. And the same sacrament which, by God's appointment, is the *bath*[b] in which we are *washed* from the *guilt* of our sins, is, by the same appointment, the *grave*[c], in which our old nature is buried, and from which we are raised again unto newness of life. "If any man be *in Christ*, he is a *new creature*," he has passed into an entirely new state of existence, he has a new life, in a new world, with new relation-

[a] Rom. vi. 1, 2.   [b] Acts xxii. 16. Tit. 3. 5.   [c] Rom. vi. 4.

ships, new desires, new hopes, new fears, new faculties. Once, he was an alien from the commonwealth of Israel, and a stranger from the covenants of promise[d]; now he is a fellow-citizen of the saints and of the household of God[e]; he was sometimes far off, now in Christ Jesus he is made nigh by the blood of Christ[f]. He was sometimes darkness, now he is light in the Lord[g]. He was the slave of sin[h]—sold under sin[i]—led captive by Satan at his will[k]—now sin has no more dominion over him[l]; for the law of the Spirit of life in Christ Jesus hath made him free from the law of sin and death[m]. Thus, every way, old things are passed away, all things are become new; and all things are of God, who hath reconciled us to Himself by Jesus Christ, and hath blessed us with all spiritual blessings in Him.

And yet it is the great unhappiness of the most of us, that we pass through life without any adequate conception, in many cases without any thought at all, of the high privileges which belong to us, and of the grace and strength treasured up for us, in Christ—ours to use to God's glory, or to neglect to our own condemnation. It was the knowledge of our proneness this way which led the Apostle to pray for his converts, (and he mentions it in that Epistle which more than any other is full of the great subject of our union with Christ,) that God would

---

[d] Ephes. ii. 12.   [e] Ephes. ii. 19.   [f] Ephes. ii. 13.
[g] Ephes. v. 8.   [h] John viii. 34. 2 Pet. ii. 19.   [i] Rom. vii. 14.
[k] 2 Tim. ii. 26.   [l] Rom. vi. 14.   [m] Rom. viii. 2.

give unto them the Spirit of wisdom and revelation in the knowledge of Him, the eyes of their understanding being enlightened, that they might know what is the hope of His calling, and what the riches of the glory of His inheritance in the saints; and what the exceeding greatness of His power to them who believe, according to the working of His mighty power, which He wrought in Christ, when He raised Him from the dead, and set Him at His own right hand in the heavenly places[n]. Assuredly unless we do know and consider these great gifts, we shall never rise to high attainments in the divine life. But it is the prevailing fault, whether from sloth, or unbelief, or a worldly spirit, or the low standard which we set ourselves and countenance in others, that we toil feebly on, beset with doubts, complaints, and scruples, to the end of our course, instead of arising in the full confidence of faith, and going cheerfully on our way, strong in the grace that is in Christ Jesus. Nor is it too much to say, that numbers, if they were asked the question which St. Paul asked the disciples at Ephesus, "Have ye received the Holy Ghost since ye believed?" might answer, as far as to any practical purpose they are acquainted with Him, almost in the very words of those disciples, "We have not so much as heard whether there be any Holy Ghost[o]."

This then is the point to which our enquiry has now brought us. We have considered the provision

[n] Ephes. i. 17—20.   [o] Acts xix. 2.

which God's rich mercy hath made for our deliverance from the *guilt* of sin. We are now to consider the provision which the same rich mercy hath made for our deliverance from its *power*. The *principle* of this deliverance is contained in this simple truth: that whosoever is truly united to Christ—a living member of His mystical body—is a *partaker of the Spirit of Christ*. It was the Holy Spirit who united us to Christ in the first instance—and it is by the indwelling of the same Spirit in our hearts, now that we are united to Him, that our union is maintained and preserved, insomuch that should that blessed Being be provoked to abandon us, our union with Christ is at an end.

Thus then, when God adopts a man into His family, and gives him an inheritance among his children, He does not leave him to continue such as he was before: but He endues him with grace whereby he may walk worthy of his high calling, and grow in meetness for the heavenly home which He destines for him. By nature we are altogether sinful; there is no health, no life in us; we are dead in trespasses and sins: by grace, we are partakers of a new principle—a divine principle— a principle of life and holiness. Not indeed that the new principle destroys and annihilates the old, in this present life. The two coexist together in the Christian while he continues on earth. The flesh lusteth against the Spirit, and the Spirit against the flesh. In those who are not under the influence of divine grace—there is but one of these principles—the flesh reigns supreme. And in heaven again, there will be but one of these principles—the Spirit will reign supreme. But here on earth they are both found in every true servant of God. But how found? Not in a state of peace, but of warfare. And if the Christian is prospering in the divine life, then the Spirit is gaining victory after victory over the flesh. The new principle of holiness is spreading and increasing and strengthening itself, while the old principles of sin is losing ground, and becoming weaker and weaker day by day[p].

For it should be added, that although Scripture expressly speaks of the new nature, as given to all who are truly united to Christ, yet its whole tenour goes upon the supposition that that heavenly principle needs to be cherished and put forth and exercised. Thus in the very passage where it is declared so expressly that "our old man is crucified with Christ," and we are enjoined to "reckon ourselves to be dead indeed unto sin, but alive unto God through Jesus Christ our Lord," the Apostle mingles

---

[p] "Ita quamvis ibi (in Baptismo) peracta fuerit plena peccatorum remissio, remansit tamen, qua proficeretur in melius, adversus catervas desideriorum malorum in nobis ipsis utique tumultuantium vigilanter exserenda et instanter exercenda luctatio, propter quam dicitur etiam baptizatis 'Mortificate membra vestra quæ sunt super terram;' et, 'Si Spiritu facta carnis mortificaveritis, vivetis;' et 'Exuite vos veterem hominem.'" August. contr. Julian. Pelag. lib. vi. §. xviii.

exhortations with his declarations and injunctions; "Let not sin therefore reign in your mortal body that ye should obey it in the lusts thereof. Neither yield ye your members as instruments of unrighteousness unto sin: but yield yourselves unto God, as those that are alive from the dead [q]." The truth is, that while the Holy Spirit dwells in all Christ's members, all are not equally under His influence. His presence with us is vouchsafed according to our faithfulness. We may neglect, grieve, quench, do despite to, and utterly drive from us the Spirit of grace, or we may cherish His sacred influence, and stir up the gift of God which is within us, and be filled more and more with the Spirit, being renewed, day by day, in the likeness of Him that created us, and so changed into the same image from glory to glory even as by the Spirit of the Lord.

This may suffice for a *general* view of our condition such as it is *in Christ*. I shall proceed to follow it out into detail, shewing in each of the particulars, which were mentioned, on a former occasion, as indicating the sad effects of the fall, how Christ is the remedy which the abounding love of God has provided for the misery entailed upon us by the sin of Adam.

1. Foremost in the long train of evils which followed upon the fall is *ignorance*. Man lost the knowledge of God, and of his true good. His understanding became darkened; and (what made

[q] Rom. vi. 12, 13.

his case past hope) " he *loved* darkness rather than light." Thus it is with every man in his natural state. There may be great knowledge of the things of this world, great shrewdness—wit—genius—learning;—and yet the knowledge of those truths, which, above all others, we are concerned to know, may be wanting, nay, despised and counted foolishness. Indeed in nothing are the humiliating effects of the fall more apparent than in the perversion of the understanding, whereby great mental powers and acquirements are made, when they are not sanctified, obstacles in the way of divine knowledge instead of helps to it. " Ye see your calling, brethren," writes the Apostle, " how that not many wise men after the flesh—not many mighty, not many noble are called; but God hath chosen the foolish things of the world to confound the wise;........and things which are despised hath God chosen, yea and things which are not, to bring to nought things that are[r]."

As then ignorance of God and of the things of God and the love of that ignorance are the foremost in the long train of evils which Adam's sin brought upon his race; so the knowledge of God and of the things of God and delight in that knowledge, and a thirst for larger and larger supplies of it, are the precursors of whatsoever blessings God bestows upon us in Christ. Light was the first thing created in the natural world. It is the first in the spiritual.

[r] 1 Cor. i. 26—28.

And this knowledge God communicates to us by producing in us the spirit and temper of little children. "I thank thee, O Father, Lord of heaven and earth, because Thou hast hid these things from the wise and prudent, and *hast revealed them unto babes*[a]." A deep sense of our own ignorance—willingness to be taught—submission of the understanding to the divine word, lie at the foundation of it. The great truths of the Gospel were, in St. Paul's day, as foolishness in the world's eyes. And so they still are, till men are brought to receive the truth in the love of it. Then, long cherished prejudices melt away, the obstacles which pride and regard for human opinion had raised, are removed, and men are willing to become fools that they may become wise.

Thus the Christian is renewed in knowledge, after the image of Him that created him[b]. And if he is faithful to the light given, he goes on increasing in knowledge day by day. By the study of God's word, by the observation of God's providence, by watching the motions of his own heart, by holding communion with God in prayer and other divine ordinances, by intercourse with his fellow-Christians—his acquaintance with religious truth is not only enlarged and deepened, but becomes more heartfelt and experimental. Once he had heard of God by the hearing of the ear, but now his eye seeth Him. Once, eternal things had no charm for him, his thoughts

[a] Matt. xi. 25.   [b] Col. iii. 10.

were engrossed with the matters of time and sense, now he rejoiceth at God's word as one that findeth great spoil", and he counts all things but loss for the excellency of the knowledge of Christ Jesus his Lord˟. Or if he have not reached this standard, it is what he is continually striving after, and making nearer and nearer approaches to.

If it be asked how the Christian obtains his knowledge? He has it *from Christ* his Head, who is made unto Him of God wisdom, and in whom are hid all the treasures of wisdom and knowledge. And the Holy Spirit is his Teacher; whose office it is to receive of the things of Christ, and to shew them unto His peopleˠ. The natural man receiveth not the things of the Spirit of God, for they are foolishness unto Him; neither can He know them, because they are spiritually discerned. But he that is spiritual judgeth all things. And he hath received the Spirit which is of God, that he may know the things which are freely given us of God˟. But yet while the Holy Spirit is his teacher—diligence and pains-taking are no less necessary on his part, than in the case of human learning. Rather indeed they are more necessary, for a man has to attend to his heart as well as to his understanding, lest the one should come under the influence of some corrupt bias, and so the other be warped from the truth. Solomon's directions for the study of divine wisdom imply all this: " My son, if

---

" Ps. cxix. 162.   ˟ Phil. iii. 8.   ˠ John xvi. 14.
˟ 1 Cor. ii. 12—15.

thou wilt receive my words, and hide my commandments with thee, so that thou incline thine ear unto wisdom, and apply thy heart to understanding, yea if thou criest after knowledge, and liftest up thy voice for understanding; if thou seekest her as silver, and searchest for her as for hid treasures, then (and not otherwise) shalt thou understand the fear of the Lord, and find the knowledge of God[a]."

Thus then in respect of his *understanding*, the Christian is a new creature in Christ.

2. And it is the same with respect to his *affections*. God is dethroned in the heart of the natural man. He is not loved; He is not feared. Other lords beside Him have the dominion. Man lives to himself and to the world. And the God in whose hand his breath is, and whose are all his ways, he does not glorify.

But it is otherwise with him, who is under the influence of Christ's Spirit. God, who, before, was regarded with indifference, or as an object of dread, if not of secret dislike, is now seen, in Christ, *as a Father*. " Because ye are sons," says the Apostle, " God hath sent forth the Spirit of His Son into your hearts, crying Abba, Father[b]." And the Christian learns to draw nigh to Him with the confidence of a child, (though tempered with holy awe and lowly reverence,) as remembering that He is his Father *which is in heaven*. He now sees God every where, and recognises His hand in every occurrence, and

[a] Prov. ii. 1—5. [b] Gal. iv. 6.

wonders that he did not before; and is ready to say, as Jacob when he awoke from his sleep, "Surely the Lord is in this place, and I knew it not[e]." Now, God is both loved and feared; and faith, while it apprehends, more and more, His infinite goodness and His infinite majesty, increases both affections. And with these is joined trust and alliance, so that he who once perhaps was liable to be disquieted and filled with anxious fears, is now enabled to cast all his care upon God, (knowing that He careth for him)—his care not only for things temporal, but for things spiritual also. And thus the peace of God keeps his heart, so that like a citadel garrisoned by Almighty strength, it may laugh at foes without. And yet further, the remembrance of God's great mercies in Christ Jesus begets thankfulness, and thankfulness stirs up to holy obedience. And the more he serves God, the more he loves God, and the more he loves, the more he serves.

And while the love of *God* is thus shed abroad in the Christian's heart by the Holy Spirit which is given him, the love of *man* follows in its train. The Christian learns to love all men, because all are in one sense the objects of his Father's love; but Christ's servants most, for they are so in an especial sense.

In these respects then, as regards his affections, the Christian is a new creature in Christ. Old things

[e] Gen. xxviii. 16.

are passed away, all things are become new. Once, he was swallowed up in his own petty concerns, engrossed with self, or at most looking no further than to the little circle in which he moves. Now, his heart is warmed with the love of God and the love of man. God's glory, Christ's honour, the Church's prosperity, the welfare spiritual and temporal of all around him, affect him sensibly. He offers up those petitions in the Lord's prayer—" Hallowed be Thy Name, Thy kingdom come, Thy will be done in earth as it is in heaven"—with a depth and earnestness of feeling which before he could not have realized. And his actions correspond to his feelings. He lays himself out, and exerts himself and denies himself in doing so, to further the cause of God and the welfare of men by all means possible.

Perhaps there is nothing in which the change which has passed upon him is more sensible, than in his view of prayer and the use he makes of it. Real, earnest prayer, is the first symptom of spiritual life. There was a time when he knew nothing of this. When prayer, if resorted to at all, was resorted to as the last resource, a sort of forlorn hope, when other hopes failed. He had no delight in it, he knew nothing of its spirit, he had no consciousness of the sweet and blessed privilege which it offers of communion with God, of the comfort which it ministers in sorrow, the strength in weakness, the decision in difficulty, or of its chastening, tranquillizing influence in joy. But now he has been taught something of its efficacy. And instead of its being his last resource, it is his first. Nothing is now begun to his mind which has not been begun with prayer. And having once commended himself and his affairs to his Father's care, he is enabled to leave them calmly in His hands, however dark and gloomy the prospect may be. Why should he be anxious? Did ever faith and waiting upon God fail of their reward?

And here again, if it be asked, Whence is this change? How comes it, that he who once cared not for God, neither was God in all his thoughts, now loves God with childlike affection, and fears Him with holy fear? How comes it, that he who was once absorbed in himself, now almost forgets himself in his thoughtfulness for others? How comes it that he who was once a stranger to prayer, now counts prayer his privilege and joy? How comes it, that he who was once apt to be harassed and disquieted by the prospect of dangers, can now look forward with calmness and confidence, in the full assurance that all shall eventually be well?—The answer is still the same. He is a new creature *in Christ*. And all these blessed dispositions have been wrought in him by the Spirit of Christ. Not that he has reached this measure of attainment at once, or without effort. It is what he has been long aiming at and striving after, and now that he has reached it, he forgets what is behind, and thinks only of further progress.

3. Another respect in which the Christian has undergone a change is in *the government of himself, and the subjection of the lower appetites to reason and conscience.*

In nothing are the sad consequences of the fall felt more sensibly than in the rebellion of the lower appetites. Even the natural conscience has light sufficient to discern that the harmony of the divine laws is broken, and that man is not what he ought to be in this respect. Good is approved, but not followed; evil hated, but not shunned. Man is sometimes deliberately and with full consciousness his own enemy: and at others he is borne along in spite of himself, all his higher thoughts and purposes of good swept away by the torrent of corruption. And the knowledge of God's law, if it checks the torrent for a moment, checks only to swell and increase its force. "I delight in the law of God after the inward man," says the Apostle, " but I see another law in my members warring against the law of my mind, and bringing me into captivity to the law of sin which is in my members. O wretched man that I am! who shall deliver me from the body of this death[d]!"

Christ shall deliver thee. The law of the Spirit of life in Christ Jesus hath made thee free from the law of sin and death. "For what the law could not do, in that it was weak through the flesh, God sending His own Son in the likeness of sinful flesh,

[d] Rom. vii. 22—24.

and for sin, condemned sin in the flesh, that the righteousness of the law might be fulfilled in us, who walk not after the flesh, but after the Spirit[e]." So that in this respect also, the Christian is a new creature in Christ. Grace is given him whereby he may bring under and subdue the flesh; and in proportion as he is faithful to that grace will be his success. Not that he may hope to *annihilate* his enemy on this side of heaven. While he carries about a mortal body, that body must be the scene of unceasing conflict[f]. If one evil habit be for a time overthrown, another rises in its stead—new circumstances bring to light oftentimes corruptions, of the very existence of which within us we were not aware. Is thy servant a dog that he should do this? we should have been disposed to ask, till the event proved that, but for divine grace, there is nothing so vile which we might not be led on to do. We may not hope then to *annihilate* the evil which is inwrought within us. But we may

---

[e] Rom. viii. 2—4.

[f] " Quid aliud in mundo quam pugna adversus diabolum quotidie geritur? quam adversus jacula ejus et tela conflictationibus assiduis dimicatur? Cum avaritia nobis, cum impudicitia, cum ira, cum ambitione congressio est: cum carnalibus vitiis, cum illecebris sæcularibus assidua et molesta luctatio est. Obsessa mens hominis et undique diaboli infestatione vallata vix occurrit singulis, vix resistit. Si avaritia prostrata est, exsurgit libido; si libido compressa est succedit ambitio; si ambitio contemta est, ira exasperat, inflat superbia, vinolentia invitat, invidia concordiam rumpit, amicitiam zelus abscindit." Cyprian. de Mortalitate.

hope by God's grace to keep it in check, and to bring it into subjection, and this increasingly, if only we are faithful to the grace given us[g]. But this faithfulness implies the most unwearied diligence, watchfulness, self-discipline, and steady resistance to our natural sloth. And unwillingness to put forth such strenuous efforts, and to continue in them unto the end, is the cause of the frequent failures and shameful discomfitures of which we have so often to complain. God is not wanting to us, but we to ourselves; and being wanting to ourselves we are wanting to God also. For allowed negligence and indulged sloth destroy the simple childlike trust in God, and confidence in His help, and consequent believing earnest application to Him for His grace, which are the sinews of the Christian's strength.

4. There is yet another respect in which the

---

[g] " Quamdiu ergo peregrinantes a Domino per fidem ambulamus, non per speciem, unde dictum est, 'Justus ex fide vivit,' hæc est nostra in ipsa peregrinatione justitia, ut ad illam perfectionem plenitudinemque justitiæ, ubi in specie decoris ejus jam plena et perfecta charitas erit, nunc ipsius cursus rectitudine et perfectione tendamus, castigando corpus nostrum et servituti subjiciendo, et eleemosynas in dandis beneficiis, et dimittendis quæ in nos sunt commissa peccatis, hilariter et ex corde faciendo, et orationibus indesinenter instando; et hæc faciendo in doctrina sana, qua ædificatur fides recta, spes firma, charitas pura. Hæc est nunc nostra justitia, qua currimus esurientes et sitientes ad perfectionem plenitudinemque justitiæ ut ea postea saturemur." S. August. de Perfec. Justit. §. viii.

Christian has undergone a change. When Adam fell, he brought both himself and his whole race under the power of Satan. Thenceforward Satan became the god of this world; and he still rules in the plenitude of his power in the hearts of those who know not God.

But Christ hath broken the tyrant's yoke. He first met and overcame the evil one Himself; and now, in Him, His people are armed for the conflict, and strengthened to resist and subdue the enemy. The world is still under Satan's sway. But God hath gathered His people out of the world in one sense, while He still leaves them in it in another. He hath gathered them out of the world, in that He hath delivered them from the power of darkness, and translated them into the kingdom of His dear Son; setting them in His Church, across whose hallowed bound Satan's sway does not extend. He still leaves them in the world, for His Church is still sojourning on earth, and they are in the world, like men in a garrison in an enemy's country—safe while they remain within the walls of the city of God, but in peril the instant they wander forth.

The condition of the Christian then in respect of Satan is, that as he renounced him in his baptism, so he has been formally delivered from his power. He is not *of* that world, which lieth in wickedness and is under the dominion of the wicked one. He has been turned from darkness to light, and from the power of Satan unto God. He is one with Christ and Christ with him, and therefore he has Almighty strength engaged in his defence. He is one with Christ and Christ with him, and therefore he is a partaker of the Spirit of Christ, and by that Spirit he is enabled for whatsoever conflicts with the evil one he may have to enter upon. But conflict he must look for, as long as he continues in the Church militant here below. Most distinct and emphatic are the warnings, given us in Holy Scripture to this effect—though they who are most concerned in them treat them too often as though they meant nothing. It is not a little remarkable that St. Paul closes that Epistle, in which of all others he speaks most largely of the glorious privileges which we have in Christ, by reminding those to whom he writes of the enemy they have to contend with and the warfare that awaits them, and shews them the armour with which they must array themselves for the conflict. And no general ever addressed his soldiers on the eve of battle in words which could give a more lively idea of the formidable nature of the struggle in which they were about to engage, or the momentous issue that was at stake, or the necessity for unwearied exertion, than that which the Apostle's exhortation conveys[h].

The difference between the Christian and the man who has no part in Christ, is simply that which our Lord describes in His parable. In the one, the strong man armed keepeth his palace, and his goods

[h] Ephes. vi. 10—20.

are in peace: Satan rules with unresisted sway. In the other, a stronger than the strong man has come upon him and overcome him, and taken from him all his armour wherein he trusted, and divided his spoils. But yet the strong man is still permitted to be at large, and the Christian has need of all his vigilance to keep himself from again falling under his power; and not of his vigilance only, but of that better strength which is treasured up for him in Christ, who shall ere long so wholly bruise Satan under the feet of His servants, that he shall never again rise up to molest them.

In these various respects then is the Christian *a new creature* in Christ. He is renewed in *knowledge*. He is renewed in his *affections*. The power of *indwelling sin* is broken. He is delivered from *the yoke of Satan*. And all this by virtue of his hidden union with Christ, and the grace and strength ministered to him by the Spirit of Christ. And he has *motives* to obedience now which he had not formerly. For fear he has love, because the love of God is shed abroad in his heart by the Holy Spirit which is given him; and yet he has fear too; but the fear of a son, not of a slave. For the spirit of bondage, he has the spirit of freedom. Instead of a reluctant constrained service, which seemed to be measured by the standard, what is the least which is required of me? he now runs the way of God's commandments, because God hath set his heart at liberty; and the question which he asks is no longer what is the least which is required, but what shall I render unto the Lord, for all His benefits towards me?

And the *effects* in his life and conversation are answerable, in exact proportion to the care with which he maintains his union with his Lord, and the fidelity with which he yields himself to the guidance of the Holy Spirit. His faith may fail, like that of the Israelites, when they should have marched forward to take possession of the land of Canaan, and in this way he may look off from Christ; or he may lean upon himself, and go forth in his own strength, like Samson, when the Lord had withdrawn from him the superhuman aid with which He had been wont to strengthen him, and in this way again he may look off from Christ; or, on the other hand, he may be slothful and indolent, neglecting the Apostle's caution, to watch and be sober, and so grieve that blessed Spirit who has vouchsafed to take up his abode within him—in any of which cases, discomfiture and shame are sure to follow. But let him only be true to his Lord and to himself, and he shall go from strength to strength, gaining fresh victories over sin, growing in conformity to the divine image, and bringing forth more and more abundantly the fruits of righteousness which are by Jesus Christ, to the glory and praise of God.

Such is the provision which God has graciously made for the restoration of that divine image which Adam lost. As in Christ we have deliverance from the guilt of sin, so in Christ we have deliverance from its power. And the one deliverance is inseparably connected with the other. Whom God justifies, them He also glorifies, adorning them with the graces of the Spirit here[a], as earnests and forecasts of that perfect holiness with which He will array them hereafter, when He shall present His church unto Himself a glorious church, not having spot or wrinkle or any such thing.

And this blessed consummation God's faithful servants in all ages have longed for and pressed after to the end of their earthly pilgrimage, as the highest object of their most deeply cherished desires; not counting themselves even to the last day of their sojourn here to have attained, or to be already perfect, but following after, if that they might apprehend that for which they have been apprehended of Christ Jesus; and thus forgetting those things which are behind, and reaching forth unto those which are before, they have pressed towards the mark, for the prize of their high calling of God in Christ Jesus[b].

The true Christian then is not merely *accounted* righteous, but he has a *principle of righteousness* implanted in his heart, which brings forth the fruit of actual righteousness in his life and conversation, according as time and opportunity are given; and thus he is justly called and really *is* righteous. And

---

[a] So the Apostle's meaning is interpreted by Chrysostom, Theodoret, Œcumenius, and Theophylact; see Whitby, Preface to the Ep. to the Galatians.   [b] Phil. iii. 12—14.

this righteousness is indispensable to his admission into that holy heaven, where the people shall be all righteous^c, and into which nothing that defileth shall enter^d.

And here we are again led to the question which was the subject of our consideration in the preceding discourse; whether our inherent righteousness can form the ground of our acceptance with a righteous God. It was there shewn from the *direct* teaching of Scripture, that our justification consists not in our being *made* but in our being *accounted* righteous. The same conclusion is forced upon us by the consideration of the actual nature of the inherent righteousness which we have. True though that righteousness is, and well-pleasing to God in Christ, it is not sufficient to stand the severity of God's righteous judgment, much less to merit the reward of eternal life.

And yet Bellarmine does not scruple to maintain, that the righteousness of the Christian, the righteousness infused into him by the Holy Spirit—whether the *habitual* righteousness communicated in the first instance, or the *actual* righteousness which is its fruit—may be such as to preclude the necessity of our having recourse to the imputation of Christ's righteousness^e.

---

^c Isaiah lx. 21.   ^d Rev. xxi. 27.

^e Bellarm. de Justificat. lib. ii. c. 7. " Dicunt (adversarii) imputationem hanc propterea necessariam esse, non solum quod

But is this the teaching of God's word, or in accordance with the experience of God's Saints?

"Behold, I Paul say unto you," the Apostle writes to the misguided Galatians, "that if ye be circumcised, Christ shall profit you nothing. For I testify again to every man that is circumcised, that he is *a debtor to do the whole law*. Christ is become of no effect unto you, whosoever of you are justified by the law; ye are fallen from grace[f]." And does not the Apostle's argument hold in full force, though the law by which justification is sought, be no longer the Jewish law with its burthensome ceremonial; but the law which is the guide of the Christian's conduct, and the rule by which he will be judged? Whosoever will be justified by the law, whatever law that be, *makes himself a debtor to do the whole law*. That his righteousness is a true righteousness, that it is wrought in him by Christ's Spirit, that it is well-pleasing unto God for Christ's sake, these considerations will not avail him in the position in which he

vere peccatum in nobis perpetuo hæreat, sed etiam quod justitia nostra inhærens non tam sit perfecta, ut simpliciter et absolute justificet. At *causam istam* facile refutabimus, si Scripturis sanctis adversarii fidem habere voluerint. Nam justitia inhærens, sive renovatio interior in fide, spe, et charitate, potissimum sita esse cognoscitur.......Quare *si probaverimus fidem, spem, et charitatem in hac vita posse esse perfectam*, probatum quoque erit, non esse necessariam imputationem justitiæ Christi. And he then proceeds to adduce arguments, such as, in his judgment, are sufficient to prove, that faith, hope, and charity may be in perfection even in the present life.

[f] Gal. v. 2—4.

has placed himself. He has removed his cause out of that court in which God could be just and at the same time the justifier of him that believeth in Jesus, and has placed it where God can have respect to nothing but the work done; and where the question is, not *by whose aid* that work has been done, but *what is the standard* which it has reached? Is the righteousness attained a *perfect* righteousness?

And what is the unvarying testimony both of Scripture and experience on this point? If regard be had to the existence of a living principle of righteousness, nothing can be more plain than that such a principle is found in all God's servants, by reason of which they are justly called and really are righteous. But if the question be whether this their righteousness is so perfect that it can endure the severity of God's strict judgment, then do they all, with one voice, disclaim such a righteousness, and they truly the most earnestly who approach the nearest to it. "Whom though I were righteous," says one speaking of God, "yet would I not answer," as though not daring to rest on his righteousness, " but I would make supplication to my judge;" and with good reason, for he adds presently, " If I justify myself, mine own mouth shall condemn me: if I say I am perfect, it shall also prove me perverse.... If I wash myself with snow water, and make my hands never so clean; yet shalt thou plunge me in the ditch, and mine own clothes shall abhor me[g]." Such was Job's

[g] Job ix. 15, 20, 30, 31.

estimate of his own righteousness; and the Psalmist's was the same of his. He will not even mention it, but like Job, betakes himself to make supplication unto his Judge. "Enter not into judgment with thy servant, for in thy sight shall no man living be justified." "If Thou, Lord, shouldest mark iniquities, O Lord, who shall stand? But there is forgiveness with Thee, that Thou mayest be feared[h]." And if

[h] Ps. cxliii. 2. Ps. cxxx. 3, 4. on the latter of which passages St. Augustine comments, " Ecce aperuit de quo profundo clamaret. Clamat enim sub molibus et fluctibus iniquitatum suarum. Circumspexit se, circumspexit vitam suam; vidit illam undique flagitiis et facinoribus coopertam: quacunque respexit, nihil in se bonum invenit, nihil illi justitiae serenum potuit occurrere. Et cum tanta et tam multa peccata undique et catervas scelerum suorum videret, tanquam expavescens, exclamavit, ' Si iniquitates observaveris, Domine, Domine, quis sustinebit?' Non dixit ' Ego non sustinebo,' sed ' quis sustinebit?' Vidit enim prope totam vitam humanam circumlatrari peccatis suis, accusari omnes conscientias cogitationibus suis, non inveniri cor castum praesumens de sua justitia. Si ergo cor castum non potest inveniri, quod praesumat de sua justitia; praesumat omnium cor de misericordia Dei, et dicat, ' Si iniquitates observaveris, Domine, Domine, quis sustinebit?"

"Venturus est Dominus, et inventurus peccata tua; quod perfecta autem justitia vixisti non inventurus. Homicidia forte, gravia sunt enim et valde majora, non est inventurus; adulterium non est inventurus, furta non est inventurus, rapinam non est inventurus, maleficia non est inventurus, idololatriam non est inventurus; non est ista inventurus. Nihil ergo est inventurus? Audi sermonem Evangelii: ' Qui dixerit fratri suo, Fatue.' Ab istis etiam peccatis linguae minutissimis quis abstinet? Sed forte dicis, Parva sunt. Si parvum tibi videbatur aut modicum fratri dicere,

we pass to the New Testament, we find St. Paul acknowledging that he has not yet attained, neither is already perfect[i]; and St. James declaring, that in many things we offend all[k]; and St. John warning us, that if we say that we have no sin we deceive ourselves, and the truth is not in us[l]. On which passage St. Augustine remarks, (quoting it purposely to shew that entire freedom from sin is not to be attained by the Christian in this life,) " the Apostle's words are, not, If we say we *had* no sin," i. e. in our unregenerate state, but, " If we say we *have* no sin," *now* that we are born again in Christ, " we

---

' Fatue,' vel Gehenna ignis videatur tibi magna; si contemnebas minus peccatum, vel pœnæ magnitudine deterrere. Sed dicis, Minora sunt, minuta sunt, sine quibus non potest esse ista vita. Congere minuta, et faciunt ingentem acervum. Nam et grana minuta sunt et tamen massam faciunt: et guttæ minutæ sunt, et flumina implent, et moles trahunt. Ideo et ille considerans quam multa minuta peccata quotidiana committat homo, si nihil aliud, vel per cogitationes et linguam, attendit quam multa sint: et si attendit quam minuta sint, videt per multa minuta fieri acervum magnum, et non quasi peccata sua pristina cogitans, sed ipsam fragilitatem humanam, jam ascendens clamat, ' De profundis clamavi ad te Domine; Domine, exaudi vocem meam. Fiant aures tuæ intendentes in vocem deprecationis meæ. Si iniquitates observaveris, Domine, Domine, quis sustinebit?' Vitare possum homicidia, adulteria, rapinas, perjuria, maleficia, idololatriam; numquid et peccata *linguæ?* numquid et peccata *cordis?* Scriptum est, ' Peccatum iniquitas est.' ' Quis' ergo ' sustinebit, si tu iniquitates observaveris?' Si nobiscum severus judex agere volueris, non misericors pater, quis stabit ante oculos tuos ?" S. August. in Psalm cxxix. §. 2 & 5.

[i] Phil. iii. 12.   [k] James iii. 2.   [l] 1 John i. 8.

deceive ourselves[m]." And to close these testimonies, we find our Lord in the prayer which He gave His disciples, and which He intended for their use, whether in the exact words, or as a summary of their wants, as long as they should remain on earth, teaching us to pray daily for the forgiveness of our trespasses, and thereby implying that we should daily need forgiveness.

And if it be replied, that such expressions as these now quoted refer to smaller sins, *venial*[n] as

[m] " Quisquis dicit post acceptam remissionem peccatorum ita quemquam hominem juste vixisse in hac carne, vel vivere, ut nullum habeat omnino peccatum, contradicit Apostolo Joanni qui ait. ' Si dixerimus quia peccatum non habemus, nos ipsos seducimus, et veritas in nobis non est.' Non enim ait ' *habuimus*,' sed ' *habemus*.' Quod si quisquam asserit de illo peccato esse dictum, quod habitat in carne mortali nostra secundum vitium quod peccantis primi hominis voluntate contractum est, cujus peccati desideriis ne obediamus, Paulus Apostolus præcipit; non autem peccare, qui eidem peccato, quamvis in carne habitanti, ad nullum opus malum omnino consentit, vel facti, vel dicti, vel cogitati, quamvis ipsa concupiscentia moveatur, quæ alio modo peccati nomen accepit, quod ei consentire peccare sit, nobisque moveatur invitis; subtiliter quidem ista discernit; sed videat quid agatur de Dominica oratione, ubi dicimus ' Dimitte nobis debita nostra:' quod, nisi fallor, non opus esset dicere, si nunquam vel in lapsu linguæ, vel in oblectanda cogitatione, ejusdem peccati desideriis aliquantulum consentiremus." S. August. de Perfec. Justit. §. xxi.

[n] See Concil. Trident. Sess. vi. c. xi.—Bellarmine, after St. Thomas, draws a subtle distinction between *peccata contra legem* and *peccata præter legem*, classing " venial" sins under the latter head; and he censures Vega and other Romish writers for acknowledging them to belong to the former, a concession, he says, which almost

they are termed, without which it is not pretended that the Christian can live; even so, enough is conceded to spoil our inherent righteousness as to any fitness it may have for standing the severity of God's judgment. That which is venial and therefore *admits* of pardon, does also by the very force of the term *need* pardon. And what then becomes of that righteousness which consists in "*doing the whole law*," where we are constrained to *sue for forgiveness for the breach of the law?*

But let us take heed lest we suffer ourselves to be beguiled by words. Doubtless there are *degrees* of guilt, and all sins are not of equal magnitude, but the *least* sin is no otherwise venial than as remitted through the Saviour's blood; and the *greatest is* venial, (if we except that one for which our Lord tells us there is no forgiveness,) when that blood which cleanseth from all sin is applied to cleanse it.

The doctrine of the possibility of our reaching such a state of sinlessness as that which has been referred to, springs naturally out of another doctrine which the Church of Rome has authoritatively sanctioned, pronouncing an anathema on those who deny

obliges them to admit the argument drawn by their adversaries from such passages as James iii. 2. and 1 John i. 8.—Bellarm. de Justificat. l. iv. c. 14. If that argument needed extrinsic support, it could not have any more forcible than that furnished by such a concession on the part of some, and such a distinction to evade that concession, on the part of others of its opponents. See Bp. Davenant's remarks on Bellarmine's distinction, De Justit. Actual. c. xlviii.

it; viz. that every thing which has really and properly the nature of sin is taken away in baptism. So that even concupiscence, though left, for the trial of the Christian, is not strictly sin in the regenerate. It is called sin in Scripture, (the decree allows,) but it is so called, not because it *is* sin strictly speaking, but because it *comes of sin* and *leads to sin*°.

° Concil. Trid. Sess. v. §. 5. " Hanc concupiscentiam, quam aliquando Apostolus peccatum appellat, sancta Synodus declarat, Ecclesiam Catholicam nunquam intellexisse peccatum appellari, quod vere et proprie in renatis sit; sed quia ex peccato est, et ad peccatum inclinat." The decree is couched in some places in the language of St. Augustine; and that Father is claimed by Romish writers as teaching its doctrine in express words. St. Augustine's meaning is, not that concupiscence is not sinful in the regenerate, but that it *is not imputed* for sin. It was forgiven in Baptism; and if it were possible that thenceforward it should not produce actual sin, it would not again be laid to the Christian's charge; and would not therefore, in St. Augustine's judgment, (see the quotation at p. 151.) need the petition, " Forgive us our trespasses," in reference to it. " Ad hæc respondetur, dimitti concupiscentiam carnis in baptismo, non ut non sit, sed *ut in peccatum non imputetur.* Quamvis autem reatu suo jam soluto, manet tamen, donec sanetur omnis infirmitas nostra, proficiente renovatione interioris hominis de die in diem, cum exterior induerit incorruptionem. Non enim substantialiter manet, sicut aliquod corpus aut spiritus: *sed affectio est quædam malæ qualitatis,* sicut languor. Non ergo aliquid remanet, *quod non remittatur;* cum fit, sicut scriptum est, ' Propitius Dominus omnibus iniquitatibus nostris;' sed donec fiat et quod sequitur, ' Qui sanat omnes languores tuos, qui redimit de corruptione vitam tuam, manet in corpore mortis hujus carnalis concupiscentia. Cujus *vitiosis desideriis* ad illicita perpetranda non obedire præcipimur,

Yet surely, even at first sight, that which *the Apostle calls sin*—and so calls, because it *comes of sin*, and *leads to sin*—which is the *daughter* of sin, and, where time is given, the *mother* of sin—cannot be other than sin in the strictest sense. The decree grounds its assertion on another, that God *hates* nothing in the regenerate—for there is no condemnation to those who are indeed buried with Christ by baptism unto death. It is true there is no condemnation to them; but this is not *because they have no sin*, (which, if they should say, an Apostle tells us, the truth would not be in them,) but because God beholding them in Christ *does not impute sin* to them. That cannot but be hateful in itself and hateful in God's sight, how much soever it may be kept in check, which, lurking in man's heart, is ever prompting him to rebel against his Creator's laws, and prevents him from loving God, as he ought to love God, with all his heart, and with all his soul, and with all his strength[p]. The serpent still lives and retains both its malice and its venom, though its head be trampled upon. Yet even if the question were waived, as to whether concupiscence is sin, till

---

ne regnet peccatum in nostro mortali corpore." August. De Nuptiis et Concupiscentia, lib. i. c. xxv. See other quotations from St. Augustine on this subject in the notes towards the close of Sermon VII.

[p] " Nam cum est adhuc aliquid carnalis concupiscentiæ quod vel continendo frenetur, non omni modo ex tota anima diligitur Deus." August. de Perfect. Just. §. viii.

it is complied with, where is he who has been so faithful a steward of God's grace, and who has maintained so strict a watch over his heart, that even for a single day he has not had occasion to offer up the petition in reference to the day—Forgive us our trespasses, as we forgive them that trespass against us?

This argument St. Augustine repeatedly urges in his controversies with the Pelagians, in proof that not even the regenerate; for whose use the Lord's Prayer is intended are free from sin. And they who need daily to sue for forgiveness must rest upon another righteousness than their inherent righteousness when they stand before the righteous Judge, sitting upon His throne of judgment.

And thus much indeed he teaches in express terms. "Whatever measure of righteousness a man may have," he says, "let him bethink himself, whether there will not be somewhat worthy of blame to be found in him, which escapes his own eye, when the righteous King shall sit on His throne, whose knowledge no sins can escape—no not even those of which it is said, Who shall understand his errors? When therefore the righteous King shall sit upon His throne, who shall boast that his heart is pure? or who shall boast that he is free from sin? Who, but those who would glory in their own righteousness, not in the mercy of their Judge[q]?" It is

[q] "Quantalibet justitia sit præditus homo, cogitare debet, ne aliquid in illo, quod ipse non videt, inveniatur esse culpandum,

plain by this in what court he would desire to be tried. Not in that where man must stand upon his own righteousness, though wrought in him by the operation of the Holy Ghost, but in that, where God is just, and the justifier of him that believeth in Jesus; and where the plea must be, Enter not into judgment with thy servant, O Lord, for in thy sight shall no man living be justified.

And no doubt this is what in many cases really earnest and sincere men are brought to when they apprehend that great and dreadful judgment to be at hand, however they may have shrunk from it or disputed against it in their day of health and prosperity. The near prospect of eternity enables them to see things in their due proportions. Sin is then beheld in its undisguised hatefulness; and their own righteousness, how highly soever they might have been disposed to esteem it, shrinks up into its true size. "Howsoever," says Hooker, " men, when they sit at ease, do vainly tickle their hearts with the wanton conceit of I know not what proportionable correspondence between their merits and their rewards, which in the trance of their high speculations, they dream that

---

cum rex justus sederit in throno, cujus cognitionem fugere delicta non possunt, nec illa de quibus dictum est, ' Delicta quis intelligit?' 'Cum,' ergo, ' rex justus sederit in throno, quis gloriabitur castum se habere cor? aut quis gloriabitur mundum se esse a peccato.' Nisi forte isti qui volunt in sua justitia, non in ipsius judicis misericordia gloriari?" S. August. de Perfect. Justit. §. xv.

God hath measured, weighed, and laid up as it were in bundles for them: notwithstanding, we see by daily experience, in a number even of them, that when the hour of death approacheth, when they secretly hear themselves summoned forthwith to appear and stand at the bar of that Judge, whose brightness causeth the eyes of the Angels themselves to dazzle, all these idle imaginations do then begin to hide their faces, to name merits then is to lay their souls upon the rack, the memory of their own deeds is loathsome unto them, they forsake all things wherein they have put any trust or confidence, no staff to lean upon, no ease, no rest, no comfort then, but only in Jesus Christ [r]."

" It is not in question," says Bishop Andrewes, pressing the same point, " whether we have an inherent righteousness or no: or whether God will accept or reward it: but whether that must be our righteousness *coram Rege justo judicium faciente.* Which is a point very material, and in no wise to be forgotten: for without this, if we compare ourselves with ourselves, what heretofore we have been, or if we compare ourselves with others, as did the Pharisee, we may take a fancy perhaps, and have some good conceit of our inherent righteousness. Yea if we be to deal in schools by argument or disputation, we may peradventure argue for it, and make some show in the matter. But let us once be brought and arraigned *coram rege justo sedente in Solio,* let us

[r] Hooker on Justification, §. 21.

set ourselves there, we shall then see that all our former conceit will vanish straight, and righteousness in that sense (that is, an inherent righteousness) will not abide the trial."

And presently afterwards he adduces those well-known propositions of Bellarmine's, in which, after asserting confidently in the first that a man may place confidence in merits, he descends in the second to *some confidence,* and that " if he is *sure* they *are* such ;" and then in the third, after better bethinking himself, it may be, of the Judge sitting in His throne, he spoils all. " Because we cannot be sure of our own righteousness—and for fear of vain glory—it is safest to place all our confidence only in God's mercy." " Mark his *misericordia,*" adds Bishop Andrewes, " and that he declineth the *judicial* proceeding—and mark his *reason,* because his righteousness is such as he is *not sure of it,* nor dare not put any trust in it, nor plead it *coram rege justo judicium faciente.* Which is enough, I think, to shew, when they have forgot themselves a little out of the fervour of their oppositions, how light and small account they make of it themselves, for which they spoil Christ of one half of His name[a]."

To sum up what has been said: Every Christian, who is, what his name imports, a living member of Christ's mystical body, has a *true inherent righteousness infused into him by that Spirit of holiness which flows to him from Christ, and connects him with*

[a] Bp. Andrewes's Sermon on Justification in Christ's Name.

Christ. He is not merely *accounted* righteous, but he really *is* righteous; and he is so in exact proportion to the measure in which the Holy Spirit dwells within him. He may grieve the blessed Being who has vouchsafed to take up His abode within him, and provoke him first to withhold His influence, and eventually, to withdraw it altogether. But if he is faithful to the grace given him, the principle of spiritual life which he has in Christ, becomes stronger and more vigorous, and the old nature which he derived from his first father, is increasingly weakened and subdued. He loses more and more the likeness of the first Adam; and he is transformed more and more into the likeness of the second Adam. And thus he is ever advancing towards that *perfect* righteousness wherewith Christ shall one day array all His Saints, when He shall present them to Himself holy and unblamable and unreprovable in His sight, not merely accounting them such, but, of His great mercy, both making and keeping them such.

But, on the other hand, this inherent righteousness, whatsoever measure of it we may have attained, well-pleasing though it be to God in Christ, and indispensable to our admission into heaven, *is not sufficient* to stand the severity of God's righteous judgment, and cannot be our justification in His sight. If we *must* claim heaven *on the ground of merit*—the *reward* being infinite the *merit* must be infinite; and where shall we find an infinite *merit*, but in His righteousness, whose sufferings provided for our sins an infinite *satisfaction*? "If in that the blessed Saints themselves," says Bishop Andrewes, "(were their sufferings never so great, yea though they endured never so cruel martyrdom,) if all those could not serve to satisfy God's justice for their sins, but it is the death of Christ must deliver them; is it not the very same reason, that were their merits never so many, and their life never so holy, yet that by them they could not, nor we cannot, challenge the reward, but it is the life and obedience of Christ that, *de justitia*, must procure it for us all?"

Nor is it merely a question of words, whether we rest our hopes of acceptance with God simply and at once upon Christ, or indirectly upon Him through the inherent righteousness which He works in us by His Spirit. "The Pelagians," says Hooker[1], "being over-great friends to nature, made themselves enemies unto grace, for all their confessing that men have their souls and all the faculties thereof, their wills and all the ability of their wills, from God. And is not the Church of Rome still an adversary unto Christ's merits, because of her acknowledging (i. e. for all she acknowledges) that we have received the power of meriting by the blood of Christ?" We cannot substitute in Christ's place even the works wrought in us by Christ's Spirit, but we so far lay another foundation than the Apostles laid, and preach another Gospel than the Apostles preached.

[1] Hooker on Justification, §. 33.

SERMON V.

FAITH.

"As our natural life begins and is maintained by bodily taste, so is the new man framed and nourished in us by this taste spiritual; which only rightly apprehends the nature, worth, and qualities, of heavenly mysteries, itself consisting in a temper of mind symbolizing with divine goodness, or with the heavenly mind of the second Adam. Our souls and affections, thus affected, have the same proportion to the several branches of God's will revealed, that every sense or faculty hath to its proper object; and this apprehension of our spiritual food by a proper, distinct, symbolical, conceit of its goodness, is the last and most essential difference wherein the nature of faith, as Christian, consists; which cannot possibly be wrought but by the Spirit of God. For as the object is, such must the assent be—supernatural." Jackson on Justifying Faith, §. i. chap. 9.

Heb. xi. 1.

Faith is the substance of things hoped for, the evidence of things not seen.

If the New Testament were placed in the hands of one who had been previously unacquainted with it, he could not fail to be struck with the importance attached by it in every part to *Faith*. Few things probably would strike him more. If miracles are to be wrought, faith is represented as required on the part of those who are to be benefitted by them. If prayer is to be effectual, faith is spoken of as the very soul of prayer, without which it cannot prevail, and with which nothing is too great for it to achieve. And with regard to the Gospel and its blessings, not one of them but is connected in the most explicit manner with faith. By faith we are first engrafted into Christ; and Christ dwells in our hearts by faith[a]. We become the sons of God by faith[b]. We become partakers of the Spirit by faith[c]; God cleanses our hearts by faith[d]; we overcome the

[a] Eph. iii. 17. [b] Gal. iii. 26. [c] Gal. iii. 14.
[d] Acts xv. 9.

world by faith[e]; we are saved by faith[f]. When the Baptist bare witness to our Lord, he testified, "He that believeth on the Son hath everlasting life, and he that believeth not the Son shall not see life, but the wrath of God abideth on him[g]." And the preaching both of our Lord and of His Apostles echoes on the same testimony to the end of the inspired volume.

But of all the blessings vouchsafed to us through the Gospel, none is more frequently spoken of in connexion with faith, than Justification. St. Paul especially again and again refers to the relationship between them, and, on more than one occasion, treats of it of set purpose. There might seem therefore at first sight, little room for controversy on a subject so frequently and so fully dwelt upon. And indeed, in the acknowledgment, as far as the form of words is concerned, that we are justified by faith, all who profess to take Scripture for their rule, are agreed. But when we come to the meaning of the words, and proceed to enquire, Wherein our justification consists—whether it is a righteousness infused into us or imputed to us: What is the nature of the faith which justifies—whether it is simply the assent of the understanding to certain truths, or whether its seat is in the will and the affections: and lastly, What is the connexion between faith and justification, or, in other words, How it is that faith justifies—whether as dis-

---

[e] 1 John v. 4. [f] Rom. x. 9. [g] John iii. 36.

posing towards justification, as being the first of a series of good works, or rather habits of holiness, which God crowns with His favour; or as virtually containing within itself the whole circle of Christian graces; or as leading us straight to Christ, with a hearty and unreserved consent to the Gospel Covenant, that we may receive in and from Him that righteousness which we have not, and cannot have, of ourselves—we enter upon a wide field of enquiry—so wide, that under the same form of words, scope seems to have been found for every variety of opinion: though, many times perhaps, in spite of apparent discrepancies, men have been nearer to each other, than, for want of thoroughly understanding each other's meaning, they may have seemed to be. And yet, when the grave importance of the subject is considered, and its immediate bearing upon our eternal interests, it is obvious that error or misapprehension cannot be of trivial moment.

The first of these questions relating to the nature of justification, has been already considered. And thus far, a *general* answer has been returned to the question, How shall sinful man be justified before God? In prosecuting the subject, my aim has been throughout to view it, not as though it were isolated and detached, but rather as a part, intimately connected with other parts, of one large and comprehensive whole. And the same course must still be pursued. Whatsoever blessings we either have or hope for pertaining to life and godliness, are given us in Christ. Justification is one of these, intimately connected with the rest, but yet not to be confounded with them, much less to be regarded as though it comprised them all. It is not (according to the pervading principle of a recent work on the subject[b]) identical with our union with Christ, or equivalent to the indwelling wherewith Christ dwells within us by His Spirit, but it is one of the unfailing fruits of that union, one of the inseparable effects of that indwelling. Being one with Christ and Christ with us, God looks upon us no longer as we are in ourselves, the guilty and defiled children of Adam, but as we are in Christ, free from all stain of past sin. And our sanctification is derived from the same source. For being one with Christ, and Christ with us, we are made partakers of Christ's Spirit, and endued with a new principle of life and holiness. And thus the two blessings are inseparably connected, though yet essentially distinct. Whom God justifies, them He also glorifies[b], adorning them with the graces of His Spirit here, both as infallible evidences that He has received them into His favour, and also as qualifications for that eternal weight of glory, which He has in store for them hereafter, and of which they are even now pledges and earnests.

But it is to be considered further, how we are first brought into a justified state, and how that state is continued and preserved. And thus we are led

[b] Newman's Lectures on Justification.

from the more *general* portion of the subject, to the consideration of the *particular relationship* in which justification stands connected with faith, with baptism, and with obedience. For with all of these it is plainly connected. " Go ye into all the world," said our Lord to His Apostles, when sending them forth as His ambassadors to their fellow men, " Go ye into all the world, and preach the Gospel to every creature. He that believeth and is baptized shall be saved; but he that believeth not shall be damned[i]." Here are faith and baptism declared to be necessary in order to our entrance upon a state of salvation, or, in other words, seeing that salvation is but justification perfected, upon a state of justification. " Go ye and teach all nations, baptizing them in the name of the Father, and of the Son, and of the Holy Ghost; teaching them to observe all things, whatsoever I have commanded you[k]." Here is obedience implied as the very end for which we are admitted into that state. Our present business must be with Faith; and the questions we shall have to consider are those which have been already hinted at: I. What is the nature of the faith which justifies? and II. What is the connexion between that faith and justification? though it is only the former of these on which I propose to enter in the present discourse.

i. " He that cometh to God," says the Apostle to the Hebrews, " must believe that He is, and that

---

[i] Mark xvi. 15, 16.   [k] Matt. xxviii. 19, 20.

He is a rewarder of them that diligently seek Him[l]." Faith in the being of God, and in His moral government, lies at the foundation of religion. Take this away, and natural religion as well as revealed falls to the ground. But we cannot come unto God except through Christ, nor through Christ, but by the Spirit. Faith therefore in Christ, as the appointed Mediator between God and man, and in the Holy Spirit, as in Him, who must both dispose and enable us to come unto God through that Mediator, is no less necessary than faith in God. And thus, from the very reason of the case, all the three Persons of the sacred Trinity, and each in His several office, are alike the objects proposed to our belief, if we would have access to God here, and be admitted into His glorious presence hereafter[m].

But further, it is not enough to believe merely in the existence of God and of His moral government of the world, nor that we have access to Him through Christ and by the Holy Spirit. It has pleased Him to reveal to us in the Scriptures a great variety of particulars, which it concerns us to know respecting Himself and His service, His gracious purposes towards us, and His will concerning us. And these likewise, even the whole compass of revealed truth, are necessary, in the very reason of things, to be believed, if we would approach Him acceptably, and approve ourselves before Him. In some particulars

[l] Heb. xi. 6.
[m] See Butler's Analogy, part ii. c. 1. §. 2.

indeed, ignorance, or error, or unbelief, may possibly be of less consequence than others; yet seeing it has pleased Almighty God to make a revelation to man, there can be no part of that revelation, which it does not most deeply concern us to accept; and doubtless there are some parts of it of such vital consequence, that the rejection of them must be fatal to our eternal happiness, inasmuch as it precludes us from the use of those means which He has appointed to be used on our parts for the attainment of happiness.

If we look to the actual teaching of the New Testament, we shall find that the faith to which such great and blessed effects are attributed is described, as to its subject-matter, in various ways. Sometimes it is spoken of simply as faith in God, faith in Christ, faith in the Name of Christ,—" It was not written for Abraham's sake alone, that his faith was imputed to him (for righteousness), but for us also, to whom it shall be imputed, if we believe on Him that raised up Jesus our Lord from the dead[a]." " He that believeth on Him is not condemned; but he that believeth not is condemned already, because he hath not believed in the Name of the only-begotten Son of God[o]." At other times it is described as the belief that Jesus is the Christ, the Son of God, and the like. Such was St. Peter's celebrated confession so highly commended by our Lord, " Thou art the Christ, the Son of the living God[p];" and Martha's,

[a] Rom. iv. 23, 24.   [o] John iii. 18.   [p] Matt. xvi. 16.

"Lord, I believe that Thou art the Christ, the Son of God, which should come into the world[q]." Such is St. John's account of the Christian's faith, in closing his Gospel; "These are written, that ye might believe that Jesus is the Christ, the Son of God, and that believing ye might have life through His Name[r];" and again in his first Epistle, "Who is he that overcometh the world, but he that believeth that Jesus is the Son of God[s]?" Such was the eunuch's profession of faith previously to his baptism; "I believe that Jesus Christ is the Son of God[t]." Elsewhere we find the addition of some other articles of chief importance: as the death and passion of Christ, "Whom God hath set forth to be a propitiation through faith in His blood[u];" the resurrection of Christ, "If thou shalt confess with thy mouth the Lord Jesus, and shalt believe in thy heart that God hath raised Him from the dead, thou shalt be saved[x]." At other times again we have it spoken of complexly and in a larger sense, as belief of the truth[y], belief of the Gospel[z], belief in Christ's words[a], receiving the word of Christ[b], receiving the word of God[c], &c. Yet it is with the belief of the simple truths first referred to, such as that Jesus is the Christ, the Son of God, that He died and was buried, and rose again for us, that we find the bless-

[q] John xi. 27.   [r] John xx. 31.   [s] 1 John v. 5.
[t] Acts viii. 37.   [u] Rom. iii. 25.   [x] Rom. x. 9.
[y] 2 Thess. ii. 12.   [a] Mark i. 15.   [b] John v. 47.
[h] Acts xvii. 11.   [c] Acts xi. 1.

ings of salvation and eternal life explicitly connected[d]. And in accordance with this teaching, the profession of faith which the Church has required in all ages in order to Baptism, has consisted of but few articles, those namely which relate to the Persons of the sacred Trinity, and other points of primary importance. Not that others also are not necessary, but that these are the foundation of all, which being once laid, the whole superstructure of revealed truth is in the way to be built up. He that denies these is an infidel; he that perverts them, a heretic; he that believes them in his heart, and confesses with his mouth, and shews forth the influence of them in his life and conversation, is a Christian indeed.

Such is faith as to its subject matter. The truth that Jesus is the Son of God is the centre; and around this, springing from it and depending upon it, is gathered the whole circle of Christian doctrine. This is that good deposit which St. Paul committed to Timothy[e]; that form of sound words which he exhorted him to hold fast[f]: that faithful word, which he reminded Titus a bishop must keep[g]. This is that faith which himself both received and kept, and by keeping attained unto everlasting life.

But to come more immediately to the point we

---

[d] See Matt. xvi. 16, 17. John xx. 31. 1 Cor. xv. 2—4. &c.
[e] 2 Tim. i. 14.　　　[f] 2 Tim. i. 13.　　　[g] Tit. i. 9.

have in hand—the nature of that faith by which we are justified before God.

Justifying faith has been defined in various ways. By some it is made to consist in the *assurance* that our sins are forgiven, and that we are received into God's favour through Christ. And men have carried this view so far, that they have almost denied that a man had faith, in its strictly Christian sense, if he could not feel confident of his acceptance. But surely this account of faith has no foundation in Scripture. The word of God sets forth God's gracious offers of mercy in the general. It declares that "God is not willing that any should perish, but that all should come to repentance[h];" that it "is a faithful saying, and worthy of all acceptation, that Christ Jesus came into the world to save sinners[i]." But it no where assures any man in particular that he is forgiven and accepted. If he has a true and living faith, he is so doubtless. But his being so is the consequence of his faith, and his assurance that he is so must depend upon the reason he has for believing that his faith is what it ought to be. Others again make justifying faith to consist in *trust*. And trust indeed is inseparable from it; but so also are hope and fear, and other affections, according to the various objects about which it is conversant. If God's mercy in Christ Jesus be the object, then doubtless faith takes the form of trust;

[h] 2 Pet. iii. 9   [i] 1 Tim. i. 15.

but if heaven and its eternal joys be the object, then it takes the form of desire or hope; or, if the dreadful consequences of falling from God be the object, then it takes the form of fear. And the like may be said of *obedience*, which is another word put by some into the definition of justifying faith. Obedience is the fruit of faith, and wherever faith is genuine and time and opportunity are given, it will be sure to spring from it; but the two notions are perfectly distinct, nay so distinct, that to confound them goes nigh to subvert the terms of the Gospel Covenant.

" Faith," says the Apostle to the Hebrews, describing faith in general, but yet with an especial regard to that faith by which the just shall live, of which he had spoken in the preceding verse, and the mention of which gave occasion to his description, " Faith is the substance of things hoped for, the evidence of things not seen[k]." " It is as firm a persuasion of the existence of the things which are the objects of hope, as if we had them already in possession; of the reality of things which are invisible, as if they were actually present to the eye[l]." It is, in fact, the soul's eye, so to speak, by which we see what with the bodily eye we cannot see; the soul's ear, by which we hear what with the bodily ear we cannot hear; the soul's hand, by which we handle

---

[k] Heb. xi. 1.

[l] Bishop of Lincoln's Charge, (1843,) p. 28. See Chrysost. in Heb. xi. 1, 2.

what with the bodily hand we cannot handle. If we examine the various instances of faith adduced by the Apostle, we shall find, that in every case the notion conveyed is that of a firm persuasion, a cordial assent, in respect of matters beyond the reach of sense, such as in matters which come within the range of the senses, would be produced by actual sight, or hearing, or contact: and this persuasion and assent manifesting themselves variously according to the various subjects with which they were conversant. "Through faith we understand that the worlds were framed by the word of God, so that things which are seen were not made of things which do appear[m]." Here is assent simply. "By faith Noah, being warned of God of things not seen as yet, moved with fear, prepared an ark to the saving of his house, by the which he condemned the world, and became heir of the righteousness which is by faith[n]." Here is the firm persuasion of the truth of God's threatenings manifesting itself in a salutary provision against the impending judgments. "By faith Abraham, when he was called to go out into a place which he should after receive for an inheritance, obeyed, and he went out, not knowing whither he went[o]." Here is the firm persuasion of the truth of God's promise, manifesting itself in implicit and unquestioning obedience. "These all died in faith, not having received the promises, but having seen them afar off,—seen them with the eye

[m] Heb. xi. 3, 4.   [n] Ibid. v. 7.   [o] Ibid. v. 8.

of faith—and were persuaded of them, and embraced them, and confessed that they were strangers and pilgrims on the earth[p]." Here again is the same firm persuasion of the truth of God's promises—His promises of a heavenly country—manifesting itself in the earnest embracing of them, and unwearied patience in the pursuit of them. "By faith Abraham, when he was tried, offered up Isaac, and he that had received the promises offered up his only-begotten son, (on whom all those promises depended,) accounting that God was able to raise him up even from the dead[q]." Here was the firm persuasion both of the truth of the promises respecting his seed, which he had already received, and also of God's Almighty power to restore his son to him even from the dead: yea, and that He would do so, rather than one jot or one tittle of those promises should fail; and all this manifesting itself in one of the most wonderful instances of unhesitating and self-denying obedience, which the world ever saw.

In Romans iv. St. Paul adduces Abraham's faith on another occasion, in a passage in which he is expressly treating of the subject of justification. Abraham, says he, " against hope believed in hope, that he might become the father of many nations, according to that which was spoken, So shall thy seed be. And being not weak in faith, he considered not his own body now dead, when he was about a hundred years old, neither yet the deadness

[p] Heb. xi. 13.   [q] Ibid. v. 17—19.

of Sarah's womb: he staggered not at the promise of God through unbelief, but was strong in faith, giving glory to God: and being fully persuaded that what he had promised he was able also to perform'." Here again we have the same pervading idea—a firm persuasion both of the truth of God's promise, and of His ability to perform that promise, though most improbable to reason, and contrary to all experience. The Apostle himself makes the application; " Therefore it was imputed to him— this simple faith in God's word and belief in His power was imputed to him—for righteousness. Now it was not written for his sake alone that it was imputed to him; but for us also, to whom it shall be imputed, if we believe on Him that raised up Jesus our Lord from the dead'."

These are instances of faith as manifested by the saints of the Old Testament,—of faith too, as it is expressly declared, more or less connected with their justification and acceptance with God. And the faith more peculiarly belonging to the New Testament is described by the same characteristics. In its essential quality, a firm persuasion of the truth revealed and a cordial assent to it, it is still the same. Comparing our Lord's declaration to Martha and Martha's reply, we have belief in Jesus, belief to which the promise of eternal life is annexed, expressed in the acknowledgment, " I believe that Thou art the Christ, the Son of God, which should

' Rom. iv. 18—21.   ' Rom. iv. 22—24.

come into the world`ᵗ`." "If ye believe not that I am He," said our Lord to the Jews, "ye shall die in your sins`ᵘ`;" where that which was lacking on their parts was the persuasion of the truth which our Lord referred to, the belief that He was the Christ. Doubtless the bare admission of that truth would not have saved them; but what we are at present concerned to remark is, that the faith, by which we are delivered from wrath and condemnation, is described not as trust, or assurance, or obedience, but simply as the belief that Jesus is the Christ. To the same purpose are those declarations of St. John in his first Epistle, "Whosoever shall confess that Jesus is the Son of God, God dwelleth in him, and he in God`ˣ`." "Whosoever believeth that Jesus is the Christ, is born of God`ʸ`." "Who is he that overcometh the world, but he that believeth that Jesus is the Son of God`ᶻ`." Where the blessings of fellowship with God, the new birth, and victory over the world, are severally connected with the simple belief in those great and central truths, that Jesus is the Christ, the Son of God.

If there be one passage in which more than any other the nature of justifying faith is treated of of set purpose, it is Romans x. St. Paul is contrasting the righteousness which is of the law with the righteousness which is of faith. "Moses," says he, "describeth the righteousness which is of the law,

---

`ᵗ` John xi. 25—27.   `ᵘ` John viii. 24.   `ˣ` 1 John iv. 15.
`ʸ` 1 John v. 1.   `ᶻ` 1 John v. 5.

That the man which *doeth* these things shall live by them. But the righteousness which is of faith speaketh on this wise, Say not in thy heart, (as though doubting the great truths of Christ's incarnation and resurrection,) Who shall ascend into heaven, that is, to bring Christ down from above, or, Who shall descend into the deep, that is, to bring up Christ again from the dead. But what saith it? The word is nigh thee, even in thy mouth and in thy heart, that is, the word of faith, which we preach, That if thou shalt confess with thy mouth the Lord Jesus, and shalt believe in thy heart that God hath raised Him from the dead, thou shalt be saved. For with the heart man believeth unto righteousness, and with the mouth confession is made unto salvation[a]." Where, as in the passages before referred to, the faith by which we are justified is described simply as belief. A different truth indeed is specified as the subject matter to be believed, but the nature of the faith is the same.

In accordance with this view of the nature of faith, we find the Apostles in their preaching, as recorded in the Acts, aiming steadily at this one object, to persuade those whom they addressed of the great truths of the Gospel, such as that Jesus is the Christ, that God hath raised Him from the dead, that remission of sins is freely offered in His name to all who shall believe on Him, that He is appointed of God to be the Judge of quick and dead,

[a] Rom. x. 5—10.

and the like; and then, on their professing their belief, they straightway baptize them, as Philip did the Eunuch, thereby formally consigning to them the justification of which by faith they were already heirs.

And the faith which the Apostles sought to produce in others, was the hidden but effectual stay of their own spiritual life. "We walk by faith," says St. Paul, "not by sight[b]." "We look not at the things which are seen, but at the things which are not seen; for the things which are seen are temporal, but the things which are not seen are eternal[c]." "The love of Christ constraineth us, because we thus judge, that if one died for all, then were all dead; and that He died for all, that they which live should not henceforth live unto themselves, but unto Him which died for them, and rose again[d]." Here is still the same firm persuasion of the reality of these great verities, on which the Christian's hope is built. This was the spring of their unwearied labours, this was the stay which supported them under their manifold and all but overwhelming sufferings.

I may add, as a confirmation of the view now taken, that the faith, which our Lord required in those who sought His miraculous aid, for the removal of diseases and other evils pertaining to this life, seems to have consisted simply in the belief of His divine power. "Believe ye *that I am able to do this?*" was His question to the two blind men who

[b] 2 Cor. v. 7.   [c] 2 Cor. iv. 18.   [d] 2 Cor. v. 14, 15.

sought of Him the gift of sight: "*According to your faith* be it unto you[e]." And the centurion's faith, which He so highly commended, was altogether of the same character; "Speak the word only, and my servant shall be healed[f]." Like faithful Abraham, whose true son he thus proved himself, though an alien by birth, he was strong in faith, giving glory to God, being fully persuaded that diseases were Christ's servants, ready to come or go at His bidding.

It is plain then, from what has been said, that the notion, which is usually attached to faith in Scripture, when that faith is spoken of to which is annexed the gift of righteousness and the promise of eternal life, is simply belief in the great truths which are revealed in the Gospel, a firm persuasion of their certainty, and a cordial assent to them. There may be passages in which the word faith is used in a larger or a derived sense, still, this, which has been dwelt upon, as it is its proper, so it is its ordinary, signification[g].

ii. But yet it is not less plain, that the bare assent of the understanding to the truth, that Jesus is the Christ, and the truths connected with it, is not sufficient to justify us in God's sight. So far Simon

---

[e] Mat. ix. 28, 29.   [f] Mat. viii. 8.
[g] See Barrow's Sermons on the Creed, Serm. iv. Of Justifying Faith: and Whitby's Preface to his Commentary on the Epistle to the Galatians.

Magus believed, and yet he continued in his sins; so far those among the chief rulers believed of whom St. John speaks, who yet, for fear of the Pharisees, and because they loved the praise of men more than the praise of God, did not confess Christ, and their faith profited them nothing[h]. So far the very devils believe and tremble. We must seek further therefore for the properties of that faith of which such great things are spoken in Scripture, and to which such blessed effects are attributed. In its essence, it is simply *belief*—belief in the revelation which God has made to us by Christ. But yet, as we have seen, a man may have faith thus far, and yet have neither part nor lot in the blessings which Christ hath purchased for us. What further characteristic is there then of that faith by which we are first justified, and eventually saved?

I answer *generally*, that though, strictly speaking, faith in the first instance is simply belief, and has its seat in the understanding, yet, that it may justify, *it must also influence the will and the affections*. This was in reality what was lacking in the faith of the persons referred to, *an earnest affection* for that truth of which in their minds they were persuaded. They believed the truth, as far as regards a cold and lifeless assent, but they did not love the truth.

If man were not fallen from that righteousness in which he was originally created, the will and the understanding would invariably go together; faith could not

[h] John xii. 42, 43.

be an idle and inefficacious principle,—a mere speculation, resting in the mind, and exercising no influence upon the life and conversation. It would be impossible for a man to admit the persuasion that there is a heaven and a hell, that in his natural state he is lost, subject to condemnation, and in danger of eternal misery; that God, of His great mercy, hath provided a way of escape; that He so loved the world, that He gave His only-begotten Son, that whosoever believeth on Him should not perish, but have everlasting life; that the Lord of glory took our nature upon Him and was made man, and, after a life of suffering and sorrow, submitted to a shameful death, that He might atone for our sins; that He afterwards rose again and ascended into heaven, and that He shall come again at the last day to judge the whole race of mankind, and to give to every man according to his works, so that they who have done good shall go into life everlasting, and they who have done evil into everlasting fire—it would be impossible, if we were not miserably fallen, for a man to assent to these great truths, and yet live on in ungodliness. But yet experience shews us that men may and do assent to them, and live so notwithstanding.

The truth is,—and it is a truth which it deeply concerns us to bear in mind,—that *faith is God's gift*. Not only does the Lord give the word, by the hearing of which faith comes, but He also prepares the heart, by the gracious influences of His Spirit, to receive that word as into good ground, so that it may not lie there barren and unproductive, but may spring up and bear fruit. For lack of this preparation, which lack was yet their own fault, many among the Jews did not yield even a bare assent to the truth. The heavenly Sower scattered the good seed of the word upon their hearts, but it was caught up and borne away as soon as it fell. They *would* not believe, because they loved darkness rather than light; and *because they would not*, "therefore," so God ordained in just judgment, "they *could* not." Though our Lord "had done so many miracles before them, yet they believed not on Him, that the saying of Esaias the Prophet might be fulfilled which he spake: Lord, who hath believed our report, and to whom hath the arm of the Lord been revealed? *Therefore they could not believe*, because that Esaias said again, He hath blinded their eyes and hardened their heart, that they should not see with their eyes, nor understand with their heart, and be converted, and I should heal them[i]." For lack of this preparation, numbers at this day, though living in a Christian country, reject Christianity, and numbers are led away by what the Apostle describes as damnable heresies[k], God sending them strong delusion that they should believe a lie, because they received not the love of the truth that they might be saved[l]. We little consider how much we stand in need of God's grace, even that we may yield a cordial assent to the truth,

[i] John xii. 37—40.   [k] 2 Pet. ii. 1   [l] 2 Thess. ii. 10, 11.

apart from the influence which that assent may have upon our wills and affections [m].

And if we look to this latter also, and have regard not only to a right belief—right as to its subject matter—but a right belief rightly received, still more is God's preventing grace needed. St. John after mentioning in the passage just quoted one class of the Jews who did not believe on our Lord in any sense, speaks immediately afterwards of another class, who did believe on Him, but because of the Pharisees did not confess Him, "for," he adds, "they loved the praise of men more than the praise of God [n]." Here was the good seed, not carried away as soon as sown, as in the former case, but yet equally unproductive to any practical purpose, because not received into an honest and good heart—a heart, like Lydia's, opened by the Lord, and prepared for its reception by the Holy Spirit. "I thank Thee, O Father, Lord of heaven and earth," were our Saviour's words in reference to the faith of which we speak, "because Thou hast hid these things from the wise and prudent, and hast revealed them unto babes. Even so, Father, for so it seemed good in thy sight [o]." If God's grace be withheld, even the soundest and most accurate form of doctrine, though intelligently discerned, and cordially assented to, will prove of no efficacy; if vouchsafed, even the few simple but pregnant truths

[m] See Barrow of Justifying Faith, Works, vol. iv. p. 338, 339.
[n] John xii. 42, 43.   [o] Matt. xi. 25, 26.

which constitute the main points of the Christian's faith, imperfectly apprehended, it may be, but received with the whole heart, will give the child more understanding than his teachers, and will make the rude unlettered peasant wise unto salvation.

Thus then though faith has its seat in the understanding, yet it avails nothing, *unless it pass from thence to the will and the affections.* And this would seem to be what St. Paul alludes to, when he tells the Corinthians, " My speech and my preaching was not with enticing words of man's wisdom, but in demonstration of the Spirit and of power, that your faith should not stand in the wisdom of men, but in the power of God[p]." Human learning might enlighten the understanding, and human eloquence convince the reason, but there needed another Teacher and another Orator, to illuminate and affect the heart, and without this, he well knew, nothing was done to any purpose.

And as the faith by which we are justified influences the will and the affections, it must needs manifest itself, as circumstances arise, in the various acts which have their source in these. And hence it is not unfrequently spoken of as though it were identical with these acts, or rather with the habits from which they proceed[q]; though, if we would speak accurately, we must distinguish it from them.

[p] 1 Cor. ii. 4, 5.

[q] Thus St. Augustine—" Ille credit in Christum, qui et sperat in Christum et diligit Christum." De Verbis Dom. Serm. 61 " Inseparabilis est bona vita a fide quæ per dilectionem operatur;

Thus it produces repentance, yet it is not repentance; it works by love, yet it is not love; it is the spring of all holy obedience, yet it is not obedience; it leads to assurance, yet it is not assurance. It assumes the forms of hope and trust, yet, in strictness, it is distinct from hope and trust.

When, for example, God declares by His prophet, " I will pour upon the house of David, and upon the inhabitants of Jerusalem, the Spirit of grace and of supplications, and they shall look upon me whom they have pierced, and they shall mourn for him as one mourneth for his only son, and shall be in bitterness for him, as one that is in bitterness for his first-born[r]," here is faith manifesting itself under the form of contrition and penitence. Faith is the eye with which they look, sorrow and brokenness of spirit the effects which follow upon looking. When Abraham unhesitatingly obeyed the command to offer up his only son, in whom all the wondrous

---

imo vero ea ipsa est bona vita." De Fide et Oper. §. xxiii. And to the same purpose, in the Homilies, Faith is described to be " not only the common belief of the articles of our faith, but also a sure trust and confidence of the mercy of God through our Lord Jesus Christ, and a stedfast hope of all good things to be receeived at God's hand," &c. Yet presently afterwards, hope, trust, and other graces, are spoken of so as to imply, that, though inseparable from a true lively and Christian faith, they are yet distinct from it. " This faith *is not without* hope and trust in God, *nor without* the love of God and our neighbour, *nor without* the fear of God, *nor without* the desire to hear God's word, and to follow the same in eschewing evil, and doing gladly all good works." The first part of the Sermon of Faith.

[r] Zech. xii. 10.

promises which God had made him centered, here was faith manifesting itself under the forms both of trust and hope and obedience; of trust, in that it still leaned confidently on God's promise; of hope, in that it hoped against hope, that in some mysterious way his son should yet be restored to his arms; of obedience, in that it complied, without a murmur and without delay, with that strange and, to all but such faith as Abraham's, incredible, command. And, in short, the exploits of that glorious army of saints and martyrs which the Apostle enumerates in Heb. xi, are nothing else than so many instances of faith manifesting itself in different ways according to the different circumstances which called it forth, yet still distinct from its manifestations.

But though faith is, in strictness, distinct from the habits of repentance, love, obedience, hope, trust, &c. yet when circumstances permit, it invariably produces them, and so far is inseparable from them. For example, " repentance toward God, and faith toward our Lord Jesus Christ[s]" go hand in hand in the Apostle's preaching, and they will also in our experience, if we have either in reality. That heart cannot duly have received the truth, in which the love of sin still reigns. And if, after the truth has been received, the love of sin be again admitted, faith, as to its efficacy toward justification, is so far subverted. St. Paul bids Timothy hold faith and a good conscience, and he adds, that some, having

[s] Acts xx. 21.

put away the latter, concerning faith have made shipwreck[t]. Faith first makes the conscience good, and then lives in keeping it so.

Again, when the Apostle would describe the faith by which we are justified, distinguishing it from a dead and unprofitable faith, he describes it as working by love[u]. Love—love to God and love to man for God's sake, is the natural result of faith, (if we may use the word *natural* where we speak of grace,) *when received into a heart prepared by God's Spirit for its reception.* " We love Him," says St. John, " because He first loved us;" and it is by faith we apprehend His love, and, apprehending it, are stirred up to love Him in return. And loving Him in sincerity, we cannot choose but love our brethren also. For " he that loveth Him that begat, loveth Him also that is begotten of Him[x]." And seeing that love is the fulfilling of the law, and that faith " worketh by love," we may understand, at least in one sense, the Apostle's meaning, when he puts and answers the question; " Do we then make void the law through faith? God forbid: yea, we establish the law[y]."

Again, trust or affiance in God is another property inseparable from a true and lively faith. To trust Him, and repose ourselves with full confidence upon His love and mercy, is the necessary result of what the Scriptures teach us of His gracious dealings

[t] 1 Tim. i. 19.   [u] Gal. v. 6.   [x] 1 John v. 1.
[y] Rom. iii. 31.

with us and purposes towards us in Christ Jesus, when received into a heart prepared by divine grace, and made susceptible of holy influences. And indeed of all the habits which spring from faith, unless indeed we except hope, trust seems to resemble it the most. To believe God's word, when that word is the word of promise, and we interested in the promise, is but one degree removed from trusting it. Still, however, though faith and trust seem almost to coincide here, they are really distinct. Faith is the cause, trust the effect, and so only one of many characteristics by which a true and living faith is distinguished from the mere assent of the understanding[z].

[z] " Confidence, *fiducia*, or trust, is so nearly allied to faith, that some include it in the essence or formal signification of the word in the learned tongues: which opinion may seem to have some countenance in the book of Homilies. But what there is said of faith to this purpose, is a popular description, not an accurate or artificial definition: like as also we may not think the author of those Homilies meant formally and essentially to define faith, when he saith that *faith is a firm hope*, for so in the same place doth he describe it. And to speak the truth, he that puts *fiducia* in the essential definition of faith, and leaves *hope* out, had need of as much cunning as he that should undertake to make payment of ten pounds and subtract seven." Jackson on Justifying Faith, sect. i. ch. 10.

Much stress has been laid upon the expressions, " believing *in* or *on* God," " believing *in* or *on* Christ," as though they necessarily involved the idea of *trust*. Yet St. John uses this very term of those whose faith, whatever it was, allowed of their denying Christ. " Many," says he, " of the chief rulers *believed*

And the same holds of obedience, and of the assurance of God's favour. Obedience, like trust, is one of the immediate fruits of faith, and assurance follows upon obedience. Where faith does justify, it takes the form of trust, though not of trust only, but of other habits also as circumstances arise. Wherever faith does justify, it inevitably produces obedience, at least, if time and opportunity admit, and obedience, as it is persevered in and gives evidence of the truth and reality of the faith from

---

on him, ἐπίστευσαν εἰς αὐτόν, but because of the Pharisees they did not confess Him, lest they should be put out of the synagogue, for they loved the praise of men more than the praise of God." John xii. 42, 43. And though *trust* is frequently implied, as are also hope and love and other graces, in such expressions, as St. Augustine often remarks, (see quotations in Bp. Pearson on the Creed, Art. I. note *i.* p. 29.) yet in strictness, these are rather the inseparable effects of a true and lively faith, than parts of faith itself. And though in *popular* language we may well describe faith by its effects, yet if we would speak accurately, we must restrain our definition within narrower bounds. " Quid est credere in Deum? Credendo amare, credendo diligere, credendo in eum ire, et ejus membris incorporari. August. in Joan. Tract. 29. Which doctrine of St. Augustine's being taken notice of by Peter Lombard, hath since been continued by the Schoolmen. And Aquinas, bringing all three under one act of faith, hath been contradicted by Durandus: Credere in Deum non est præcise actus fidei, sed fidei et caritatis simul; et sunt etiam plures, et non unus actus tantum: by whose subtle but yet clear determination, as many of his are beyond the rest of the Schools, whatsoever is added by the preposition to *believe*, appears not to be a part of belief, but an act superadded to the act of faith." Bp. Pearson on the Creed, Art. I. note *i.* on p. 29.

which it springs, issues in assurance; so verifying the prophet's words, "The work of righteousness shall be peace, and the effect of righteousness quietness and assurance for ever [a]."

To sum up what has been said: Faith, in the first instance, has its seat in the understanding; and it consists, so far as it comes under the description of a Christian's faith, in the belief of those truths, which Christ has revealed to us—first those concerning Himself, such as His divine nature, His incarnation, His death and passion, His atonement, His resurrection, His ascension, His second coming to judge the world, and then whatsoever other truths spring from and depend upon these. But though the understanding is, in the first instance, the seat of faith, yet faith avails nothing, and has no efficacy towards justification, unless its influence extend to the will and the affections. This it is which distinguishes the faith by which cometh salvation from the faith of wicked men and devils.

And this faith is *God's gift in both respects*. And we cannot otherwise obtain it, except God give it to us. And as Solomon says of wisdom [b], It is a point of wisdom to know whose gift wisdom is, so it is a point of faith to believe whose gift faith is. And unless we take this circumstance into consideration, and keep it distinctly before us, we shall not in any wise form a right conception of the nature of faith. Many of the errors which have arisen respecting it,

[a] Isaiah xxxii. 17.   [b] Wisd. viii. 21.

have had their origin in no other source than this, that its divine origin has been overlooked.

But yet, while we speak of faith as God's gift, let us not forget that it rests with us, whether we will receive it in the first instance, or, having received it, whether we will cherish it, that it may increase and become stronger and more vigorous. "How can ye believe," was our Lord's expostulation with the Jews, "which receive honour one of another, and seek not the honour that cometh from God only[c]!" And it was their condemnation, that, when light was come into the world, they loved darkness rather than light, because their deeds were evil[d]. *Wilful* blindness tends to bring on *judicial* blindness: whereas, on the contrary, faithfulness to present light, whatever that light may be, will be recompensed with more light. "Whosoever hath, to him shall be given, and he shall have more abundance; but whosoever hath not, from him shall be taken away even that he hath[e]."

How deeply it concerns us to cherish, by all possible means, this precious gift of faith, will be evident if we consider its unspeakable importance in the economy of our salvation. Whatever be its office in the work of our justification, we cannot be justified without it in the first instance, nor retain a justified state afterwards. Nor is it less necessary to our sanctification. Our devotedness to God's service, our self-denial, our diligence, our watchfulness, our

[c] John v. 44.   [d] John iii. 19.   [e] Matt. xiii. 12.

zeal, and all our other graces, will droop or flourish exactly in proportion as the hidden life of faith within us is languid or vigorous.

It is a remarkable feature of the present time, that so small a portion of public attention is attracted to the evidences of religion. Many of us must remember, when, to judge by the discourses which were heard, and the books which were written, it seemed to be one of the engrossing subjects of the day. We may thank God, so far as this is an index of the state of the public mind, for the change which has taken place; though, alas! in one respect it has been too much like the change from a foreign war to a civil. Yet let us not suppose, that the bulwarks which were raised in other days against the assaults of infidelity may be safely neglected. We little know how soon they may be needed again. And even though they be not needed against external assaults, our great adversary well understands how to assail the faith of those whom he would ensnare or harass, from within.

And if he does not attempt to rob us of our faith altogether, let us not forget that he may steal the jewel, while he leaves the casket. He may suffer us to retain a cold and lifeless assent to the truth, while the will and the affections, into which, through that assent, the truth ought to have passed, remain uninfluenced. Good need have we therefore to offer up the Apostles' supplication, "Lord, increase our faith:" good need have we to use with unwearied diligence the means by which faith may be increased, especially to study much, and with much prayer and devout meditation, that holy book which God has given us for its nourishment and support; nor less to cultivate that inward witness of the Spirit, which Christ has left to His people that He may testify of Him.

SERMON VI.

THE CONNECTION BETWEEN FAITH AND JUSTIFICATION.

" We are accounted righteous before God, only for the merit of our Lord and Saviour Jesus Christ, by Faith, and not for our own works or deservings: wherefore, that we are justified by Faith only is a most wholesome doctrine, and very full of comfort." Art. xi.

" It is a childish cavil wherewith, in the matter of Justification, our adversaries do so greatly please themselves, exclaiming that we tread all Christian virtues under our feet, and require nothing in Christians but faith, because we teach, that faith alone justifieth. Whereas by this speech we never meant to exclude either hope or charity from being always joined, as inseparable mates, with faith in the man that is justified; or works from being added as necessary duties required at the hands of every justified man: but to shew, that faith is the only hand which putteth on Christ unto Justification, and Christ the only garment, which, being so put on, covereth the shame of our defiled natures, hideth the imperfections of our works, preserveth us blameless in the sight of God, before whom otherwise the weakness of our faith were cause sufficient to make us culpable, yea to shut us from the kingdom of heaven, where nothing that is not absolute can enter." Hooker on Justification, §. 31.

Rom. iv. 16.

It is of faith, that it might be by grace.

It is impossible to read the New Testament without noticing, that a most important function is assigned to faith in the economy of our salvation. And the writers of the New Testament refer us back to the Old[a], as teaching, if less frequently, yet not less unequivocally, the same doctrine respecting it: the Law—that faith is imputed for righteousness[b]; the Prophets—that the just shall live by faith[c]; and both the Law and the Prophets furnishing a great cloud of witnesses to its purifying and sanctifying efficacy, when received into a heart which God has prepared for its reception.

Faith indeed has to do with both justification and sanctification. The question to which we come to-day, is, What is its office in respect to our justification? How is it that faith justifies us? or, to speak more accurately, seeing that it is God that justifieth, How is it that we are justified by faith?

[a] Rom. iii. 21, 22.   [b] Rom. iv. 3. Gen. xv. 6.
[c] Rom. i. 17. Hab. ii. 4.

What is the connection between faith and justification?

Nor is this a mere speculative question, which it matters little how we answer, or whether we leave it unanswered altogether. No question can well be of trivial moment, where salvation is concerned: and this least of all so, which bears so closely upon the foundation on which our eternal hopes must rest, that it amounts to nothing less than whether we are really building on that foundation or not. True it is that thousands of God's saints have journeyed to their blessed home in every age, who never paused to ask the question; and, if they had asked it, perhaps would have paused again before they could have given the true answer. But their lives were an unceasing answer. They wrought righteousness, yet they put no trust in their righteousness, but rested all their hopes of acceptance on His righteousness, in whom they had learnt to trust. And if we are sure that we are following in their steps, we may be sure that virtually we have the true answer. But yet to have the true answer explicitly as well as virtually, is itself, under God, no little help towards our following in their steps; as certainly to have a wrong answer may divert our course altogether, and lead us in the opposite direction to that in which they have gone and we would go.

I answer *generally* then, that we are justified by faith, in that by faith we are united to Him in whom alone we can have either justification or any other blessing pertaining to life and godliness. The connexion between faith and the union which we have with Christ, is expressly referred to in the Apostle's prayer for the Ephesians, that Christ may dwell in their hearts by faith[d]; and it is implied in many other passages, in which, though our union with Christ is not expressly spoken of, yet its effects, this of justification among them, are referred to faith as the instrumental cause.

Still however the question recurs, What is the office of faith, whether in respect of our union with Christ directly, or, through that union, of our justification?

The doctrine of the Church of Rome, as set forth in the decrees of Trent[e], is, that we are justified by faith, in that faith is the first of a series of habits, such as fear, hope, love, repentance, and others, which constitute, as far as the habit is concerned, that inherent righteousness, in which, as she teaches, our justification consists. There is no sense then in which, according to this view, we can be said, in the language of our Article, to be justified by faith only. In fact, we are justified by the other habits referred to at least as much as by faith, by love, even more so. In one word, our justification consists in an inherent righteousness, and we are justified by faith, because faith is the first step towards the formation of that righteousness[f].

[d] Eph. iii. 17.   [e] Concil. Trid. Sess. vi. c. 6. 7. 8.
[f] " Per fidem ideo justificari dicimur, quia fides est humanæ

But it has been already shewn, that we cannot stand before God in an inherent righteousness; that, according to St. Paul's plain and unequivocal teaching, our justification consists in our being accounted righteous, God beholding us, not as we are in ourselves, the guilty and defiled children of Adam; but as we are in Christ, free from all stain of past sin. And if so, the basis on which this theory rests is overthrown, and some other office must be found for faith, than that of leading the way in that series of holy habits which are supposed to form our justification.

If instead of justification, the Church of Rome

---

salutis initium, fundamentum et radix omnis justificationis." Concil. Trid. Sess. vi. c. 8. " Adversarii, *sola fide* justificationem acquiri sive apprehendi docent: Catholici contra, ac praesertim Synodus ipsa Tridentina, quam omnes Catholici ut magistram sequuntur, (Sess. vi. cap. 6.) septem actus enumerat, quibus impii ad justitiam disponuntur, videlicet fidei, timoris, spei, dilectionis, pœnitentiæ, propositi suscipiendi sacramenti, et propositi novæ vitæ atque observationis mandatorum Dei." Bellarm. de Justif. lib. i. c. 12. " Fides justificat vel disponendo ad justitiam et inchoando justitiam formalem, secundum Catholicos, vel apprehendendo justitiam Christi, secundum hæreticos." Ibid. lib. iv. c. 18. " Ex hoc principio (sc. causam formalem justificationis non esse justitiam quæ est in Christo, vel solam remissionem peccatorum, sed justitiam in nobis realiter inhærentem) evidenter sequitur, non solam fidem per modum dispositionis justificare. Nam justitia ista realis et inhærens non debet apprehendi per fidem, sed infundi per gratiam. Ad hanc autem infusionem disponit quidem actus fidei, sed disponunt etiam actus timoris, pœnitentiæ, aliarumque virtutum, sed præter cæteros actus dilectionis sine dubitatione disponit." Ibid. lib. i. c. 18.

had used the word *sanctification*, there would have been no ground left for dispute in the matter. For whatever she teaches of faith in respect of *inherent righteousness*, we may safely admit, as long as that inherent righteousness is not made *the ground of our acceptance* with God. Faith truly does lead the way in the formation of the Christian character, as St. Peter teaches us, when he bids us " add to our faith virtue, and to virtue knowledge, and to knowledge temperance, and to temperance patience, and to patience godliness, and to godliness brotherly kindness, and to brotherly kindness charity [g]." But that character, when in its utmost perfection on earth, falls short of that standard which it must reach, if we would make it the ground of our acceptance with a righteous God sitting upon His throne of judgment [h].

Another account of the office of faith, in respect of our justification, is, that we are justified by faith, in that faith is the parent, so to speak, of all Christian graces and good works [i]. And this is virtually the

[g] 2 Peter i. 5—7.

[h] " Quid enim perfectius quidve excellentius in veteri populo sacerdotibus sanctis? Et tamen eis præcepit Deus sacrificium primitus pro suis offerre peccatis. Et quid sanctius in novo populo Apostolis? Et tamen præcepit eis Dominus in oratione dicere, ' Dimitte nobis debita nostra.' Omnium igitur piorum sub hoc onere corruptibilis carnis et in istius vitæ infirmitate gementium spes una est, quod advocatum habemus ad Patrem Jesum Christum justum, et ipse est exoratio peccatorum nostrorum." August. contra duas Epist. Pelag. lib. iii. §. v.

[i] See Bp. Bull, Harmon. Apostol. Diss. Prior. c. 2. §. 10.

same as saying, that we are justified by obedience, by that obedience, which faith contains within itself and will manifest in works, as time and opportunity are given.

The chief difference between this theory and that of the Church of Rome appears to lie, first, in the different senses attached to the word justification; the Church of Rome, as has been said, understanding it of an *infused quality*, an *inherent* righteousness; those who adopt this theory, of an *extrinsic* righteousness, a righteousness *accounted*[k]. Both agree in representing faith as justifying *as a work*. The one class would speak of it rather as one good work among many, and therefore as merely contributing its share towards our justification; the other, as the parent of all good works both habitual and actual. Both agree in ascribing, in the matter of our justification, the same kind of causality to works as to faith: only on this point again they differ, and it must be confessed to be a most material difference, that while Romish writers universally maintain the *merit* of good works, and most of them, with the distinction, that those done before justification deserve grace *de congruo*, and those done after justification deserve grace here and eternal life hereafter *de condigno*[1],

[k] Bp. Bull, Harmon. Apost. Diss. Prior. c. 1.

[1] "Catholici omnes agnoscunt opera bona justorum esse meritoria vitæ æternæ, sed tamen aliqui censent non esse utendum his vocibus *de condigno* et *de congruo*, sed absolute dicendum opera bona justorum esse meritoria vitæ æternæ, ex gratia Dei. Alii volunt opera bona justorum esse meritoria de condigno, largo

they who embrace the view referred to earnestly disclaim the idea of merit altogether[m].

But there is this fatal objection to every system, which rests our justification, in the ordinary sense which that word bears in Scripture, upon the ground of our obedience, whether habitual or actual, that it runs counter to the whole spirit of St. Paul's argument in those Epistles where he treats of justification of set purpose. Nothing can be more plain than

modo, ita ut hoc condignum respectu condigni proprie sumpti possit dici congruum, respectu congrui proprie sumpti possit dici condignum. Communis autem sententia Theologorum admittit simpliciter meritum de condigno." Bellarm. de Justific. lib. v. c. 16. Bellarmine thus distinguishes *meritum de congruo* from *meritum de condigno:* " Etiamsi est (meritum de congruo) a Deo, tamen non est a Deo intus inhabitante per gratiam justificantem, sed extrinsecus excitante et adjuvante, ut Augustinus docet in Epist. 105, et praeterea est a Deo incipiente et inchoante, nondum complente et perficiente: proinde est meritum inchoatum et imperfectum, et habet aliquam dignitatem et proportionem ad suum finem, sed non tantam quantam requirit meritum de condigno. Denique deest, ut diximus, pactum proprie dictum, sine quo nullum potest esse meritum ex justitia sive de condigno." De Justif. lib. i. c. 21.

[m] " Aure atque animo abhorreat (lector) ab isto Pontificiorum quorundam (quorundam, inquam, quia quosdam aliter sentire ingenue fatendum est) perniciosissimo errore, qui bonis justorum operibus ex condigno, hoc est, propter intrinsecam eorum bonitatem ac dignitatem, praemium caeleste deberi, asserere non verentur. Certe enim qui ejusmodi operum meritum adstruunt, Christianorum nomen haud sunt meriti: ac fidenter pronuntiare ausim, vix ac ne vix quidem gratiam Christi sensisse aut novisse, qui horrendam istam opinionem animo penitus imbiberunt." Bp. Bull. Harmon. Apostol. Diss. Post. c. xviii. §. 4.

that the point at which he aims throughout is to shut out works, not indeed from forming an indispensable part of the Christian life, from being the necessary fruits of our faith, but *from the office of justifying.*

I. In the Epistle to the Romans, St. Paul has in view the case of those who are seeking justification *in the first instance;* and his object is to shew, that no man can stand before God on the ground of his own righteousness: and for this reason, because no man has a righteousness of his own which is sufficient to endure the severity of God's righteous judgment. Even Abraham, eminent saint as he was, was justified not by works, but by faith, the Scripture testifying of him, that he *believed* God, and it was *counted* to him for righteousness[n].

Now surely the whole tone and spirit of this reasoning would seem to be opposed to the view, which represents faith as justifying either as a good work, one among many good works, or as containing within itself the whole circle of Christian graces. And that this is not only apparently but really so, will be evident if we look more closely into the Apostle's argument. It is true, the works which he has primarily in view are works done in a state of nature, and without the aid of divine grace; but the point I urge is, that *his argument concludes equally against all works,* whether actual or habitual,

[n] Rom. iv. 3.

whether wrought in the unassisted strength of nature, or by the aid of divine grace, so *far forth as they are the ground of our acceptance with God.*

He shews, for instance, at great length^o, that "all have sinned, and come short of the glory of God;" that therefore none can claim justification as a matter of *debt*. If we are justified, it must be *freely*, of God's mere grace and bounty, and in such a way as shall leave no room for boasting. "Where is boasting?" he asks. "It is excluded. By what law? Of works? Nay, but by the law of faith. Therefore we conclude that a man is justified by faith without the deeds of the law^p." But if faith itself be regarded as a work, or as the parent of all good works, do not we, in effect, represent the Apostle as building again with one hand, what he had, the moment before, destroyed with the other? Do not evangelical works, if they are rested upon as the ground of our acceptance, claim justification as a matter of debt, not accept it as of free grace, and so furnish occasion for boasting, which it is the object of the Gospel to exclude?

And this is yet further evident from the instance of Abraham's faith, which the Apostle has selected, and his remarks upon it. "If Abraham were justified by works," he says, "he hath whereof to glory^q." And this surely, whether his works were works of nature, or works of grace, for even as works of grace they were his own, though ultimately referrible to

^o Rom. i. ii. iii.   ^p Rom. iii. 27, 28.   ^q Rom. iv. 2.

God, in like manner as, so far as they were works of nature, they were God's, though mediately wrought by himself. And it is to be observed, that Abraham had already by faith, as the Apostle to the Hebrews declares, left the land of his fathers, at God's call, and gone out into a place which he should after receive for an inheritance, not knowing whither he went[r]. So that if works proceeding from faith might afford matter for glory, Abraham had whereof to glory. Yet even these works are shut out, that righteousness may be bestowed upon him as a free gift, to which he can put in no claim, not as a matter of debt. "Abraham *believed* God, and it *was counted* to him for righteousness. Now to him that worketh is the reward not reckoned of grace but of debt, but to him that *worketh not, but believeth* on him that justifieth the ungodly, *his faith is counted for righteousness*[s]." And yet, as we have seen, Abraham had wrought, and wrought by faith, and such works as might well, if any works might, afford matter for glory[t]. This reasoning of the Apostle seems conclusive against all works, so far forth as they are the ground of our acceptance, evangelical as well as moral. And

---

[r] Heb. xi. 8.   [s] Rom. iv. 3—5.

[t] "Τὸ μὲν γὰρ ἔργα μὴ ἔχοντα ἐκ πίστεως δικαιωθῆναί τινα, οὐδὲν ἀπεικός· τὸ δὲ κομῶντα ἐν κατορθώμασι μὴ ἐντεῦθεν, ἀλλ' ἀπὸ πίστεως, γενέσθαι δίκαιον, τοῦτο ἦν τὸ θαυμαστὸν καὶ μάλιστα τῆς πίστεως τὴν ἰσχὺν ἐμφαῖνον. Διὸ δὴ τοὺς ἄλλους παραδραμὼν πάντας, ἐπὶ τοῦτον (τὸν Ἀβραὰμ) ἀνάγει τὸν λόγον." Chrysost. in Rom. Hom. viii. §. 1.

if against evangelical works in act, then against the habit, whether it be faith or charity, from which they spring.

And it is surely a confirmation of this view, that, as Waterland[u] observes after Whitby, in the particular instance of Abraham's faith, which the Apostle has chosen, though Abraham had faith *before* what was said of his justification in Gen. xv. and *afterwards* more abundantly when he offered up his son Isaac, yet neither of those instances was pitched upon by the Apostle as fit for his purpose, because in both obedience was joined with faith; whereas here was a pure act of faith without works. " Fear not, Abram," God had said to him, " I am thy shield, and thy exceeding great reward." On which Abraham answers, as though, for an instant, his faith had lost its accustomed tone, " Lord God, what wilt Thou give me, seeing I go childless?....Behold, to me Thou hast given no seed, and, lo, one born in my house is mine heir. And, behold, the word of the Lord came unto him, saying, This shall not be thine heir: but he that shall come forth out of thine own bowels shall be thine heir. And He brought him forth abroad, and said, Look now toward heaven, and tell the stars, if thou be able to number them: and He said unto him, So shall thy seed be." Incredible promise, to one that was now far advanced in years, and yet had no child! But Abraham's faith rose to meet it. " He believed in the Lord, and he counted it to him for

---

[u] On Justification, Works, vol. ix. p. 455.

rightcousness." He had believed *before*, as we have seen, and manifested his faith by his ready and unquestioning obedience. He believed *afterwards*, and manifested his faith by the same ready and unquestioning obedience, only in a far greater trial; yet with neither of these does the inspired writer of the book of Genesis connect the imputation of righteousness. The instance he selects, is one of faith manifesting itself simply in receiving and embracing God's word, because it is God's, however incredible to reason, and contrary to experience; and St. Paul, his express object being to shew that we are justified by faith and not by works, chooses the same instance which Moses had done before him. It is surely not a little remarkable, that if he had meant to exclude only such works as are done by the unassisted strength of nature, he should thus studiously pass over, and, by thus passing over, apparently exclude, such signal instances of works springing from faith, as he had ready to his hand. And still more so, when we find him proceeding to another instance of faith, precisely similar to the one he had already dwelt upon, and dwelling upon that in like manner, and declaring of it likewise, as he had done of the former, that it was imputed to Abraham for righteousness. "Being not weak in faith," he says, referring to his faith in receiving God's promise of a son, repeated at the institution of circumcision, " he considered not his own body now dead, when he was about a hundred years old, neither yet the deadness of Sarah's womb;

he staggered not at the promise of God through unbelief, but was strong in faith, giving glory to God, and being fully persuaded, that what He had promised He was able also to perform. And therefore it was imputed to him for righteousness. Now it was not written for his sake alone that it was imputed to him, but for us also, to whom it shall be imputed if we believe on Him that raised up Jesus our Lord from the dead[a]."

It may be urged, indeed, that St. James refers to one of these very instances of faith manifesting itself in obedience, which St. Paul passes over, alleging it as a proof that a man is justified by works, and not by faith only. But this only makes St. Paul's choice of the instances he has chosen, and his silence as to the others, the more marked. St. Paul had one object in view, and he chose those instances which bore upon his object. St. James had a different object, and he chose those which bore upon his. The instances which St. Paul chose, were precisely such as served to shew that we are justified by faith without works, so far as the ground of our acceptance with God is concerned; those which St. James chose were precisely such as served to shew, that though we are justified by faith, yet it is not by a faith which is barren and unproductive, but which shews itself, when time and opportunity are given, in actual righteousness.

As a further proof that evangelical works, or works

[a] Rom. iv. 18—24.

which are the fruit of faith, are excluded from the office of justifying, as well as works done by the unassisted strength of nature, may be added St. Paul's contrast between the righteousness which is of the law and the righteousness which is of faith in Romans x. " Moses," he says, " describeth the righteousness which is of the law," that is, the method of justification proposed under the law, " That the man which doeth those things shall live by them[x]." And do not we in effect make the Gospel method of justification, to all practical purposes, the same as that proposed under the law, if we suppose the declaration of the Gospel also to be, the man that doeth those things shall live by them, and this, though with more abundant grace, yet with higher requirements? But let us hear the terms in which the Apostle describes the Gospel method of justification. " The righteousness which is of faith," he says, " speaketh on this wise: Say not in thine heart, (as though doubting the great truths referred to,) who shall ascend into heaven? or who shall descend into the deep?....But what saith it? The word is nigh thee, even in thy mouth and in thy heart, that is, the word of faith which we preach, That, if thou shalt confess with thy mouth the Lord Jesus, and shalt believe in thy heart that God hath raised Him from the dead, thou shalt be saved. For with the heart man believeth unto righteousness, and with the mouth confession is

[x] Rom. x. 5.

made unto salvation[y]." Here is faith—faith in its simplest form, not indeed unaccompanied by the confession of Christ before men, and, if so, not unaccompanied by baptism, and surely not less unaccompanied, as time and opportunity allow, by good works;—but yet *as to the ground of our acceptance before God*, expressly opposed to whatsoever works may be imagined as included in the declaration, "The man that doeth those things shall live by them[z]."

In the Epistle to the Galatians, St. Paul has in view the case of persons who had already been brought into a state of justification, but were in danger of losing it, not indeed by resting upon evangelical works, but by looking upon obedience to the Jewish law as a necessary complement to the Gospel. And here also, his arguments conclude equally against works proceeding from faith, so far

[y] Rom. x. 6—10.

[z] " Μὴ τοίνυν φοβηθῇς, φησὶν, ὡς τὸν νόμον παραβαίνων, ἐπειδὴ τῇ πίστει προσῆλθες· τότε γὰρ αὐτὸν παραβαίνεις, ὅτε δι' αὐτὸν τῷ Χριστῷ μὴ πιστεύσῃς· ὡς, ἂν πιστεύσῃς αὐτῷ, κἀκεῖνον ἐπλήρωσας, καὶ πολλῷ πλέον ἢ ἐκέλευσε· πολλῷ γὰρ μείζονα δικαιοσύνην ἔλαβες......Ἵνα γὰρ μὴ λέγωσιν Ἰουδαῖοι, πῶς εὗρον μείζονα δικαιοσύνην οἱ τὴν ἐλάττω μὴ εὑρόντες; λέγει λογισμὸν ἀναντίρρητον, ὅτι κουφοτέρα αὕτη ἡ ὁδὸς ἐκείνης. Αὕτη μὲν γὰρ πλήρωσιν ἀπαιτεῖ πάντων· Ὅταν γὰρ ποιήσῃς πάντα, τότε ζήσεις· ἡ δὲ ἐκ πίστεως δικαιοσύνη οὐ τοῦτο λέγει, ἀλλὰ τί; Ἐὰν ὁμολογήσῃς ἐν τῷ στόματί σου Κύριον Ἰησοῦν, καὶ πιστεύσῃς ἐν τῇ καρδίᾳ, ὅτι ὁ Θεὸς αὐτὸν ἤγειρεν ἐκ νεκρῶν, σωθήσῃ." Chrysost. in loc.

forth as they are the ground of our acceptance, as against works done before the grace of Christ and in a state of nature. He refers to the same instance of Abraham's faith as in the Epistle to the Romans, " Even as Abraham believed God, and it was accounted to him for righteousness. Know ye therefore that they which are of faith, the same are the children of Abraham." He contrasts the righteousness which is of the law and the righteousness which is of faith in the same way as in the Epistle to the Romans, " As many as are of the works of the law are under the curse, for it is written, Cursed is every one that continueth not in all things which are written in the book of the law to do them. But that no man is justified by the law in the sight of God, it is evident, for, The just shall live by faith; and the law is not of faith, but, The man that doeth them shall live in them[a]." We have indeed in these two brief sentences from the Old Testament the respective characteristics of legal and evangelical righteousness. " The man that doeth these things shall live in them,"—this is the righteousness of the Law; " The just shall live by faith,"—this is the righteousness of the Gospel. Substitute obedience for faith, even the obedience which is the fruit of faith, and you again bring back the law, not only with its requirements, but with its threatenings. " Stand fast therefore," the Apostle proceeds both to exhort and warn the Galatians, " in the liberty wherewith Christ

[a] Gal. iii. 6—12.

hath made us free, and be not entangled again with the yoke of bondage. Behold, I Paul say unto you, that, if ye be circumcised, Christ shall profit you nothing. For I testify again to every man that is circumcised, that he is a debtor to do the whole law[b]." And surely the same reason and the same exhortation and warning are equally applicable to those who are substituting the obedience which comes of faith in the place of faith, or rather of that better righteousness, which is appropriated by faith. Whosoever seeks justification by works, even by evangelical works, obliges himself to perfect obedience, and thus entangles himself again in that yoke of bondage from which Christ came to set him free. Christ is become of no effect to him, now that he seeks to be justified by obedience. He has removed his cause out of that court in which God could be just and the justifier of him that believeth in Jesus, and has placed it where, besides a perfect inherent righteousness, there can be no other alternative than condemnation.

Thus then while the immediate object of St. Paul, in the Epistles which have been referred to, is to shut out from the office of justifying works done in a state of nature, and without the aid of divine grace,

---

[b] Gal. v. 1—3. "Ὁ περιτεμνόμενος τὸν νόμον κύριον ποιεῖ· κύριον δὲ εἶναι νομίζων, καὶ ἐκ τοῦ μείζονος αὐτὸν παραβαίνων μέρους, ἐκ δὲ τοῦ ἐλάττονος τηρῶν, πάλιν ὑπὸ τὴν ἀρὰν ἑαυτὸν τίθησιν· ὑποβάλλων δὲ ἑαυτὸν τῇ ἀρᾷ, καὶ διακρουσάμενος τὴν ἀπὸ τῆς πίστεως ἐλευθερίαν, πῶς δύναται σωθῆναι;" Chrysost. in Gal. v. 2.

his arguments conclude equally against *all* works, both actual and habitual, and consequently against both the notions of faith which have been mentioned, both that which represents it as justifying in that it is one among other works, which God crowns with His favour; and that which represents it as justifying in that it is the parent, so to speak, of all works. We must seek therefore some other account of the office which faith bears in the matter of our justification.

Yet before we do so, the question must not be passed by, How is the exclusion of works—evangelical works as well as those done in a state of nature—from the office of justifying, to be reconciled with St. James's declaration, that a man is justified by works and not by faith only[c]? It would be presumptuous to suppose that a question of so great difficulty as that to which this virtually amounts— how, what seem to be discrepancies in the teaching of St. Paul and St. James are to be reconciled—can, at this day, after having been so long at issue, be set at rest to the satisfaction of opposing parties. Yet if the circumstances under which the Apostles respectively wrote, and the persons whom they respectively had in view, be taken into consideration and duly weighed, much of the real difficulty of the question vanishes. St. Paul was intent upon guarding the doctrine of justification by faith from perversion on one side, St. James from perversion

[c] James ii. 24.

on the opposite. St. Paul had to deal with those who magnified works, and made faith of little or no account; St. James with those who magnified faith, and made works of little or no account. It is not strange therefore, if, in guarding against opposite extremes of error, each extreme one of fearful peril, and such as drew to itself, for the time, almost exclusive attention, the two Apostles should have used language, which, apart from this consideration, it might be difficult to reconcile. Yet were they both guided by the same Spirit, and both teach, whatsoever mode of reconciling them we adopt, the same doctrine. Does St. Paul declare, in express terms, that works done *before* the grace of Christ cannot put away God's wrath and endure the severity of His judgment, and does the whole tenour of his discourse conclude with equal force against works done *after* grace and *by* grace, so far forth as they are available to the same end, so that from first to last, we must be content to rest upon Daniel's plea[d], and sue for acceptance, not for our righteousnesses, whether legal or evangelical, but for God's great mercies? This is St. James's doctrine also. " So speak ye," he says, " and so do, as they that shall be judged by the law of liberty. For he shall have judgment without mercy that hath shewed no mercy; and mercy rejoiceth against judgment[e]:" which plainly implies, that if God enter into judgment with His servants, judging them not by a law of liberty, a liberal and generous law, wherein " mercy rejoiceth against

[d] Dan. ix. 18.   [e] Jas. ii. 12. 13.

judgment," but according to strict justice, dealing forth to them judgment without mercy, no man living shall be justified. So that all will need a better plea than their own inherent righteousness, even though that be a righteousness wrought in them by God's Spirit, and though that also must be present, in that great and dreadful day, when the righteous King shall sit upon His throne, and when they who make mention of God's righteousness only, shall find that God has not forgotten theirs, and they who make mention of their own, that it is in God's esteem of no account. Does St. James again warn men, in the plainest and most earnest language, that "faith, if it hath not works, is dead, being alone[f]," and that such a faith can neither justify in the first instance, nor save at the last? And does not St. Paul urge the very same truth, with the same plainness, and the same earnestness? Jealous as he is in shutting out works from the office which belongs to faith, he is not less jealous in guarding against the idea that the faith by which we are justified can be severed from works. "In Jesus Christ," he says, "neither circumcision availeth any thing, nor uncircumcision, but faith which worketh by love[g]." "What shall we say," he asks in another place, anticipating the objection, which he foresaw would be urged, as indeed it has been repeatedly, against his doctrine, "shall we continue in sin (seeing that we are justified by faith) that grace may abound? God forbid: how shall we that are dead to sin, live any longer therein? Know

---

[f] James ii. 17.   [g] Gal. v. 6.

ye not, that so many of us as were baptized into Jesus Christ were baptized into His death? Therefore we are buried with Him by baptism into death; that like as Christ was raised up from the dead by the glory of the Father, even so we also should walk in newness of life[h]." The faith by which we are justified leads us as earnestly to contend against the dominion of sin, as to flee from its condemnation. And it does not more surely lead us to Christ for the one, than, in Christ, to the Holy Spirit for the other.

When therefore we find the two Apostles, while they harmonize most entirely in their doctrine, as they must needs do, who were both taught by the same divine teacher, using terms, which, taken literally and in the same sense, appear inconsistent with each other, it can only be, that they use one or more of those terms in different senses. One principle of harmonizing the Apostles is based on the supposition, that "*works*" is the equivocal term. And it is contended, that the works, which St. Paul excludes from the office of justifying, are not evangelical works, but such only as are done in our own unassisted strength[i]. But the whole tenour of St. Paul's argument, if what has now been urged be conclusive, shuts out evangelical works as well as others from this office, in St. Paul's sense of the word "*justify*." Our best works are insufficient to

[h] Rom. vi. 1—4.
[i] See Bp. Bull, Harmon. Apostol. Diss. Poster. c. 6. &c.

form the ground of our acceptance with Him, who is of purer eyes than to behold iniquity. Yet are works, notwithstanding, indispensable at our hands—*the habit* which shall produce them, from the first, and *the works themselves*, as time and opportunity are given—indispensable, not as the ground of our acceptance, and such as shall enable us to claim heaven as a debt, but yet as the very end for which we have been created in Christ Jesus, and as constituting that holiness without which no man shall see the Lord—indispensable therefore *as conditions* of our acceptance. And this consideration leads to what might seem a truer and more satisfactory mode of reconciling the apparent discrepancies in the two Apostles, namely, if we understand St. Paul to use the word "*justify*" in what, through his use of it, who uses it so frequently, has come to be looked upon as its strictly proper sense, namely, of God's accounting righteous those who in themselves are unrighteous; St. James in a larger and more comprehensive sense, as having respect, at the same time, to those habits and works of righteousness, which necessarily accompany justification. This is Waterland's[k] principle of reconciling the apparent discrepancies, and it has the advantage of doing so without in any wise impairing those great doctrines, which the two Apostles were severally watching over with such earnest watchfulness.

Yet, whatever principle of interpretation we adopt,

[k] See Waterland on Justification, Works, vol. ix. p. 458.

it concerns us to remember, that it is of far greater consequence to us, and perhaps a safer employment, and one more in accordance with the reverence due to God's word, to strive rightly to apprehend the teaching of each Apostle, especially so far as it was designed to guard against the errors which each had in view, than to endeavour to limit or extend the terms used by one, so as to bring them into harmony with the terms used by the other. Each calls our attention to a great practical truth,—the one, *that we need a better righteousness than our own in which to stand before God;* the other, *that without a righteousness of our own, we shall never be admitted into His presence.* And the Church has been reminded too often in her history, that the warning neither of the one nor of the other Apostle was superfluous, and again and again has she had cause to bless God, whose good providence and watchful care have provided her with both.

I have already dwelt longer on this point than my space allows: yet let us not leave it without remarking the admonition which this seeming discrepancy in the language of the two Apostles suggests, that we take heed how we put an ill construction upon doctrinal statements, though they be not framed exactly according to our own model, when they may in any wise bear a sound one. We see that there is a sense, in which it is good divinity to say, that we are justified *by faith without works;* and that there is a sense, in which it is good divinity to say, that we are justified *by works and not by faith only*. Of course, both cannot be true in the same sense, and it can be no light error to hold either in a wrong sense. But let him who holds the one soundly, be thankful that he does so, and strive to hold it practically also: but let him take heed how he condemns his neighbour, who holds the other, when he is not sure that he holds it unsoundly.

II. We have seen then that our best works cannot stand before God, and endure the severity of His judgment. We need a better righteousness in which to appear before Him, in whose sight the heavens are not clean, and who chargeth even His angels with folly,—even His righteousness who is " made unto us of God wisdom, and righteousness, and sanctification, and redemption, that, according as it is written, He that glorieth let him glory in the Lord[l]."

And this brings us to the point to which we tend. Here is the precise office of faith in the matter of our justification. We are justified by faith, because faith, instead of holding out something of our own to rest upon, whether pointing to works done, or calling our attention to itself as the root and foundation of all works, remits us simply and at once to Christ, who is " the LORD our righteousness[m]," that we may receive in Him and from Him, what we have not, and cannot have, of ourselves, both that perfect

---
[l] 1 Cor. i. 30, 31. [m] Jer. xxiii. 6.

righteousness of justification which we may boldly plead before God, and also that inherent, though as yet imperfect, righteousness of sanctification which shall qualify us for admission into His presence.

That this is really the office of faith in the matter of our justification, will be plain if we consider the language of Scripture on the subject.

Observe, first, the reasons which are assigned by the Apostle why justification should be by faith rather than by works: the one, *that our salvation may be of grace;* the other, *that boasting may be excluded.*

1. " If they, which are of the law, be heirs," he says, " faith is made void, and the promise made of none effect: because the law worketh wrath; for where no law is, there is no transgression." And this holds, be it observed, not only of the Jewish law, which the Apostle had primarily in view, but of every law, setting forth the declaration of God's will. Every law of a righteous God must work wrath to those, who, while they are under it, and are to be judged by it, are continually coming short of its requirements, unless they have transferred their cause into that court where " mercy rejoiceth against judgment," and where God can be " just, and, at the same time, the justifier of him which believeth in Jesus." " Therefore," the Apostle continues, seeing that the law, so far from saving, only worketh wrath, and maketh God's promise of none effect,—" therefore *it*

is of faith, that it might be by grace, to the end the promise might be sure to all the seed; not to that only which is of the law, but to that also which is of the faith of Abraham, who is the father of us all[n]."

But does not "*grace*" mean *grace infused?* No; for the Apostle had said, but a few verses before, "To him that worketh is the reward not reckoned *of grace*, but *of debt*[o];" where "*grace*" plainly signifies *a thing freely given*, without claim or just demand, as opposed to that which is due. "The Apostle," says Hooker, "as if he had foreseen, how the Church of Rome would abuse the world in time by ambiguous terms, to declare in what sense the name of grace must be taken, when we make it the cause of our salvation, saith, 'He saved us according

---

[n] Rom. iv. 14-16. "Εἰ γὰρ οἱ ἐκ νόμου κληρονόμοι, κεκένωται ἡ πίστις, Ἵνα γὰρ μή τις λέγῃ, ὅτι καὶ πίστιν δυνατὸν ἔχειν καὶ νόμον τηρῆσαι, δείκνυσιν ὅτι ἀμήχανον. Ὁ γὰρ ἐχόμενος τοῦ νόμου ὡς σώζοντος, ἀτιμάζει τῆς πίστεως τὴν δύναμιν. Διό φησι, Κεκένωται ἡ πίστις· τουτέστιν, οὐ χρεία τῆς κατὰ χάριν σωτηρίας· οὐδὲ γὰρ δύναται τὴν ἰσχὺν τὴν ἑαυτῆς ἐπιδείξασθαι................Ὁ νόμος ὀργὴν κατεργάζεται...Εἰ δὲ ὀργὴν κατεργάζεται καὶ παραβάσει ὑπευθύνους ποιεῖ, εὔδηλον ὅτι καὶ κατάρᾳ· οἱ δὲ κατάρᾳ καὶ τιμωρίᾳ καὶ παραβάσει ὄντες ὑπεύθυνοι, οὗτοι οὐ κληρονομεῖν ἄξιοι, ἀλλὰ τοῦ δίκην διδόναι καὶ ἐκβάλλεσθαι. Τί οὖν γίνεται; Ἔρχεται ἡ πίστις ἐφελκομένη τῇ χάριτι, ὥστε τὴν ἐπαγγελίαν εἰς ἔργον ἐξελθεῖν. Ὅπου γὰρ χάρις, συγχώρησις· ὅπου δὲ συγχώρησις, οὐδεμία κόλασις· κολάσεως δὲ ἀνῃρημένης, καὶ δικαιοσύνης ἐπιγενομένης ἀπὸ τῆς πίστεως, οὐδὲν τὸ κωλῦον κληρονόμους ἡμᾶς γενέσθαι τῆς ἐπαγγελίας τῆς ἀπὸ τῆς πίστεως. Διὰ τοῦτο οὖν ἐκ πίστεως, φησίν, ἵνα κατὰ χάριν." Chrysost. in loc.

[o] Rom. iv. 4.

to His mercy p,' which mercy, though it exclude not the washing of our new birth, the renewing of our hearts by the Holy Ghost, the means, the virtues, the duties, which God requireth of our hands which shall be saved, yet is it so repugnant unto merits, that to say we are saved for the worthiness of any thing which is ours, is to deny we are saved by grace. Grace bestoweth freely, and therefore justly requireth the glory of that which is bestowed. We deny the grace of our Lord Jesus Christ; we abuse, disannul, and annihilate the benefit of His bitter passion, if we rest in these proud imaginations, that life is deservedly ours, that we merit it, and that we are worthy of it q." Salvation then is " of faith, that it may be by grace," according to the prophet's proclamation, " Ho every one that thirsteth, come ye to the waters, and he that hath no money; come ye, buy and eat; yea, come, buy wine and milk without money and without price r." And the office of faith in the matter is, that it believes God's promise, and embraces it, or, to use the prophet's image, that it believes the gracious proclamation, and comes to the waters. " If," said our blessed Lord to the Samaritan woman, " thou knewest the gift of God, and Who it is that saith to thee, Give Me to drink, thou wouldest have asked of Him, and He would have given thee living water s." Faith was what she lacked, and had

p Tit. iii. 5.   q Hooker on Justification, §. 34.
r Isaiah lv. 1.   s John iv. 10.

she had faith, her faith would have obtained the precious gift, not by working, but by asking. And yet it would have wrought too, if it had asked in the sincerity of an honest and true heart.

2. But again, justification is said to be by faith, in order to shut out boasting. "By grace are ye saved, through faith, (and that not of yourselves, it is the gift of God,) *not of works, lest any man should boast*[t]." Do we wish a practical commentary upon this passage? We have it in the parable of the Pharisee and the Publican. "God, I thank Thee that I am not as other men are, extortioners, unjust, adulterers, or even as this publican. I fast twice in the week, I give tithes of all that I possess." Here is the boasting which would claim heaven as a debt. "God be merciful to me a sinner." Here is the simple faith, which will make mention of God's righteousness only, and casts itself upon the mercy of its Judge. And our Lord Himself witnesses of him who spake these words, that "he went down to his house justified rather than the other[u]." So far are the Gospels and the Epistles from speaking a different language from each other, as some have insinuated, on this great subject. Whoever would obtain the gift of life must sue for it as a sinner, not demand it as a debt: but though as a sinner,—not as a sinner who loves his sin and would fain continue in it, but who hates sin, and longs to be free from it, and comes to the Saviour that he may be free, with full

[t] Eph. ii. 8, 9. [u] Luke xviii. 11—14.

purpose of heart, that, by God's grace, sin shall no more have dominion over him. "Where is boasting then?" the Apostle asks. "It is excluded. By what law? Of works? Nay, but by the law of faith[x]." Faith would not exclude boasting, if it justified us as itself a work, or as the root and foundation of all works. It is *both* indeed; but yet it is not in either of these characters that it justifies us; but because it sends us straight to Christ, that we may be found in Him, not having our own righteousness, which is of the law, but that which is through the faith of Christ, the righteousness which is of God by faith[y].

3. But yet further, the very objections which, in St. Paul's day, were urged against his doctrine, or which he foresaw were likely to be urged against it, strongly confirm the view which has been taken, inasmuch as they are precisely such as were likely to be urged on the supposition that that view is the true view. A system, of which the basis was justification *by works* whether legal or evangelical, was hardly the one to suggest the calumny, that it held the principle that we are to " do evil that good may come[z];" or, which is but the same slander under another form, that we are to " continue in sin that grace may abound[a]." But such was a very natural, though a very wicked, misrepresentation of a system, which taught, that we are justified by faith, because

[x] Rom. iii. 27.   [y] Phil. iii. 9.   [z] Rom. iii. 8.
[a] Rom. vi. 1.

faith leads us to put aside all confidence in our own good deeds, and to rest all our hopes of acceptance on the righteousness of Christ. And it may be added, that even the abuse of St. Paul's doctrine, which, as is generally thought, drew forth St. James's caution, is itself a witness to the view which has been contended for. For that abuse was hardly likely to have grown out of a system, which represented faith as justifying, either as being one among other good works, or as being the well-spring and fountain of all good works.

4. However, not to rest more on this argument than it will bear, I would observe further, that Scripture, when referring to the office of faith in the matter of our justification or salvation, (and the one is only the complement of the other,) speaks of it repeatedly in a great variety of ways, but with a remarkable harmony of purpose, as the *instrument* by which we become cognizant of and appropriate to ourselves spiritual blessings, in like manner as the senses are instruments by which we become cognizant of and appropriate to ourselves the things of sense around us. And I mention it the rather, because there have been those who have spoken slightingly of the term " instrument," as applied to faith, and have censured the use of such metaphorical language as would describe it as the *hand* by which we lay hold on Christ, or the *eye* by which we behold Him, not considering that on such subjects our language must be metaphorical, and forgetting the many

instances of such language occurring in Scripture. Thus, for example, faith is represented repeatedly as holding the same office in respect of the spiritual world, which the eye does in respect of the material. The figure is of frequent occurrence in the account of faith given in Heb. xi.; as where it is said of the elder saints, that they " all died in faith, not having received the promises, but *having seen* them afar off, and were persuaded of them and embraced them[b]." In accordance with this language, we find our Lord saying to the Jews, " This is the will of Him that sent Me, that every one which *seeth the Son and believeth on Him*, may have everlasting life, and I will raise him up at the last day[c];" and more plainly still, in his discourse with Nicodemus, " As Moses lifted up the serpent in the wilderness, even so must the Son of Man be lifted up, that whosoever believeth in Him should not perish, but have eternal life[d]." The dying Israelites were healed by looking, and they who are perishing by the bite of a more deadly serpent are saved by believing; sight was the instrument in the one case, faith is the instrument in the other. Again, the Apostle says of faith in a more general sense, referring to the whole course of the Christian's conversation, " We walk by faith, not by sight[e];" and in accordance with

[b] Heb. xi. 13. Ἡ πίστις τοίνυν ἐστὶν ὄψις τῶν ἀδήλων, φησὶ, καὶ εἰς τὴν αὐτὴν τοῖς ὁρωμένοις φέρει πληροφορίαν τὰ μὴ ὁρώμενα. Chrysost. in Heb. xi. 1.

[c] John vi. 40.   [d] John iii. 14, 15.   [e] 2 Cor. v. 7.

this figure, we find our Lord telling the Jews, in the very same passage in which he had spoken of faith as the *eye* by which we *behold* Christ, "He that *cometh* to Me shall never hunger, and he that believeth on Me shall never thirst[f];" where *believing*, in the one clause, is expressed by *coming*, in the other. And thus the gracious invitation, which we have elsewhere, "*Come* unto Me, all ye that labour and are heavy laden, and I will give you rest[g]," is addressed directly to faith; and faith accepts it by coming, that she may have rest[h]. Once more, when our Lord tells the Jews in the passage just referred to, "I am the bread of life, he that cometh to Me shall never hunger, and he that believeth on Me shall never thirst;" and presently afterwards, "I am the living bread which came down from heaven, if any man *eat* of this bread he shall live for ever, and the bread which I will give is my flesh, which I will give for the life of the world[i];" though it cannot be doubted, but that He here intimated that mystical feeding upon His Body and Blood, which should afterwards be vouchsafed to His servants in the holy

---

[f] John vi. 35.   [g] Matt. xi. 28.

[h] "Non ad Christum ambulando currimus, sed *credendo;* nec motu corporis, sed voluntate cordis accedimus. Ideo illa mulier, quae fimbriam tetigit, magis tetigit quam turba quae pressit. Ideo Dominus dixit, 'Quis me tetigit?' Et mirantes discipuli dixerunt, 'Turbae te comprimunt, et dicis, Quis me tetigit?' Et ille repetivit, 'Tetigit me aliquis.' Illa tangit, turba premit. Quid est 'tetigit' nisi *credidit?*" August. in Joan. Tract. xxvi. §. 3.

[i] John vi. 51.

Supper, yet did He not less plainly signify, that the mean whereby the Body of Christ is received and eaten, and the Blood of Christ received and drunk, whether in the Lord's Supper or otherwise, is faith[k].

In all these instances we have faith represented as bringing us into communion with Christ, and appropriating to us the blessings which He has purchased for us, not as a good work, one among many good works, nor as the basis and foundation of all good works; but simply as an *instrument*— the *eye*, by which we behold Him; the *foot*, by which we go to Him and approach Him; the *mouth*, by which we feed upon Him, to the strengthening and refreshing of our souls[m].

---

[k] "*Credere* in eum hoc est manducare panem vivum. Qui *credit* manducat: invisibiliter saginatur, quia invisibiliter renascitur. Infans intus est, novus intus est, ubi novellatur ibi satiatur." August. in Joan. Tract. xxvi. §. 1.

[m] "I am sensible that some very eminent men have expressed a dislike of the phrase of the *instrumentality* of faith, and have also justly rejected the thing according to the false notions which some have conceived of it. It cannot, with any tolerable sense or propriety, be looked upon as an instrument of *conveyance* in the hand of the efficient or principal cause; but it may justly and properly be looked upon as *the instrument of reception in the hand of the recipient*. It is not the mean by which the grace is *wrought, effected,* or *conferred;* but it may be and is *the mean by which it is accepted or received:* or, to express it a little differently, it is not the instrument of justification in the *active* sense of the word; but it is in the *passive* sense of it." Waterland, Summary View of Justification, Works, vol. ix. p. 451. "By this

How entirely the view, which has now been taken of the office of faith in respect of our justification, is the view which our own Church commends to us, will be evident from the following passage from the Homily which she refers to in her Article on Justification. If the passage be a long one, its direct bearing upon this deeply important subject must be my excuse for reading it entire. " First you shall understand, that in our justification by Christ, it is not all one thing, the office of God unto man, and the office of man unto God. Justification is not the office of man, but of God; for man cannot make himself righteous by his own works, neither in part nor in the whole; for that were the greatest arrogancy and presumption of man that Antichrist could set up against God, to affirm that a man might by

---

speech (that faith alone justifieth) we never meant to exclude either hope or charity from being always joined as inseparable mates with faith in the man that is justified; or works from being added as necessary duties required at the hands of every justified man : but to shew that *faith is the only hand* which putteth on Christ to justification, and Christ the only garment which, being so put on, covereth the shame of our defiled natures, &c." Hooker on Justification, §. 31. " Accipere hoc donum dicimus *manu fidei* quæ applicat nobis Christi justitiam, non ut nostra fiat per modum *infusionis* aut *inhæsionis* sed per modum *imputationis*. Atque demiror Papistas non posse intelligere quomodo per fidem Christi justitia nobis applicetur, qui putant se intelligere, quomodo, per indulgentias pontificias, Christi et sanctorum merita sive vivis sive mortuis assignentur." Bishop Davenant, de Justitia habituali, c. xxiii.

his own works take away and purge his own sins and so justify himself. But justification is the office of God only, and is not a thing which *we render unto Him*, but which *we receive of Him;* not which we *give* to Him, but which we *take* of Him by His free mercy, and by the only merits of His most dearly beloved Son, our only Redeemer, Saviour, and Justifier, Jesus Christ: so that the true understanding of this doctrine, We be justified freely by faith without works, or that we be justified by faith in Christ only, is not, that this our own act to believe in Christ, or, this our faith in Christ, which is within us, doth justify us and deserve our justification unto us, (for that were to count ourselves to be justified by some act or virtue that is within ourselves,) but the true understanding and meaning thereof is, that although we hear God's word and believe it, although we have faith, hope, charity, repentance, dread and fear of God within us, and do never so many good works thereunto, yet we must renounce the merit of all our said virtues, of faith, hope, charity, and all our other virtues and good deeds, which we either have done, shall do, or can do, *as things that be far too weak and insufficient and imperfect* to deserve remission of our sins and our justification; and therefore we must trust only in God's mercy, and that sacrifice which our High Priest and Saviour Jesus Christ, the Son of God, once offered for us upon the Cross, to obtain thereby God's grace and remission as well of our original sin in baptism, as of all actual sin committed by us after our baptism, if we truly repent and turn unfeignedly to Him again. So that as St. John Baptist, although he were never so virtuous and godly a man, yet in this matter of forgiving of sin, he did put the people from him, and appointed them unto Christ, saying thus unto them, Behold, yonder is the Lamb of God, which taketh away the sins of the world; even so, as great and as godly a virtue as the lively faith is, yet it putteth us from itself and remitteth or appointeth us unto Christ for to have only by Him remission of our sins or justification. So that our faith in Christ, as it were, saith unto us thus: It is not I that take away your sins, but it is Christ only; and to Him only I send you for that purpose, forsaking therein all your good virtues, words, thoughts, and works, and only putting your trust in Christ[n]."

Such is the language of the Homily on the subject; and if we should be asked for a witness from the elder Church, let it be the following passage of Clemens Romanus. "The ancient Patriarchs," he says, "were all greatly glorified and magnified, not for their own sake, or for their own works, or for the righteousness which they themselves wrought, but through His good pleasure. And we also being called through His good pleasure in Christ Jesus are not justified by ourselves, neither by our own wisdom, or knowledge, or piety, or the works which we have done in holiness of heart, but

[n] Homily of Salvation, part 2.

by that faith by which Almighty God justified all from the beginning°."

° Clem. Rom. ad Corinth. Ep. i. c. 32. Πάντες οὖν ἐδοξάσθησαν καὶ ἐμεγαλύνθησαν, οὐ δι' αὐτῶν, ἢ τῶν ἔργων αὐτῶν, ἢ τῆς δικαιοπραγίας ἧς κατειργάσαντο, ἀλλὰ διὰ τοῦ θελήματος αὐτοῦ. Καὶ ἡμεῖς οὖν διὰ θελήματος αὐτοῦ ἐν Χριστῷ Ἰησοῦ κληθέντες, οὐ δι' ἑαυτῶν δικαιούμεθα, οὐδὲ διὰ τῆς ἡμετέρας σοφίας, ἢ συνέσεως, ἢ εὐσεβείας, ἢ ἔργων ὧν κατειργασάμεθα ἐν ὁσιότητι καρδίας· ἀλλὰ διὰ τῆς πίστεως, δι' ἧς πάντας τοὺς ἀπ' αἰῶνος ὁ παντοκράτωρ Θεὸς ἐδικαίωσεν. "Here it is observable," Waterland remarks, (Works, vol. ix. p. 453.) on quoting this passage, "that the word *faith* does not stand for the whole system of Christianity, or for Christian belief at large, but for some particular self-denying principle, by which good men, even under the patriarchal and legal dispensations, laid hold on the mercy and promises of God, referring all, not to themselves or their own deservings, but to Divine goodness in and through a Mediator. It is true, Clemens elsewhere, and St. Paul every where, insists upon true holiness of heart, and obedience of life, as indispensable *conditions* of salvation or justification; and of that, one would think there could be no question among men of any judgment or probity: but the question about *conditions* is very distinct from the other question about *instruments*, and therefore both parts may be true, viz. that faith and obedience are equally *conditions*, and equally indispensable where opportunities permit; and yet faith over and above is emphatically *the instrument* both of *receiving* and *holding* justification, or a title to salvation.

"Σὺ δέ μοι σκόπει πῶς πανταχοῦ τὰ δύο τίθησι, καὶ τὰ παρ' αὐτοῦ καὶ τὰ παρ' ἡμῶν. Ἀλλὰ τὰ μὲν αὐτοῦ ποικίλα καὶ πολλὰ καὶ διάφορα· καὶ γὰρ ἀπέθανε δι' ἡμᾶς, καὶ κατήλλαξεν ἡμᾶς, καὶ προσήγαγε καὶ χάριν ἔδωκεν ἄφατον· ἡμεῖς δὲ τὴν πίστιν εἰσηνέγκαμεν μόνον." Chrysost. in Rom. Hom. ix. St. Augustine expresses the same doctrine in words singularly resembling those of St. Clement in the passage quoted in the text. Referring to the Pelagian teaching, that the saints of the Old

The sum of what has been said is this: In the soul's first quickening into spiritual life, the *law*

Testament had attained perfection of righteousness, he says, Quantælibet fuisse virtutis antiquos prædices justos, *non eos salvos fecit nisi fides Mediatoris, qui in remissionem peccatorum sanguinem fudit.* Ipsorum enim vox est, 'Credidi, propter quod locutus sum.' Unde ait et Apostolus Paulus: 'Habentes autem eundem spiritum fidei, secundum quod scriptum est, Credidi, propter quod locutus sum: et nos credimus, propter quod et loquimur.' Contra duas Epist. Pelag. lib. i. §. xxi.

In the third book of the same treatise St. Augustine sets forth the same doctrine more at length: " Aiunt etiam (Pelagiani) ' quod omnes Apostoli vel Prophetæ non plene sancti definiantur a nobis, sed in comparatione pejorum minus malos eos fuisse dicamus: et hanc esse justitiam cui Deus testimonium perhibet, ut quomodo dicit propheta, justificatam Sodomam comparatione Judæorum, sic etiam nos criminosorum comparatione dicamus sanctos aliquam exercuisse virtutem.' Absit ut ista dicamus: sed aut non valent intelligere, aut nolunt advertere, aut calumniandi studio dissimulant se scire quod dicimus. Audiant ergo vel ipsi, vel potius ii quos idiotas et ineruditos decipere moliuntur. *Nostra fides, hoc est catholica fides, justos ab injustis, non operum sed ipsa fidei lege discernit: quia justus ex fide vivit.* Per quam discretionem fit, ut homo ducens vitam sine homicidio, sine furto, sine falso testimonio, sine appetitu rei ullius alienæ, parentibus honorem debitum reddens, castus usque ad continentiam ab omni omnino concubitu, etiam conjugali, eleemosynarum largissimus, injuriarum patientissimus, qui non solum non auferat aliena, sed nec sua reposcat ablata, vel etiam venditis omnibus suis erogatisque in pauperes, nihil suum propriumque possideat; cum suis tamen istis velut laudabilibus moribus, si non in Deum fidem rectam et catholicam teneat, de hac vita damnandus abscedat. Alius autem, habens quidem opera bona ex fide recta quæ per dilectionem operatur, non tamen ita ut ille bene moratus, incontinentiam suam sustentat honestate nuptiarum, conjugii carnalis debitum et reddit

convinces us of our sinfulness. The language which it perpetually sounds in our ears is, " Do this and live." And the more conscience is enlightened, and the more sensible it becomes of the spirituality of

et repetit, injurias non tam patienter accepit, sed ulciscendi cupiditate fertur iratus: quamvis, ut possit dicere ' Sicut et nos dimittimus debitoribus nostris,' rogatus ignoscat: possidet rem familiarem, faciens inde quidem eleemosynas, non tamen quam ille tam largas: non aufert aliena, sed, quamvis ecclesiastico judicio non forensi, tamen repetit sua: nempe iste, qui moribus illo videtur inferior, *propter rectam fidem quæ illi est in Deum, ex qua vivit, et secundum quam in omnibus delictis suis se accusat, in omnibus bonis operibus Deum laudat, sibi tribuens ignominiam, illi gloriam, atque ab ipso sumens et indulgentiam peccatorum et dilectionem recte factorum,* de hac vita liberandus et in consortium cum Christo regnaturorum recipiendus emigrat. *Quare, nisi propter fidem, quæ, licet sine operibus neminem salvat,* (ipsa enim est non reproba fides, quæ per dilectionem operatur) *tamen per ipsam etiam peccata solvuntur, quia justus ex fide vivit:* sine ipsa vero etiam quæ videntur bona opera in peccata vertuntur; omne enim quod non est ex fide, peccatum est." August. contra Duas Epist. Pelag. lib. iii. §. v. See also August. in Psalm. cxxix. quoted above, p. 149, 150. These passages may serve to shew that St. Augustine, however he might, in many instances, use the *term justificatio* of an inherent righteousness, distinctly held the *doctrine* set forth in our Article that " we are accounted righteous before God, only for the merit of our Lord and Saviour Jesus Christ, by faith, and not for our own works or deservings." How fully St. Chrysostom held the same doctrine, will be evident to any one who will read through his Commentary on Rom. iii. iv. v. and Gal. iii. On the use of *Justificatio* and its cognates in St. Augustine and others of the Fathers, see Bp. Davenant De Justitia habituali, c. xxv.; and Barrow's Sermon " Of Justification by Faith," Works, vol. iv. p. 386.

the law rightly understood, and of its high and holy standard, reaching to the very thoughts and intents of the heart, the more it is confounded and overwhelmed with the sense of its utter inability to fulfil the requirements, and of its consequent guilt, helplessness, and misery. At this point, faith, which has indeed in no small degree conducted us thus far, enters upon its proper office. It recognises Christ in the Law, under its types and ceremonies, as the propitiation for the sins of the world; it discerns Him more plainly in the Prophets, as the promised Saviour to whom they " all give witness, that through His name, whosoever believeth in Him shall receive remission of sins^q;" it hears the Baptist declare, " Behold the Lamb of God, which taketh away the sin of the world^r;" it hears our Lord's own gracious lips declare, " Come unto Me, all ye that labour and are heavy laden, and I will give you rest^s;" it hears the Apostles declare, " Now then we are ambassadors for Christ, as though God did beseech you by us, we pray you in Christ's stead be ye reconciled to God^t." And the trembling sinner arises without delay, and comes unto Him thus witnessed to on all hands, that he may have life. But how does he come? With the purpose of continuing in sin? Nay; if his faith be the faith of God's children, the faith which is received into an honest and good heart,— honest and good, because God hath made it such,

^q Acts x. 43.
^s Matt. xi. 28.
^r John i. 29.
^t 2 Cor. v. 20.

if it be the faith that justifies, the faith that saves, he brings with him, when he comes, *a hearty and unreserved consent to the Gospel covenant in all its parts.* How could his faith be that of a true heart if it were otherwise; he not only cordially accepts eternal life and all things pertaining to eternal life, as God's free gift in Christ Jesus, but, like Saul of Tarsus, he asks, Lord, what wilt Thou have me to do"? and surrenders himself and all that he has—his soul and body, his time, his talents, his wealth, his influence, unfeignedly and unreservedly to the service of Him who loved him and gave Himself for him. If his faith does not produce one as well as the other, if it does not manifest itself in *obedience* as well as in *trust*, it is nothing worth; but yet it is neither through the worthiness of its obedience, nor the worthiness of its trust, nor any other worthiness whatsoever, that it justifies, but simply because it brings him into union with Him, who is the Lord our Righteousness.

Thus, in the language of our Article, we are justified *by faith only*, in the language of St. Paul, *by faith without the deeds of the law*: not that faith shuts out works *absolutely;* but that it shuts them out *from the office of justifying,* when we use that word, in St. Paul's sense of it, with reference to *the ground of our acceptance with God;* not again that it shuts out baptism, for this also has its place; but that so far as it is *the instrument* by which we appropriate to ourselves the blessings which God bestows upon us

---

" Acts ix. 6.   ˣ Art. xi.   ʸ Rom. iii. 28.

in Christ Jesus, so far as it leads directly to our consenting heartily, and with the full and unreserved surrender of ourselves to the Gospel Covenant, it stands alone, and no stranger intermeddleth with its joy¹.

And this doctrine, as it is " most wholesome," so is it, at the same time, " very full of comfort²."

¹ " Truth it is, that our own works do not justify us, to speak properly of our justification; that is to say, our works do not merit or deserve remission of our sins, and make us of unjust, just before God: but God, of His mere mercy, through the only merits and deservings of His Son Jesus Christ, doth justify us. Nevertheless, because faith doth directly send us to Christ for remission of our sins, and that by faith, given us of God, we embrace the promise of God's mercy and of the remission of our sins, (which thing none other of our virtues or works properly doth,) therefore Scripture useth to say, that faith without works doth justify. And forasmuch as it is all one sentence, in effect, to say, faith without works, and, only faith doth justify us, therefore the old ancient Fathers of the Church from time to time have uttered our justification with this speech; Only faith justifieth us, meaning none other thing than St. Paul meant when he said, ' Faith without works justifieth us.' And because all this is brought to pass through the only merits and deservings of our Saviour Christ, and not through our merits, or through the merit of any virtue that we have within us, or of any work that cometh from us; therefore, in that respect of merit and deserving, we forsake, as it were, altogether again faith, works, and all other virtues. For our own imperfection is so great, through the corruption of original sin, that all is imperfect that is within us, faith, charity, hope, dread, thoughts, words, and works, and therefore not apt to merit or deserve any part of our justification for us." Homily of Salvation, part 3.

² Art. xi.

While we look to our own good deeds as the ground of our acceptance before God, nothing can be more cheerless than the prospect. And the more earnest we are in striving to work out a righteousness of our own, the more deeply sensible we must be of our manifold and great deficiencies. But let Christ and His righteousness be apprehended by a true and living faith, springing up, because God has planted it there, in an honest and good heart, which has come to Christ with the cheerful confidence of one who has no reserves, and doubts neither of acceptance on Christ's part, nor of entire surrender on its own, and the soul now has that to rest upon which will not and cannot fail her. She may run the way of God's commandments, because God hath set her heart at liberty[b], delivering her from the fear of her enemies, that she may serve God in holiness and righteousness before Him all her days[c]. While, at the same time, the very consciousness she has of the infinite preciousness of the salvation she has received *in earnest*, and looks, one day, to receive *in full*, makes her walk warily and heedfully, as knowing that a deposit has been committed to her, which if she were to lose, the wealth of worlds could not compensate her for the loss.

[b] Ps. cxix. 32. [c] Luke i. 74, 75.

SERMON VII.

THE CONNECTION BETWEEN BAPTISM AND
JUSTIFICATION.

" Ille justificatur a peccato, cui, per baptismum, peccata omnia remittuntur." Ambros. apud Augustin. contra Julianum Pelagianum, lib. ii. §. v.

" Absit ut ego inanem dicerem gratiam lavacri illius, in quo renatus sum ex aqua et Spiritu, qua liberatus sum a reatu omnium peccatorum, vel quæ nascendo traxeram, vel quæ male vivendo contraxeram; qua liberor ut sciam ne intrem in tentationem, a concupiscentia mea abstractus et illectus, atque ut exaudiar dicens cum consortibus meis, ' Dimitte nobis debita nostra;' qua liberabor, ut spero, in æternum, ubi jam nulla lex in membris meis repugnet legi mentis meæ." Augustin. contra Julian. Pelagian. lib. vi. §. xiv.

" Neque hæc doctrina detrahit quicquam aut Deo aut fidei. Non Deo: quia fatemur Deum esse causam principalem, qui solus, per Verbum, fidem in nobis gignat, et in Verbo ac Sacramentis nobis offerat gratiam suam in Christo, nempe remissionem peccatorum et efficaciam Spiritus Sancti. Neque fidei derogat: quia agnoscimus illam esse unicum illud instrumentum, quo apprehendamus gratiam salutarem in Verbo et Sacramentis nobis oblatam. Tantum dicimus, quemadmodum *Fides* est quasi *manus nostra*, qua nos quærimus et accipimus, sic *Verbum* et *Sacramenta* esse quasi *manus Dei*, quibus Is nobis offert et confert quod fide a nobis petitur et accipitur." Vossius de Sacrament. vi et efficac. §. xlv.

Acts xxii. 16.

Arise, and be baptized, and wash away thy sins, calling on the name of the Lord.

Among the various arts by which our great adversary has perverted the truth whose first entrance into the world he could not hinder, none has been more successful than that by which he has contrived to thrust some one portion of it into such undue prominence as to obscure others. For a time, the portions cast into the shade have been overlooked and neglected, not without serious detriment to the whole. But their day of retribution has at length arrived, and then they have been in turn as unduly exalted as before they were unduly depressed. And thus the errors of one generation become the parents of others, the very reverse of themselves in character, which are to arise and flourish, their posthumous offspring, when they are extinct[a].

[a] " Most of the heresies and schisms of the Church have sprung up of this root, while men have made it as it were their scale, by which to measure the bounds of the most perfect religion; taking it by the farthest distance from the error last condemned. These be *posthumi hæresium filii;* heresies which arise out of the ashes of other heresies, that are extinct and amortized." Lord Bacon, on Church Controversies.

No portion of divine truth has suffered more in this way than the doctrine of Justification by Faith. The office of faith in reference to justification has at times been allowed so exclusively to fill the whole field of vision, that men have forgotten, that though in its own province it stands alone, there are other graces to be exercised, and other duties to be performed, and none of them without an important place in the economy of our salvation. "It is a branch of belief," as Hooker truly says[b], "that sacraments are in their place no less required than belief itself." And yet it has been a common thing for men so exclusively to fix their minds on the known and acknowledged necessity of faith, that they have almost or altogether lost sight of the office which the sacraments have assigned to them. And then, in turn, another generation has arisen, which has dwelt so exclusively on the sacraments and their efficacy, that men have been in danger of resting in a form of godliness, taking little care, while regard is paid to the externals of religion and to outward propriety of conduct, to cultivate that inward life of faith, without which neither religious observances nor outward propriety are of any avail.

The truth is, it is alike impossible to have a right view of the office of faith in reference to our justification, without taking into account the office of the sacraments, as to have a right view of the office of the sacraments without taking into account the office

[b] Eccles. Pol. book v. §. 60.

of faith. And he will be the safest expounder of the one, and the best maintainer of its just rights, who has the truest sense of the other's claims, and of their mutual relationship.

The office which faith bears in reference to our justification is, that it leads us simply and at once to Christ, that in Him we may obtain that righteousness which we have not and cannot have of ourselves. And in leading us to Christ, it leads us to close heartily and sincerely with the terms of the Gospel covenant, accepting Christ and whatsoever benefits are bestowed upon us through Christ, as God's gracious gift, and cordially and earnestly devoting ourselves to God's service. But the question arises, at what juncture these blessings are for the first time actually made over to us. This brings us to the consideration of that sacrament in which we have our first formal entrance into the covenant of grace, the first formal grant of remission of sins, the first formal investiture in that perfect righteousness, in which only we can hope to stand before the righteous King, when He shall sit upon His throne of judgment.

And here, I would remark, more perhaps than in any other part of our enquiry, will the advantage be felt of viewing justification as a branch of a larger subject, and not as an isolated and detached point. Justification is one of many blessings which God graciously bestows upon us in Christ, and which flow to us through our union with Him. And baptism is instrumental to our justification, precisely in the same manner and to the same extent as it is to our union with Christ. It justifies us, in whatever sense it does justify us, in that it incorporates us into Him, " who of God is made unto us wisdom, and righteousness, and sanctification, and redemption^c."

Now nothing can be more plain than that baptism is in some sort instrumental to our union with Christ. " By one Spirit," says the Apostle, " are we all baptized into one body^d." " As many of you as have been baptized into Christ, have put on Christ^e." Here the implied connection between baptism and our incorporation into Christ's body is direct. It is the Holy Spirit indeed by whom we are incorporated, but baptism is the instrument which the Holy Spirit uses, and which is therefore effectual because He uses it. Elsewhere, we find the effects of our union with Christ, and justification, or that which is equivalent to justification, among them, spoken of as produced through the instrumentality of baptism: for instance, Admission into God's kingdom, " Except a man be born of water and of the Spirit, he cannot enter into the kingdom of God^f;" Remission of sins, " Arise, and be baptized, and wash away thy sins^g;" A death unto sin, and a new birth unto righteousness, " Buried with Him in baptism, wherein also ye are risen with Him^h;" Salvation, which, in the sense in which it is used in the passages referred to, signifies

^c 1 Cor. i. 30.   ^d 1 Cor. xii. 13.   ^e Gal. iii. 27.
^f John iii. 5.   ^g Acts xxii. 16.   ^h Col. ii. 12.

our first entrance into a state of salvation, and is therefore equivalent to justification, though not without reference to that sanctification by which justification is inseparably accompanied, " Baptism doth now save us (not the putting away of the filth of the flesh, but the answer of a good conscience toward God) by the resurrection of Jesus Christ[i]."
" Not by works of righteousness which we have done, but according to His mercy He saved us, by the washing of regeneration, and renewing of the Holy Ghost[k]."

From these passages it is clear, that baptism is in some sort an instrument in effecting the union which the Christian has with Christ. To explain them so exclusively of an inward spiritual baptism, as to shut out reference to an outward material baptism, is repugnant to their plain meaning. It is true the material baptism, if it be unaccompanied by the spiritual, is but as a body without the soul; but when Scripture has so repeatedly joined the two together, how dare we hope for that which is from God, otherwise than in the use of that which is left in our own power? If baptism be a mere ceremony, why is a spiritual influence so often spoken of in connexion with it? If a spiritual influence be all that is intended in such passages, why is mention made of an outward service[1]?

---

[i] 1 Pet. iii. 21.   [k] Tit. iii. 5.

[1] " Μέλλων τοίνυν εἰς τὸ ὕδωρ καταβαίνειν, μὴ τῷ ψιλῷ τοῦ ὕδατος πρόσεχε· ἀλλὰ τῇ τοῦ Ἁγίου Πνεύματος ἐνεργείᾳ τὴν σωτηρίαν ἐκδέχου·

What then is the precise office of baptism in reference to the Christian's union with his Lord? In answering this question, I would put out of sight, in the first instance, the case of infants, and confine myself, for the sake of clearness, to that of adults, which is simpler and of more easy solution.

I. In adults, as we have seen, faith is instrumental to our incorporation into Christ, in that it leads us cordially to close with the terms of the Gospel covenant, to accept Christ as our Head in every respect, not only that we may be exalted together with Him, and glorified together, but also, if need be, as need assuredly will be, that we may suffer with Him, being conformed to Him in the likeness of His death, that we may be also in the likeness of His resurrection. It leads us, on the one hand, to accept salvation and all things necessary to salvation, as God's free and unmerited gift, bestowed upon us in Christ; on the other, to consecrate ourselves and all we have unreservedly to His service. Faith

Ἄνευ γὰρ ἀμφοτέρων ἀδύνατόν σε τελειωθῆναι. Οὐκ ἐγώ εἰμι ὁ τοῦτο λέγων, ἀλλ' ὁ Κύριος Ἰησοῦς Χριστὸς, ὁ τοῦ πράγματος τὴν ἐξουσίαν ἔχων, φησίν· Ἐὰν μή τις γεννηθῇ ἄνωθεν· καὶ ἐπιφέρει λέγων, ἐξ ὕδατος καὶ Πνεύματος, οὐ δύναται εἰσελθεῖν εἰς τὴν βασιλείαν τοῦ Θεοῦ. Οὐδὲ τῷ ὕδατι βαπτιζόμενος, μὴ καταξιωθεὶς δὲ τοῦ Πνεύματος, τελείαν ἔχει τὴν χάριν, οὐδὲ κἂν ἐνάρετός τις γένηται τοῖς ἔργοις, μὴ λάβῃ δὲ τὴν δι' ὕδατος σφραγίδα, εἰσελεύσεται εἰς τὴν βασιλείαν τῶν οὐρανῶν· τολμηρὸς ὁ λόγος, ἀλλ' οὐκ ἐμὸς, Ἰησοῦς γὰρ ὁ ἀποφηνάμενος· καί μοι λάβε τῶν λόγων τὴν ἀπόδειξιν ἀπὸ τῆς θείας γραφῆς. Cyrill. Hieros. Catechēs. iii. in Vossius. de Baptismo Disputat. 4. Thes. 8.

produces the cordial and unfeigned assent to this covenant in our hearts. And this is the main point. For without the assent of the heart, the covenant is an empty form, a dead letter. And God, who seeth the heart, might, if he had been so pleased, have required nothing beyond this inward assent; and doubtless in some extraordinary cases he does accept it as sufficient; but ordinarily, it has seemed good to him to require an outward ratification of the covenant, as well that we may thereby solemnly pledge ourselves to its observance, as that he may formally instate us in the benefits of it, and both assure us, and notify to others, that we are instated in them. This then is the precise office of baptism. "It is the solemn ratification of the great Christian covenant between God and the faithful recipient. God's gracious purpose on God's part, and faith, which itself also is God's gift, on the part of the person to be baptized, have already brought the parties to an agreement. The covenant is already made in intention; only it is not made formally. The soul is betrothed to Christ, but the marriage ceremony has not taken place. Baptism completes what was yet lacking. It is the solemn signing and sealing of the covenant by both the contracting parties. And consequently, it actually conveys and makes over to both of them the benefits to which they respectively become entitled. Thus, on the one hand, God does in and by baptism incorporate the baptized person, as a living member, into Christ's mystical body, and invest Him with the full privileges and immunities, so far as He is as yet capable of them, of that blessed fellowship. He makes him, in the well and thoughtfully chosen words of our Catechism, a member of Christ, and, because a member of Christ, the child of God, and an inheritor of the kingdom of heaven. On the other, the baptized person renounces for ever all other lords; he accepts Christ, and God, in Christ, as his only Master; and he solemnly engages himself to the performance of whatsoever duties, whether of trust, or dependence, or universal and unreserved obedience, are involved in his new relationship.

I need scarcely remark, how entirely the whole structure of our baptismal services, as well as of those of the early church, on the model of which our own are framed, is based upon the principle here set forth, that baptism is the solemn ratification of a covenant between God and the person baptized. The renunciation of the world, the flesh, and the devil, those " other lords," who formerly had dominion over us; the profession of belief in the three divine Persons of the sacred Trinity, in whose name baptism is administered; the promise of unreserved obedience to God's will thenceforward to the end of life;—all these, first solemnly required in God's behalf, as indispensable conditions in order to the administration of the sacrament, and then solemnly made on the part of the person to be baptized, and both required and made in the presence of those who stand in the twofold capacity both of " *wit-*

nesses[m]" of the transaction and of "*sureties*" for the performance of the conditions;—here is all the form and solemnity of a covenant, and nothing is wanting to complete the transaction but the solemn ratification which follows, when the baptism is administered. From that moment, he who was before spoken of as a subject of Satan's kingdom, as dead in trespasses and sins, as having no part nor lot in Christ, is regarded as regenerate, and grafted into the body of Christ's Church, as washed from all his guilt, and sanctified by the indwelling of God's Spirit, who has now vouchsafed to take up His abode within him[n]. The principle of all which is,

---

[m] So the godfathers and godmothers are called in the Service for the public baptism of such as are of riper years. "Forasmuch as these persons have promised *in your presence* to renounce the devil and all his works, to believe in God, and to serve Him; ye must remember, that it is your part and duty to put them in mind what a solemn vow, and profession, they have now made before this congregation, and especially *before you their chosen witnesses.*"

[n] "The Catechumen descends into the font a sinner, he arises purified; he goes down the son of death, he comes up the son of the resurrection; he enters in the son of folly and prevarication, he returns the son of reconciliation; he stoops down the child of wrath, and ascends the heir of mercy; he was the child of the devil, and now he is the servant and the son of God." Bede, quoted by Jer. Taylor, Works, vol. ii. p. 243. "Susceptus a Christo, Christumque suscipiens, non idem est post lavacrum, qui ante baptismum fuit, sed corpus regenerati fit caro crucifixi." Leo, Serm. xiv. de Passione, quoted by Bingham, b. xi. c. 10. §. 4.

that baptism is the solemn ratification of the great Christian covenant, and, as such, the instrument by which we are incorporated into Christ.

And that this is the true light in which baptism is to be regarded is plain from the analogy of circumcision, which occupied the same place in reference to the old covenant, which baptism does in reference to the new. Circumcision was the token of the covenant betwixt God and the children of Abraham according to the flesh; and baptism is the token of the covenant betwixt God and the children of Abraham according to the Spirit. Circumcision, in that it was the token of the old covenant, admitted those who were circumcised into all the privileges and immunities belonging to that covenant; and baptism, in that it is the token of the new covenant, invests those who are baptized, with all the privileges and immunities belonging to the new, or, to sum these up in one word, it incorporates them as living members into Christ's body.

The fathers indeed, in speaking of baptism, often use language, which might seem to put its efficacy upon another ground, besides this of its being the ratification of the Christian covenant; as though the sacramental element, straightway upon the words of consecration, underwent a change, and became, after a sort, instinct with grace and divine virtue. Thus Tertullian says, that "the Spirit descends from heaven, and resting upon the water, sanctifies it by Himself, and, being so sanctified, it imbibes the power of sanctifying°." And elsewhere they speak, as they do also of the consecrated wine in the Eucharist, as though the water, after the words of consecration, were *transelemented*, to employ an expression in frequent use with some of them, into the blood of Christ. Thus St. Jerome says of the Ethiopian Eunuch, that he " was baptized in the blood of Christ about whom he was reading ᵖ." Yet such language is obviously to be understood *mystically*, whether as regards the figure of the Saviour's blood, or that of the Holy Spirit. We are truly said to be in baptism washed in Christ's blood, yet not because the element of water is substantially changed into blood, but because the blood of Christ is really, though mystically, applied to us in that sacrament. And the Holy Spirit may, in a certain sense, be said to descend from heaven and rest upon the baptismal water, and endue it with power to sanctify, not that He thereby infuses a supernatural inherent virtue into the element, but that He is infallibly present in the sacrament to make good God's part of the covenant, and to incorporate those as living members into Christ's body, who have already cordially assented to it in their hearts ᵠ.

° De Baptismo, c. iv.

ᵖ In Esai. lviii. 7. quoted by Bingham, b. xi. c. 10. §. 4.

ᵠ Ex his colligimus, Sacramenta posse considerari trifariam: ac, pro eo, etiam triplicem esse de iis loquendi formam. Primum enim consideramus signa κατὰ φύσιν: quomodo Baptismatis aquam dicimus, et in Eucharistia panem ac vinum. Deinde attendimus

As to the view of baptism which places its efficacy on the ground of its being the ratification of the

ea opposite sive relate, ratione ejus quod significant: quomodo aqua est symbolum sanguinis Christi; panis et vinum sunt typi sive figura et imago corporis et sanguinis Christi. Adhæc in considerationem veniunt secundum conjunctionem pacti: quatenus voluntate ac promissione divina, in legitimo sacramentorum usu, concurrunt ablutio aquæ et ablutio peccatorum per sanguinem Christi; esus panis cum potu vini, et esus corporis Christi cum potu sanguinis ejus. Proprie igitur loquendo, id quod in baptismate cernimus est aqua: quod in Eucharistia panis et vinum. Sin secundo tertioque modo consideremus, locutione in sacramentis usitata aqua est sanguis Christi, panis et vinum sunt corpus Christi et sanguis ejus. Sed hoc est discriminis, quod secundo modo sic loquamur per μετανυμίαν signi; tertio autem per συνεκδοχὴν partis, quia pro toto, quod constat signo et re sacramenti, ponimus partem nobiliorem." Vossius de Sacramentorum vi et efficacia, §. lxiv. " Cum veteres aiunt sanguinem Christi et Spiritum Sanctum se aquæ miscere, populare est loquendi genus, quod ita capere oportet, quasi dicerent, quando aqua abluimur foris, oculis fidei intuendum esse sanguinem et Spiritum Christi, quia hæc cum aqua concurrunt, haud secus ac si miscerentur cum aqua. Nam dum aqua abluit corpus, etiam Christum, qui sanguinem suum effudit pro nobis, Spiritu suo in animam penetrare, suamque in ea exserere vim et efficaciam." Vossius de Baptismo Disputat. v. Thesis ii. " For even as in the Person of our Lord Jesus Christ both God and man, when His human nature is by itself considered, we may not attribute that unto Him, which we do and must ascribe as oft as respect is had *unto both natures combined;* so because in Sacraments there are two things distinctly to be considered, the outward sign, and the secret concurrence of God's most blessed Spirit, in which respect our Saviour hath taught that water and the Holy Ghost are combined to work the mystery of new birth; sacraments therefore *as signs* have only those effects

Gospel covenant, no words can set it forth more explicitly than these in which St. Bernard describes the sacraments in general: " Many things," says he, " are done simply with reference to themselves, and others with a view to others, for which they stand as signs or symbols. For instance, a ring, given simply as a ring, conveys no other gift than itself; but a ring, given to give actual possession of an inheritance, is a sign of the inheritance, it stands for it and represents it. So that he who hath received it may say, The ring is nothing, I care not for it, the inheritance is what I sought. In like manner when the Lord drew nigh His passion, He thought good to give actual possession of His grace to His disciples, by giving them some visible sign as a pledge and earnest of invisible grace....And like as

before mentioned: but of sacraments, in that by God's own will and ordinance, they are *signs assisted always with the power of the Holy Ghost*, we acknowledge whatsoever either the places of Scripture, or the authority of Councils and Fathers, or the proofs and arguments of reason which he allegeth, can shew to be wrought by them. The elements and words have power of infallible signification, for which they are called seals of God's truth; the Spirit affixed unto those elements and words, power of operation within the soul, most admirable, divine, and impossible to be expressed. For so God hath instituted and ordained, that, *together with due administration and receipt of sacramental signs, there shall proceed from Himself grace effectual to sanctify, to cure, to comfort, and whatsoever else is for the good of the souls of men.*" Hooker, Eccles. Pol. book vi. §. 6. See also Waterland on the Doctrine of the Eucharist, ch. v. Works, vol. vii. p. 94, 95.

in the things of this life, different signs are used for different purposes....so likewise in divine matters, different gifts are conveyed by different sacraments[r]."

[r] "Multa fiunt propter se tantum; alia vero propter alia designanda, et ipsa dicuntur signa et sunt. Ut enim de usualibus sumamus exemplum, datur annulus absolute propter annulum, et nulla est significatio: datur ad investiendum de hæreditate aliqua, et signum est, ita ut jam dicere possit qui accipit; Annulus non valet quicquam, sed hæreditas est quam quærebam. In hunc itaque modum, appropinquans passioni Dominus, de gratia sua investire curavit suos, ut invisibilis gratia signo aliquo visibili præstaretur. Ad hoc instituta sunt omnia sacramenta, ad hoc Eucharistiæ participatio, ad hoc pedum ablutio, ad hoc denique ipse baptismus, initium sacramentorum omnium, in quo complantamur similitudini mortis ejus.........Sicut enim in exterioribus diversa sunt signa, et, ut cœpto immoremur exemplo, variæ sunt investituræ secundum ea de quibus investimur; verbi gratia investitur Canonicus per librum, Abbas per baculum, Episcopus per baculum et annulum simul: sicut inquam in hujusmodi rebus est, sic et divisiones gratiarum diversis sunt traditæ sacramentis." Bernard. In Coena Domini. Op. vol. i. p. 87, 88. See Waterland on the doctrine of the Eucharist, (Works, vol. vii. p. 146—148.) where he quotes this passage, and enlarges upon the view given in it. " A book, a ring, a crozier, and the like, have often been made use of as instruments (of investiture.) They are not without their significancy in the way of instructive emblem: but, what is most considerable, they are instruments to convey those rights, privileges, honours, offices, possessions, which, in silent language, they point to. Those small gifts or pledges are as nothing in themselves, but they are highly valuable with respect to what they are pledges of, and what they legally and effectively convey: so it is with the signs and symbols of both sacraments......A deed of conveyance, or any like instrument under hand and seal, is not a real estate, but it conveys one; and it is, in effect, the estate itself,

But besides conveying and making over to us the benefits of the Christian covenant, baptism answers this further purpose, that it stands as a pledge and assurance to us from God, and a notification to others, that they are made over to us. God does " assure us thereby," to use our Church's language in reference to the other Sacrament, " that we are very members incorporate in the mystical body of His Son." And it is much to be remarked, how the Apostles, in writing to baptized persons, address them, on the presumption of their baptism, as in Christ. But then it is also to be remarked, that God does not leave us exclusively to the outward sign, but that as whoever is truly incorporated into Christ is incorporated by the Spirit, and whoever is truly born into God's family is born of the Spirit, so every one so incorporated and so born is sealed with the Spirit. The water and the Spirit jointly concur in incorporating us, the Spirit as the author of our incorporation, the water as the instrument in the Spirit's hands; and the water and the influences of the Spirit are also joint seals—the water outwardly upon our bodies, the Spirit inwardly upon our

---

as the estate goes along with it; and as the right, title, and property, which are real acquirements, are, as it were, bound up with it, and subsist by it."

On the *Federal* nature of Baptism, see Waterland, Doctrine of the Eucharist, ch. xi. Works, vol. vii. p. 318. Vossius de Baptismo Disp. iv. Thes. iii. and Dodwell Dissert. Cypr. Dissert. xiii. c. 21. &c.

hearts. And the outward witness is of no value, except in so far as it is confirmed by that within [s].

And I may add further, that while baptism is a pledge from God to us, that He has actually made over to us the blessings of the Christian covenant, it is, at the same time, a pledge from us to God, that we, for our parts, will be faithful to that covenant. It is our solemn oath and *sacrament*, to use the word *sacrament* in its primary sense, that henceforward Christ, and God in Christ, shall be our only Lord and Master, that we will never be ashamed of Him or His faith, that we will fight manfully under His banner against sin, the world, and the devil, and that we will continue His faithful soldiers and servants unto our lives' end [t].

We have seen now the manner in which baptism is effectual towards incorporating us into Christ. Look at it as it is in itself, and without regard to any further object, and it is a simple form, such as, in human customs, the giving of a ring, the delivery of a key, the signing of a name; but look at it as a

---

[s] "Σημεῖον γὰρ τότε τοῦτό ἐστιν, ὅταν τὸ πρᾶγμα, οὗ τοῦτό ἐστι σημεῖον, φαίνηται παρὰ σοί, τουτέστιν, ἡ πίστις· ὡς, ἂν μὴ ταύτην ἔχῃς, οὐδὲ τὸ σημεῖον λοιπὸν εἶναι σημεῖον δύναται. Τίνος γὰρ ἔσται σημεῖον, τίνος δὲ σφραγὶς, οὐκ ὄντος τοῦ σφραγιζομένου; ὡς ἂν εἰ καὶ βαλάντιον ἐπιδεικνύεις ἡμῖν σφραγῖδα ἔχον, μηδενὸς ἔνδον ἀποκειμένου· ὥστε καταγέλαστος ἡ περιτομή, τῆς πίστεως ἔνδον οὐκ οὔσης. Εἰ γὰρ δικαιοσύνης ἐστὶ σημεῖον, δικαιοσύνην δὲ οὐκ ἔχεις, οὐδὲ σημεῖον ἔχεις." Chrysost. in Rom. Hom. viii. §. 3.

[t] "Vocati sumus ad militiam Dei vivi jam tunc cum in Sacramenti verba respondimus." Tertull. ad Martyr. §. iii.

Sacrament, as the sign and seal of God's covenant with us, look at it as regards the benefits which God conveys and makes over by it to the faithful receiver, and it raises the poor outcast child of Adam from his poverty and wretchedness, and sets him with princes, yea makes him a member of Christ, and, because a member of Christ, the child of God, and an inheritor of the kingdom of heaven.

And the relation which faith bears to baptism, in working this mighty and blessed change, is, as has been already intimated, that it produces that inward assent to the covenant, without which whatever is done on our parts is an empty form. "Baptism doth save us," says the Apostle, " by the resurrection of Jesus Christ[u]," for it incorporates us into Him, that as we have been " planted together in the likeness of His death," we may be also " in the likeness of His resurrection [x]." But how does it save us?

[u] 1 Pet. iii. 21. "Baptism saves, that is, it gives a just title to salvation; which is the same as to say, that it conveys justification. But then it must be understood not of the outward washing, but of the inward, lively, faith, stipulated in it and by it. Baptism concurs with faith, and faith with Baptism, and the Holy Spirit with both; and so the merits of Christ are savingly applied. Faith alone will not ordinarily serve in this case; but it must be a contracting faith on man's part, contracting in form, corresponding to the federal promises and engagements on God's part: therefore Tertullian rightly styles Baptism 'obsignatio fidei,' 'testatio fidei,' 'sponsio salutis,' 'fidei pactio,' and the like." Waterland, Summary View of the Doctrine of Justification, Works, vol. ix. p. 441.

[x] Rom. vi. 5.

"not the putting away of the filth of the flesh," not as it is a mere external washing, "but the answer of a good conscience toward God," when the heart intends, in sincerity and truth, what the lips profess. We are "buried with Christ in baptism, wherein also we are risen with Him," writes St. Paul: but then he adds, "through the faith of the operation of God, who hath raised Him from the dead[y]," through faith, which is God's work in us: so that while, ordinarily, we can have no part nor lot in Christ, but through baptism, baptism is of no efficacy without faith[z]. It is faith which converts the simple washing into an efficacious sacrament, or, in the mystical language of the ancient writers above referred to, brings down the Holy Spirit from heaven upon the baptismal fountain, and turns the water into blood.

The consideration of the relation which faith thus bears to baptism, may serve to shew, in what sense both the word and the ministry are also spoken of as instrumental causes of our new birth; as where St. Peter says, that we are "born again not of corruptible seed, but of incorruptible, by the word of God, which liveth and abideth for ever[a]." And St. Paul tells the Corinthians, that he is their spiritual

[y] Col. ii. 12.

[z] "Ἐπὶ τούτων τὸ ὕδωρ ὕδωρ ἐστὶν, οὐδαμοῦ τῆς δωρεᾶς τοῦ Ἁγίου Πνεύματος ἐπιφανείσης." Greg. Nyssen. in Waterland, Works, vol. vii. p. 288.

[a] 1 Pet. i. 23.

father, and that in Christ Jesus he hath begotten them through the Gospel [b]. The truth is, that by the word and the ministry, or rather, as is ordinarily the case, by the ministry of the word, faith is produced. And thus the word and the ministry and baptism are all instrumental, each in its proper office, in the work of our regeneration. The word and the ministry as producing faith, and faith, as making us capable of receiving the benefit of the Sacrament. And the Holy Spirit is the author of our new birth, in that it is He who uses these instruments, and makes them effectual to our regeneration. For the word is from Him, and the ministry is from Him, and faith is from Him. And He makes the Sacrament effectual to those whom He has endued with faith, and by the Sacrament incorporates them into Christ, and transfers them from their state of nature into a state of grace [c].

---

[b] 1 Cor. iv. 15.

[c] "After the three Divine Persons, principally concurring and co-operating in man's justification, we may next pass on to the subordinate instruments: and here come in *the Ministry, the Word, and the Sacraments;* but more particularly the Sacrament of *Baptism.*..........According to the natural order of precedency, the authorized *Ministry* is first in consideration; the *Word* next; then *hearing* and *believing* with a penitent heart and lively faith; after that *Baptism, and therein the first solemn and certain reception of justification,* which is afterwards continued by the same lively faith and the use of the Word and of the other Sacrament." Waterland, Summary View of the Doctrine of Justification, Works, vol. ix. p. 435. " Sic igitur statuimus, solum quidem Christi

But the question may be asked, What is the condition of those, to whom God has already given the grace of faith, but who are not yet baptized? I answer, Their condition is an imperfect condition: their union with Christ is, as it were, in an incipient state, but it is not formally effected: they have life in some sort, but not life fully developed; the life of the womb, not the life which is given at birth. " A man begins to be a partaker of God's grace," says St. Augustine, " from the moment he begins to believe....But it is material to observe at what particular crises of time, or in the celebration of what Sacraments, grace is both more largely and more sensibly poured into the soul....Faith has its first beginnings, its conceptions, so to speak. But we need to be born, and not to be conceived only, in order to attain eternal life [d]." Baptism is the first

sanguinem nos salvare, si de meritoria salutis causa agamus; solum item Spiritum sanctum nos regenerare, si principalem regenerationis causam efficientem consideremus: sed his non excludi causas instrumentales; uti Fidem, qua meritum Christi, velut manu apprehendimus; item prædicationem Verbi et usum Sacramentorum per quæ Spiritus Sanctus in nobis operatur regenerationem et salutem nostram. Nimirum hic locum habet, quod vulgo dicitur, *subordinata non pugnare*. Quod vellem attenderent qui antiquos vel sentientes cum his, dum magnificis adeo elogiis ornant baptismum, injurios arbitrantur merito et efficaciæ servatoris nostri." Vossius de Baptismo Disputat. v. Thes. iv.

[d] " Incipit homo percipere gratiam ex quo incipit Deo credere, vel interna vel externa admonitione motus ad fidem. Sed interest quibus articulis temporum vel celebratione sacramentorum gratia

actual commencement of our new life. The state of faith and repentance before baptism is preparatory to that life, and, in adults, whose case we are now considering, indispensable to it; and doubtless, in its measure, it is a state of favour and acceptance with God: yet is it perfectly distinct from the state into which we are introduced at baptism. St. Paul gave proof both of repentance, and faith, and the purpose of a new life, when he asked the question, " Lord, what wilt Thou have me to do?" Yet it was not till three days afterwards that Ananias bade him arise, and be baptized, and wash away his sins:

---

plenior et evidentior infundatur...Fiunt inchoationes quædam fidei conceptionibus similes: non tamen solum concipi, sed etiam nasci opus est ut ad vitam perveniatur æternam." De diversis Quæst. ad Simplic. lib. i. Quæst. 2. §. 2. Tempus est ut vos exhortemur, qui adhuc estis catechumeni : *qui sic credidistis in Christum, ut adhuc vestra peccata portetis.* Nullus autem regnum cælorum videbit oneratus peccatis; quia nisi cui dimissa fuerint, non regnabit cum Christo : dimitti autem non possunt, nisi ei qui renatus fuerit ex aqua et Spiritu Sancto. August. in Joan. Tract. xi. §. 1. *Quantumcunque enim catechumenus proficiat, adhuc sarcinam iniquitatis suæ portat: non illi dimittitur nisi cum venerit ad baptismum.* Quomodo non caruit populus Israel populo Ægyptiorum nisi cum venisset ad mare rubrum, sic pressura peccatorum nemo caret, nisi cum ad fontem baptismi venerit." ibid. Tract. xiii. §. 7. " In baptism is the first formal solemn death unto sin in the plenary remission of it; which comes to the same as to say, that there also commences our justification entire: all before was but preparatory to it, as conception is to birth." Waterland, Summary View of the Doctrine of Justification, Works, vol. ix. p. 438.

and that bidding implied, that till then, he still bore the burthen of his iniquity.

Yet indispensable as baptism is to salvation under ordinary circumstances, we may not doubt, but that where men are prevented from receiving it by unavoidable necessity, the faith, which desired the sacrament, is accepted instead of the sacrament; and this, not only in the case of martyrs, baptized, as the ancients were wont to speak, in their own blood[e], but of those also, in whom, although there be not the sufferings of martyrs, there is the grace which enabled them to endure martyrdom, even that secret influence of the Spirit, by which God had already begun to draw them to Himself, and to form Christ within them. The instance of Cornelius, who, for a special reason, received those sensible gifts of the Spirit before baptism, which ordinarily were not given but to baptized persons, is a sufficient indication, that, when cause exists, God is willing to give the grace of the sacrament otherwise than in the sacrament. And it was surely to teach us the same lesson, that our Lord, after declaring the blessedness of him who should believe and be baptized, omits the reference to baptism in the clause which follows: "He that believeth and is baptized shall be saved, but he that believeth not shall be damned[f];" as though implying, that while

[e] On the belief of the ancients respecting the Baptism of blood in martyrdom, see Dodwell Diss. Cypr. Diss. xiii.

[f] Mark xvi. 16.

faith, in the case of adults, can never be dispensed with, God may and will, where, by unavoidable necessity, baptism cannot be obtained, accept the desire of the sacrament instead of the sacrament. The penitent thief had no baptism, and the death which he died was not a martyr's death; yet in his heart he believed unto righteousness, and with his mouth he made confession unto salvation. And no man ever left the earth with a surer hope of rising again to a joyful resurrection [g].

[g] " Baptism without faith cannot save a man; and by faith doth save him: and faith without baptism, where it cannot be had, not where it may be had and is contemned, may save him. That Spirit which works by means will not be tied to means." Bp. Hall's Epistles, Decade v. Ep. 4. " The Law of Christ, which in these considerations maketh baptism necessary, must be construed and understood according to rules of natural equity......And, because equity so teacheth, it is on all parts gladly confessed that there may be, in divers cases, life by virtue of inward baptism, even where outward is not found. So that if any question be made, it is but about the bounds and limits of this possibility...It hath been constantly held, as well touching other believers as martyrs, that baptism, taken away by necessity, is supplied by desire of baptism, because with equity this opinion doth best stand." Hooker, Eccles. Pol. book v. ch. 60. " Librum Ambrosii de morte Valentiniani legat,...et advertet sine dubio Sanctum homini non baptizato et mortuo fidenter de sola fide salutem præsumere et tribuere indubitanter bonæ voluntati, quod defuit facultati. Legat et Augustini de unico baptismo librum quartum.........Quantum itaque, ait, valeat, etiam sine visibili sacramento Baptismi, quod ait Apostolus, ' Corde creditur ad justitiam, ore autem confessio fit ad salutem,' in illo Latrone declaratum est. Sed tunc, inquit,

But to return: We have seen that baptism is effectual, as being the solemn ratification of the great

> impletur invisibiliter, cum mysterium Baptismi non contemptus religionis, sed articulus necessitatis excludit.' Et quidem non ignoro retractare ipsum id quod posuerat testimonium de Latrone, minusque idoneum ad comprobandam illam sententiam confiteri, eo quod sane incertum sit, utrumne fuerit baptizatus. Cæterum sententiam et audacter prosequitur, et multipliciter confirmat, nec uspiam (nisi fallor) retractasse reperies......Ab his ergo duabus columnis (Augustinum loquor et Ambrosium) crede mihi, difficile avellor. Cum his, inquam, me aut errare, aut sapere fateor: credens et ipse sola fide hominem posse salvari, cum desiderio percipiendi sacramentum; si tamen pio adimplendi desiderio mors anticipans, seu alia quæcunque vis invincibilis obviarit. Vide etiam ne forte ob hoc Salvator cum diceret, ' Qui crediderit et baptizatus fuerit salvus erit,' caute et vigilanter non repetierit ' Qui vero baptizatus non fuerit,' sed tantum, ' Qui vero,' inquit, ' non crediderit, condemnabitur;' nimirum innuens solam interdum fidem sufficere ad salutem, et sine ipsa sufficere nihil. Quapropter etsi martyrium vicem baptismi posse implere conceditur, non plane hoc facit pœna sed fides. Nam absque ipsa, quid est martyrium nisi pœna? Quæ ergo martyrio præstat, ut absque ulla dubietate pro baptismate reputetur, ipsa ita infirma et imbecillis per se erit, ut quod dare alteri valet, sola non valeat obtinere? Et prorsus sanguinis pro Christo effusio magnæ cujusdam fidei indubitata probatio est, non Deo tamen, sed hominibus. Sed quid, si Deus, qui profecto ad probandum quod vult, nullis indiget experimentis, æque magnam in corde cujuspiam in pace morientis inspicit fidem, martyrio quidem non interrogatam, martyrio tamen idoneam? Si recordatus fuerit homo necdum se salutis percepisse mysterium, et dolens, pœnitensque toto desiderio expetierit, sed assequi mortis celeritate præoccupatus nequiverit; damnabit fidelem suum Deus? damnabit, inquam, hominem pro se etiam paratum mori? Paulus dicit: ' Nemo potest dicere Dominus Jesus; nisi in Spiritu Sancto.'

Christian covenant; that as such, (speaking generally, and as yet confining our attention to the case of adults,) it is both the instrument by which we are incorporated into Christ, and also the seal by which we are assured ourselves, and notice is given to others, that we have been incorporated. The benefit which is thus conveyed, and of the conveyance of which assurance is thus given us, is, in one word, a living union with Christ.

And Justification is one of the fruits of that union, one of the subordinate benefits both conveyed and made over and also signed and sealed to us in baptism; so that, if we are incorporated into Christ's body in baptism, in that it is the solemn ratification of the great Christian covenant, we are justified on the same ground. And thus baptism is both an instrument of our justification, and also a seal to assure us that we have been justified. And the time of baptism is the date from which our justification reckons. No man ordinarily is justified before

Hunc ergo qui, in articulo mortis, non solum invocat Dominum Jesum, sed ipsius quoque toto desiderio expetit sacramentum, dicemus aut non loqui in Spiritu Sancto, et falsus erit Apostolus; aut et cum Spiritu Sancto damnari? Salvatorem habet habitantem per fidem in corde, et in ore per confessionem: et cum Salvatore damnabitur? Pro certo, cum non aliunde martyrium nisi ex fidei merito illam obtinuerit prærogativam, ut singulariter vice baptismi secure suscipiatur, non video cur non ipsa æque, et sine martyrio, apud Deum tantundem possit, cui, et sine martyrii probamento, proculdubio innotescit." Bernard. ad Hugon. de S. Vict.

baptism, and whoever receives baptism rightly, is in baptism admitted into a state of justification. But that which on our parts renders baptism effectual to the production of these blessed fruits is faith. Without faith it is an empty form, a mere bodily washing. So that if baptism is the instrument on God's part, by which He conveys the grant, faith is the instrument on ours, by which we seek for it and obtain it. And as baptism is the sole instrument in one sense, so faith is the sole instrument in the other. Nor do we at all derogate from the doctrine that we are justified by faith only, when we teach that faith attains its end for the first time in baptism [h].

The conclusion at which we have thus arrived by the consideration of the *general* benefit, (that is, our incorporation into Christ,) conveyed and made over to us in baptism, is abundantly confirmed by the language of Scripture in reference to the *particular*

---

[h] "Tantum dicimus, quemadmodum fides est quasi *manus nostra*, qua nos quærimus et accipimus; sic Verbum et Sacramenta esse quasi *manus Dei*, quibus Is nobis offert et confert quod fide a nobis petitur et accipitur." Vossius de Sacram. vi et effic. §. 45.
...... "Faith is nothing else but a hearty embracing Christianity, which first exerteth itself by open declaration and avowal in Baptism, (when we believe with our hearts to righteousness and confess with our mouth to salvation;) to that time therefore the act of justification may be supposed especially to appertain: then when the Evangelical Covenant is solemnly ratified, the grace thereof especially is conferred." Barrow of Justification by Faith, Works, vol. iv. p. 388. See also pp. 386—389. and Waterland, vol. ix. pp. 435—450.

subject of Justification. Indeed of all the blessed gifts bestowed upon us in Christ Jesus, none is more frequently connected with baptism than that plenary remission of sins in which justification consists; and that so pointedly and distinctly, that it is difficult to understand how any can receive the passages referred to, and yet evade the just conclusion, that the first grant of justification is conveyed in baptism.

When St. Peter bade the Jews on the day of Pentecost, " Repent, and be baptized for the remission of sins[1];" did not his words imply, that remission depended upon their being baptized, that their baptism was a necessary step towards attaining it, and that they should attain it on receiving baptism, provided that they brought with them the inward qualification of which he spoke? Could they have hoped for remission, if they had rested on their repentance, and despised the sacrament? And if not—then was not remission promised in the use of the sacrament? When Ananias bade Saul of Tarsus, " Arise, and be baptized, and wash away his sins," did not his words involve the same principle, viz. that remission of sins is to be had in baptism, and that the outward washing is, in the Holy Spirit's hands, effectual to cleanse the soul? Nay more, does it not imply, as has been already intimated, that though a man have faith, and repentance, and the purpose of unreserved obedience, (for all these

[1] Acts ii. 38.

St. Paul already had) yet the burthen of his sins is not removed, till he is baptized? And does not St. Paul himself teach the same doctrine, when he tells the Corinthians, that, grievously wicked as some of them had once been, they were now washed, they were sanctified, they were justified, in the name of the Lord Jesus Christ, and by the Spirit of our God[k]; evidently referring to baptism as instrumental to their justification, and to the time of baptism as the date at which their justification commenced? And does he not more plainly still teach the same doctrine, when he says of the Church, that Christ " loved it, and gave Himself for it, that He might sanctify and cleanse it with the washing of water by the word, that He might present it to Himself a glorious Church, not having spot or wrinkle or any such thing; but that it should be holy and without blemish[l]:" and again, when he reminds Titus, that God hath " saved us by the washing of regeneration and renewing of the Holy Ghost, which He shed on us abundantly through Jesus Christ our Saviour, that being justified by His grace, we should be made heirs according to the hope of eternal life[m]?" In all these places, baptism is evidently set forth as the sacrament in which we first obtain remission of sins, and enter upon a justified state; as the formal instrument by which God signs and seals the pardon of

---

[k] 1 Cor. vi. 11. [l] Eph. v. 25—27. [m] Tit. iii. 5—7.

His rebellious children, and thereby in effect both pardons them, and declares them pardoned[n].

It is almost superfluous to remark how constantly and universally this view of what may be called baptismal justification was held by the ancient Church. From East to West the confession resounded, as of one of the chief articles of the Christian faith, "I acknowledge one baptism for the remission of sins." Nor is there any doctrine, in the whole compass of Christian truth, which is more thoroughly wrought into the texture of the ancient writings. Whatever sins a man might previously have been guilty of, in baptism, it was held, he obtained plenary and entire forgiveness. And the sacrament was concluded to be both the instrument by which God conveyed the grant of forgiveness, and also the pledge by which He assured him that he was forgiven. Nor was there any case to which our Lord's commission to His Apostles, "Whosesoever sins ye remit, they are remitted unto them[o]," was held to have more direct reference than to the absolution granted in baptism. God was believed to loose in heaven that bond, which His ministers, when they administered baptism, loosed on earth[p].

Yet while the ancients spoke of baptism most

---

[n] See these passages and others considered in their bearing upon baptism, in Waterland, vol. ix. pp. 436—442.

[o] John xx. 23.

[p] See Bingham's Antiq. book xix. ch. i. §. 2.

unequivocally as the great absolution, the sacrament in which all previous sins were washed away, insomuch that the baptized person however laden with guilt when he descended into the font, came forth from it without spot or stain to sully the whiteness of his baptismal robe, they taught, not less distinctly, that such effect was wrought on those only, who brought with them the sincere repentance and lively faith, which disposed them to consecrate themselves unreservedly to God's service[q].

Thus far then we have considered the case of *adults*. And we have seen, first, from what the Scriptures teach generally of our incorporation into Christ, and then, from what they teach of Justification in particular, that baptism is ordinarily the instrument, by which God both justifies us and declares us justified; but yet that they only receive the benefit, who draw nigh with a true and lively faith. To others the sacrament is but an empty form: yea rather it is worse. In receiving it they mock God, they sin against their own souls, they contract the

---

[q] Thus St. Augustine concludes his fourth book on Baptism, " Quibus rebus omnibus ostenditur, aliud esse Sacramentum Baptismi, aliud conversionem cordis: *sed salutem hominis ex utroque compleri:* nec si unum horum defuerit, ideo putare debemus consequens esse ut et alterum desit; quia et illud sine isto potest esse in infante, et hoc sine illo potuit esse in latrone, complente Deo, sive in illo sive in isto, quod non ex voluntate defuisset: *cum vero ex voluntate alterum horum defuerit, reatu hominem involvi.* De Baptismo contra Donat. lib. iv. §. xxv.

most deeply solemn obligations, which it is possible for man to contract, little thinking it may be, that the obligation stands in full force, however they may deal by it. They have received the King's mark, and they are his sworn soldiers, whether they will serve under him or not; only if they will not, they stand thenceforward upon another footing than they who have never been enlisted under his banner.

II. But the question remains, and it is one of most deep importance to those, who, like ourselves, were baptized in infancy. Does baptism serve the same end, and has it the same effects, *in infants* as in adults? Are infants justified in baptism? Or is their justification withheld till such time as they are capable of faith and endued with faith?

This question turns in strictness upon another: Did our Lord's command to His Apostles to " baptize all nations," include infants as well as adults? If it did, no valid reason can be imagined, why the same effect should not be produced by the same sacrament in both.

And when it is considered, that our Lord spoke to those, who were already familiar both with infant circumcision, as the appointed rite for admitting the children of Jewish parents into the old covenant, and yet more with infant baptism, in the case of the children of proselytes[r], the presumption is that He

---

[r] " Baptism had been in long and common use among the Jews many generations before John Baptist came; they using

did intend His baptism to be administered to infants as well as to adults. And it is so strong a presumption, that it throws the whole burthen of proof upon those who deny the divine appointment of infant baptism. The question is, not, *Where are infants specifically named as the subjects of baptism?* but rather, *Where are they specifically excepted from the general injunction?* And when to this is added the practice of the Church from the earliest times, a practice both acquiesced in and complied with, as though no question could be moved respecting it, by those whose cause would have been signally served, could they have proved it contrary to Christ's

---

this for admission of proselytes into the Church, and baptizing men, women, and children for that end...Hence a ready reason may be given why there is so little mention of baptizing infants in the New Testament, that there is neither plain precept nor example for it, as some ordinarily plead. The reason is, because there needed no such mention; baptizing of infants having been as ordinarily used in the Church of the Jews, as ever it hath been in the Christian Church. It was enough, to mention that Christ established baptism for an ordinance under the Gospel, and then *who* should be baptized, was well enough known by the use of this ordinance of old. Therefore it is good plea—Because there is no forbidding of the baptizing of infants in the Gospel, *ergo* they are to be baptized; for that having been the common use among the Jews, that infants should be baptized as well as men and women, our Saviour would have given some special prohibition, if he intended that they should have been excluded. So that silence, in this case, doth necessarily conclude approbation to have the practice continued, which had been used of old before." Lightfoot's Harmony of the New Testament, §. ix. 3. p. 209, 210.

appointment, more convincing proof, it should seem, could hardly be desired.

Assuming then, that infant baptism is of divine appointment, what reason can be assigned, why the sacrament should not be thought to have the same efficacy in the case of infants as in the case of adults? Infants *need* the grace which adults receive in baptism as truly as adults. They need to be admitted into God's covenant; they need to be incorporated into Christ's body; they need remission of sins. And they are certainly *capable* of these benefits. Why then should the sacrament, administered to adults, be an effectual means of grace, admitting them into God's covenant, incorporating them as living members into Christ's body, and, by consequence, justifying them; while to infants, who are neither less capable, nor less in need of a vital union with Christ, and of the righteousness, which is the fruit of that union, it is an empty form, a token perhaps of a blessing to be vouchsafed at a *future* time, if repentance and faith manifest themselves, but conveying no *present* boon?' It is replied indeed, that it is for very want of these graces of repentance and faith, that the sacrament fails of its efficacy. But they who make the reply, do not consider, that the same want does not shut those infants out from heaven, who die in infancy: why then should it be thought to shut out those who live, from the benefit of baptism? If it does not hinder the one from salvation in the next life, how can it hinder the other from justification, which is the first step towards salvation, in this? God ties no man to impossibilities. Where both the subject is capable of faith, and baptism can be had, the sacrament is of no avail without faith, and faith will not suffice without baptism; but where either of these is wanting through unavoidable necessity, there we may not doubt, but that the grace of the sacrament is given, either without the sacrament, as in the case of such catechumens as are cut off, whether by martyrdom or otherwise, before they have obtained their desire of baptism, or without faith, as in the case of infants[s].

---

[s] "Sicut in latrone, quia per necessitatem corporaliter defuit (sanctificatio Sacramenti), perfecta salus est, quia per pietatem spiritualiter adfuit: sic et cum ipsa præsto est, si per necessitatem desit quod latroni adfuit, perficitur salus. Quod traditum tenet universitas Ecclesiæ, cum parvuli infantes baptizantur, qui certe nondum possunt corde credere ad justitiam, et ore confiteri ad salutem, quod latro potuit; quinetiam flendo et vagiendo, cum in eis mysterium celebratur, ipsis mysticis vocibus obstrepunt; et tamen nullus Christianorum dixerit eos inaniter baptizari." August. de Baptismo contra Donat. lib. iv. §. xxiii. "Omnino igitur eorum rejicimus sententiam, qui putant baptisma in infantibus non semper obsignare remissionem peccatorum. Quod si foret, consequeretur, sacramenta Dei in illis esse fallacia: quippe quæ gratiæ divinæ nullum ponentibus obicem non conferrent quod obsignarent. Hoc cum credere non sustineat animus, profecto non tantum ex judicio charitatis, sed etiam infallibilis charitatis, infantes baptizatos cœlo adscribimus, quotcunque priusquam ratiocinari seque actualibus polluere peccatis cœperint, de vita hac discesserint. Pro hac sententia etiam est Calvinus lib. iv. Instit. cap. 16. §. 5. 'Non enim Dominus olim circumcisione dignatus

Whatever hesitation may be felt by some in modern times, in admitting the connection between justification and baptism in the case of infants, the ancient Church knew no such scruple. Questions might be raised indeed on one or another point respecting infant baptism, but these very questions only served the more strongly to set forth, either directly or indirectly, the principle which has been contended for. Tertullian, for instance, in pursuance of a peculiar notion of his own, would have dissuaded parents from bringing their children to baptism. But the very reason he assigned— "Why should the innocence of childhood be in such haste to seek forgiveness?" while it savoured strongly of the Pelagian heresy of a later day, shews how intimately, in his mind, justification was associated with baptism. When some raised a scruple in Cyprian's time, as to whether baptism should not be refused to infants till after the eighth day from their birth, Cyprian and the Bishops in council with him gave sentence that it should on no account be refused, assigning this reason, that if persons, guilty of the most atrocious crimes, were, on believing, admitted to baptism, that therein they might obtain

est, quin eorum omnium participes faceret, quæ per circumcisionem signata tunc fuerunt: alioquin meris præstigiis ludificatus esset populum suum, si fallacibus symbolis eos lactasset: quod solo auditu horrendum.' Aliaque in hanc mentem copse habes capite et præcedenti." Vossius de Baptismo, Disput. iv. Thes. 4.

' Quid festinat innocens ætas ad remissionem peccatorum? Tertull. de Baptismo, c. 18.

forgiveness, much more surely should infants be admitted, in order to the same benefit, seeing that the sins which in them needed forgiveness were not their own but another's[u]. Again, when in the earlier stage of the Pelagian controversy, those who denied original sin, endeavoured to escape the argument with which they were pressed from the universal practice of baptizing infants, by replying that infants were baptized, not for the remission of sins, but for admission into the kingdom of heaven, into which, without baptism, both parties believed they could not enter, it was immediately rejoined, that the Church knew but one baptism, whether for adults or infants, the baptism confessed in the Constantinopolitan Creed; which implied, not only that infants have that which needs to be forgiven, but also, that, whether in infants or adults, baptism is the appointed sacrament for obtaining forgiveness[x].

---

[u] Cypr. Ep. 64. ad Fidum.

[x] " Hoc unum dicam, ut tandem finiatur oratio; Aut novum vos debere symbolum tradere, ut, post Patrem et Filium et Spiritum Sanctum, baptizetis infantes in regnum cœlorum; aut si unum et in parvulis et in magnis habetis baptisma, etiam infantes in remissionem peccatorum baptizandos in similitudinem prævaricationis Adam." Hieron. Dialog. advers. Pelagianos, lib. iii. Wall remarks on this passage, " Though St. Hierome, after having in these Dialogues largely confuted the errors of Pelagius, do insist but briefly of this proof of original sin from the baptism of infants, as being a matter which had been fully handled by St. Austin, yet this little seems to have nettled and puzzled Pelagius more

And the argument was felt to be of such force, that the Pelagians could thenceforward maintain their ground only by having recourse to subtle and disingenuous evasions, such as enabled them to reconcile the ostensible profession of the Creed with its virtual denial. Some of them granted that infants have sin, in some sort, but not original; others said, that they are indeed baptized for the remission of sins, not that they have sins of their own which need to be forgiven, but that, *whosoever has*, baptism is the appointed sacrament of forgiveness'.

than all that was said by St. Austin. The Pelagians confessed that adult persons were baptized for forgiveness of sins; but infants, having no sins, were baptized for the kingdom of heaven. This was to establish two sorts of baptism, which was contrary to that Article of the Constantinopolitan Creed then received in all the world, " I acknowledge one baptism for the remission of sins." Pelagius could never get clear from this argument. And it appears by his answer that he yielded more to the force of it than to any other." History of Infant Baptism, ch. xix. §. 26.

¹ " 'Quia non ait,' inquiunt, ' nisi quis renatus fuerit ex aqua et spiritu, non habebit salutem vel vitam æternam; tantummodo autem dixit, non intrabit in regnum Dei: *ad hoc parvuli baptizandi sunt, ut sint etiam cum Christo in regno Dei,* ubi non erunt si baptizati non fuerint.'" August. de Peccat. Mer. et Rem. lib. i. §. xxx. St. Augustine, after pressing the argument from our Saviour's words, John iii. 1—21, at some length, proceeds, " Quid de ipsa forma sacramenti loquar? Vellem aliquis istorum qui contraria sapiunt, mihi baptizandum parvulum afferret. Quid in illo agit exorcismus meus, si in familia Diaboli non tenetur? Quomodo ergo dicturus erat, eum renuntiare Diabolo, cujus in eo nihil esset? Quomodo converti ad Deum, a quo non esset aversus? *credere inter cætera remissionem peccatorum,* quæ

So unhesitatingly and without scruple was the doctrine received in ancient times, which regarded baptism, in infants, as well as in adults, as the appointed means of justification. Men might, as we have seen, in some few instances, and contrary to

illi nulla tribueretur?...Falsam igitur vel fallacem tradi parvulis baptismatis formam in qua sonaret, atque agi videretur, et tamen nulla fieret remissio peccatorum, viderunt aliqui eorum nihil exsecrabilius ac detestabilius dici posse atque sentiri. Proinde quod attinet ad baptismum parvulorum, ut eis sit necessarius, redemptione ipsis etiam opus esse concedunt, sicut cujusdam eorum libello brevissimo continetur: qui tamen ibi remissionem alicujus peccati apertius exprimere noluit. Sicut autem mihi ipse litteris intimasti, fatentur jam, ut dicis, etiam in parvulis, per Baptismum remissionem fieri peccatorum. Nec mirum: non enim redemptio alio modo posset intelligi. 'Non tamen originaliter,' inquiunt, '*sed in vita jam propria, posteaquam nati sunt, peccatum habere cœperunt,*'" Ibid. §. xxxiv. Others had recourse to the more subtle evasion referred to in the text: "Nam illud quod excogitaverunt, cum veritatis pondere premerentur, quia fidelis Dominus in verbis suis, et propterea ejus Ecclesia nullo modo fallaciter parvulos in remissionem peccatorum baptizat, sed ut fide agatur, quod agitur, utique fit quod dicitur; quod ergo excogitaverunt, cum hæc eos apertissima moles veritatis urgeret, quis non Christianus irrideat, quamlibet versutissimum cernat? Dicunt enim, ' Veraciter quidem respondere parvulos per ora gestantium, in remissionem se credere peccatorum; non tamen quia *sibi* remittantur, sed *quia credant quod in Ecclesia vel in Baptismo remittantur, in quibus inveniuntur, non in quibus nulla sunt.*' Ac per hoc nolunt ' eos ita baptizari in remissionem peccatorum, tanquam in eis fiat ipsa remissio, quos contendunt nullum habere peccatum; sed quoniam, licet sine peccato, *in eo tamen Baptismate baptizantur, quo fit in quibusque peccatoribus remissio peccatorum.*" August. Epist. 194, (alias 105,) ad Sixtum, §. x.

the voice of the whole Church, question whether infants have that which needs forgiveness; but, granting they have, there was but one opinion as to whether baptism was the sacrament of forgiveness.

And certainly the teaching of our own Church is not less clearly and unequivocally to the same effect. Throughout her service, till the baptismal element is applied, she speaks of the infant to be baptized, as sinful and defiled. But from that moment she entirely changes her language. She thanks God, that it hath pleased Him to regenerate him, to receive him for His own child by adoption, and to incorporate him into His holy Church. And all her prayer thenceforward is, that he may *continue* in this blessed fellowship, and lead the rest of his life according to this beginning.

With regard to infants dying unbaptized, the severe judgment of the ancients is well known[a]. And this, by the way, is an additional proof of the close and intimate connection believed to exist between baptism and justification; seeing that the difference in the condition of two infants, alike in all other respects, save this, that the one died with, the other without, baptism, was supposed to be no less than that the one was laid to his rest a child of light and an heir of glory, the other went down to the grave with the curse of original guilt cleaving to his

---

[a] See Bingham's Antiquities, book x. ch. 2. §. 24. and Wall's History of Infant Baptism, part ii. ch. 6.

head[b]. Our Church has both charitably and wisely abstained from pronouncing any judgment in the matter; and, while she hesitates not to declare, that " it is certain by God's word, that children which are baptized, dying before they commit actual sin, are undoubtedly saved[c]," she leaves the case of those who die unbaptized, in the obscurity in which Scripture has left it. And if we may hope confidently of the state of those adults, who, having a true and lively faith, have died without baptism, having been by unavoidable necessity precluded from the sacrament, there is surely light enough, in the midst of the darkness, to cheer the hearts of such Christian parents, as have earnestly desired baptism for their children, but, by no fault of their own, have been prevented from obtaining it[d]; while, at the same time, there is sufficient

[b] Thus St. Augustine repeatedly puts the case in his writings against the Pelagians.
[c] Service for the Public Baptism of Infants.
[d] " Sicut parvulis naturali, id est, alieno peccato obnoxiis, aliorum, id est, patronorum fides pro eis respondentium in baptismate sit ad salutem: ita parvulis, quibus baptismum denegari jussisti, parentum vel patronorum corde credentium, et pro parvulis suis fideli verbo baptisma expetentium sed non impetrantium, fides et fidelis postulatio prodesse potuerunt, dono ejus cujus Spiritus, quo regeneratio fit, ubi vult spirat." Hincmar Bp. of Rheims in Bingham, book x. ch. 2. §. 24. " That the contempt of baptism damneth, is past all doubt; but that the constrained absence thereof should send infants to hell, is a cruel rashness...... Children cannot live to desire baptism; if their parents desire it for them, why may not the desire of others be theirs, as well as,

matter both for anxious foreboding and deep and bitter self-reproach to those, who, whether through disparaging views of baptism, or inconsideration, or careless neglect, have defrauded their children of God's ordinance, and suffered them to depart they knew not whither.

The subject we have in hand has led us to consider baptism under this single aspect, as it stands connected with *Justification*. If it be enquired further, what is its office in respect of *Sanctification*, I answer, that here likewise it introduces us, so to speak, into a new world. Before baptism indeed, speaking of

according to Austin's opinion, the faith of others believing, and the mouth of others confessing?" Bp. Hall's Epistles, Dec. v. Ep. 4. " Touching infants which die unbaptized, since they neither have the sacrament itself, nor any sense or conceit thereof, the judgment of many hath gone hard against them. But yet, seeing grace is not absolutely tied unto sacraments, and besides, such is the lenity of God, that unto things altogether impossible, He bindeth no man, but where we cannot do what is enjoined us, accepteth our will to do instead of the deed itself; again, forasmuch as there is, in their Christian parents and in the Church of God, a presumed desire that the sacrament of baptism might be given them, yea a purpose also that it shall be given; remorse of equity hath moved divers of the School-divines in these considerations ingenuously to grant, that God, all-merciful to such as in themselves are not able to desire baptism, imputeth the secret desire that others have in their behalf, and accepteth the same as theirs, rather than casteth away their souls for that which no man is able to help," &c. Hooker, E. P. book v. c. 60. See the opinions of both ancients and moderns on this subject stated in Wall, part ii. ch. 6.

adults, there must have been some assistances of the Spirit, for the repentance and faith which led to baptism, were His gifts[e]. But now that we are actually incorporated into Christ, the Spirit is given after another manner. Now *He dwells within us*, the very bond of our union with Christ, and the fountain and source of the life we live in Him.

And this is the true account of that change which takes place within the Christian at his baptism. The Church of Rome would require us to believe, that nothing whatsoever which has the nature of sin is left in him. Nay, that even concupiscence which *is* left, is not sinful unless complied with[f]. And in this

---

[e] " Aliter adjuvat nondum inhabitans, aliter inhabitans. Nam nondum inhabitans adjuvat ut sint fideles, inhabitans adjuvat jam fideles." August. Ep. 194. (alias 105.) §. iv.

[f] St. Augustine is claimed by Romish writers as teaching (as, e. g. contra duas Epist. Pelagian. lib. i. §. xiii.) in express words, that concupiscence is not, strictly speaking, sin in the regenerate. What he meant was, that in them it is not sin, *because in them its guilt is cancelled.* The new-born Christian comes forth from the waters of baptism perfectly free from guilt; both original and actual. His actual sins are no longer remembered against him, neither does his original sinfulness any longer expose him to God's anger, except in so far as it issues in actual transgressions. But this is not because concupiscence is removed, or because its essential character is changed, however its force may be weakened, *but because the person in whom it is found is accepted in Christ.* " In eis qui regenerantur in Christo, cum remissionem accipiunt prorsus omnium peccatorum, utique *necesse est ut reatus etiam hujus, licet adhuc manentis, concupiscentiæ remittatur, ut in peccatum non imputetur.* Nam sicut eorum peccatorum quæ

she is consistent with herself. For the righteousness in which, according to her teaching, we must stand

manere non possunt, quoniam cum fiunt prætereunt, reatus tamen manet, et nisi remittatur, in æternum manebit; sic illius, quando remittitur, reatus aufertur. *Hoc est enim non habere peccatum, reum non esse peccati*........Nam si a peccando desistere hoc esset non habere peccata, sufficeret ut hoc nos moneret Scriptura, ' Fili, peccasti ? non adjicias iterum.' Non autem sufficit, sed addidit, ' Et de pristinis deprecare, ut tibi remittantur.' Manent ergo nisi remittantur. Sed quomodo manent si præterita sunt; nisi quia præterierunt actu, manent reatu ? Sic itaque fieri e contrario potest, *ut etiam illud maneat actu, prætereat reatu.*" August. de Nuptiis et Concupiscentia, lib. i. §. xxvi. " Dicit (Ambrosius) mortua quidem vitia per remissionem in Baptismate omnium peccatorum, sed eorum nos curare debere quodam modo sepulturam. Et in hoc ipso opere talem describit cum vitiis mortuis nos habere conflictum, ut non quod volumus agamus, sed quod odio habemus hoc faciamus: multa in nobis peccatum nobis reluctantibus operari; redivivas plerumque resurgere voluptates; luctandum nobis esse adversus carnem, adversus quam luctatus est Paulus, quando dicebat, ' Video aliam legem in membris meis repugnantem legi mentis meæ.'...Ecce quantam nos pugnam cum mortuis habere peccatis, ille strenuus Christi miles, et Ecclesiæ fidelis doctor ostendit. Quomodo enim peccatum mortuum est, cum multa operetur in nobis reluctantibus nobis ? Quæ multa nisi desideria stulta et noxia, quæ consentientes mergunt in interitum et perditionem ? Quæ utique perpeti, eisque non consentire, certamen est, conflictus est, pugna est. Quorum pugna nisi boni et mali, non naturæ adversus naturam, sed naturæ adversus *vitium, jam mortuum, sed adhuc sepeliendum*, id est omnino sanandum ? Quomodo ergo mortuum dicimus hoc peccatum in Baptismate, sicut etiam iste vir dicit, et quomodo habitare in membris fatemur, et multa operari desideria reluctantibus nobis, quibus non consentiendo resistimus, sicut etiam hic vir fatetur, nisi quia *mortuum est in eo reatu quo nos tenebat, et, donec sepulturæ perfectione sanetur, rebellat et*

before God, if we would find acceptance, must be a *perfect inherent* righteousness; and seeing that, as she justly holds, justification is conveyed in baptism, she must needs imagine a perfect inherent righteousness infused into the soul in baptism, to constitute justification. But this is not the teaching of Scripture. As far indeed as the *guilt* of sin is concerned, this is wholly taken away, when we are baptized: we are made living members of Christ's body, and " there is no condemnation to them which are in Christ Jesus." And as far as regards the *power* of sin, its dominion is broken; but then not in that the concupiscence which remains is not in its own nature sinful in us, (if it was sinful before baptism, it is surely not less sinful after, however its guilt may be cancelled by not being imputed,) but in that we are now " under grace." The Spirit of Christ dwells within us,—the principle of a new and heavenly life,—and if we will but honour His presence, and cherish His holy influences, and yield ourselves as willing instruments in His hands, we shall daily grow in conformity to that image in which man was originally created, and which it was the principal object of our Lord's coming to restore. The hea-

---

mortuum? Quamvis jam *non eo modo appelletur peccatum, quo faciat reum;* sed, quod sit reatu primi hominis factum, et quod rebellando nos trahere nititur ad reatum, nisi adjuvet nos gratia Dei per Jesum Christum Dominum nostrum, ne sic etiam mortuum peccatum rebellet, ut vincendo reviviscat et regnet." August. contra Julian. Pelagian. lib. ii. §. ix. See the note at p. 153, above.

venly leaven has been inserted into the mass, and in due time, but not the moment it is inserted, it will leaven the whole.

"As to the remission of sins," says St. Augustine, "this we have in baptism full and entire—the full and entire remission of all sins: but otherwise we are not to think that the nature and quality of the baptized person forthwith undergo a total change. Rather the first-fruits of the Spirit, then given, go on, while the new man increases day by day, gradually changing into themselves whatsoever of the old nature remains, till the whole man is at length so renewed, that even the frailness and weakness of the animal body are exchanged for the vigour and incorruption of the spiritual [g]."

[g] "Illud præcipue...attendere ac meminisse debemus, tantummodo peccatorum omnium plenam perfectamque remissionem baptismo fieri: hominis vero ipsius qualitatem non totam continuo commutari; sed spirituales primitias in bene proficientibus, de die in diem novitate crescente, commutare in se quod carnaliter vetus est, donec totum ita renovetur, ut animalis etiam infirmitas corporis ad firmitatem spiritualem incorruptionemque perveniat." De Pecc. Mer. et Rem. l. ii. §. xxvii. The same doctrine is set forth at greater length in the following passage. "Baptismus igitur abluit quidem peccata omnia, prorsus omnia, factorum, dictorum, cogitatorum, sive originalia, sive addita, sive quæ ignoranter, sive quæ scienter admissa sunt; sed non aufert infirmitatem, cui regeneratus resistit, quando bonum agonem luctatur, consentit autem, quando sicut homo in aliquo delicto præoccupatur; propter illud gaudens in actione gratiarum, propter hoc autem gemens in allegatione orationum. Ibi dicens 'Quid retribuam Domino pro omnibus quæ retribuit mihi?' hic dicens

Nor can any imaginable reason be assigned, why infants should not be thought capable of this gift of the Spirit, as well as of justification; and why therefore they should not in baptism be believed to be made partakers of the one as well as of the other. If they are incorporated as living members into Christ's body, it can only be by the indwelling of the Spirit, which connects the members with the Head. And though, while still infants, they can bring forth no fruits of actual righteousness, yet it is their peculiar blessedness, and doubly so if there

---

' Dimitte nobis debita nostra.'...............Hæc autem infirmitas, cum qua usque ad corporis mortem, defectu et profectu alternante, contendimus, (magnique interest quid vincat in nobis) regeneratione alia consumetur, de qua Dominus dicit ' In regeneratione, cum sederit hominis Filius' &c. Mat. xix. 28.......Quisquis igitur Baptismati derogat, quod modo per illud percipimus, corrumpit fidem; quisquis autem *jam nunc* ei tribuit, quod quidem per ipsum, *sed tamen postea* percepturi sumus, amputat spem. Nam si a me quisquam quæsierit, Utrum per baptismum salvi facti fuerimus; negare non potero, dicente Apostolo, ' Salvos nos fecit per lavacrum regenerationis et renovationis Spiritus Sancti.' Sed si quæsierit, Utrum per idem lavacrum *omni prorsus modo* jam nos fecerit salvos, respondebo, Non ita est. Idem quippe item dicit Apostolus, ' Spe enim salvi facti sumus. Spes autem quæ videtur, non est spes; quod enim videt quis, quid sperat? Si autem quod non videmus speramus, per patientiam exspectamus.' Salus ergo hominis in baptismate facta est, quia dimissum est quod peccati a parentibus traxit, vel quidquid etiam proprie ante Baptismum ipse peccavit: salus vero ejus tanta post erit, ut peccare omnino non possit." August. contra duas Epist. Pelagian. l. iii. §. iii.

are those around them to make them know it, as soon as they are capable of such knowledge, that they have God's Spirit with them from the first, to guide their earliest footsteps, if they will but yield themselves to His guidance, in the paths of righteousness.

Such then are the benefits of which we are made partakers in baptism,—the plenary and entire remission of all previous sin, and with this the gift of God's Spirit to renew us day by day in holiness, and conform us to the image of our divine Head. I cannot better sum them up, or confirm the doctrine which it has been my endeavour to set forth, than in these words of Hooker: "Although we make not baptism a cause of grace, yet the grace which is given men with their baptism doth so far forth depend on the very outward sacrament, that God will have it embraced, not only as a sign or token what we receive, but also as an instrument or mean whereby we receive grace, because baptism is a sacrament which God hath instituted in His Church, to the end that they which receive the same *might thereby be incorporated into Christ,* and so, through His most precious merit, obtain as well *that saving grace of imputation, which taketh away all former guiltiness,* as also *that infused divine virtue of the Holy Ghost, which giveth to the powers of the soul their first disposition towards future newness of life*[h]."

[h] Eccles. Pol. book v. c. 60. I subjoin the following passage

from Archbishop Leighton. Sacraments are " signs, but more than signs merely representing; they are means exhibiting, and seals confirming, grace to the faithful. But the working of faith, and the conveying of Christ into the soul, to be received by faith, is not a thing put into them to do of themselves, but still in the Supreme Hand that appointed them. And He indeed both causes the souls of His own to receive these His seals with faith, and makes them effectual to confirm that faith which receives them so. They are then, in a word, *neither empty signs to them who believe, nor effectual causes of grace to them who believe not....*Though they do not save all who partake of them, yet they do really and effectually save believers, (for whose salvation they are means) as the other external ordinances of God do. Though they have not that power which is peculiar to the Author of them, yet a power they have, such as befits their nature, and by reason of which they are truly said to *sanctify* and *justify*, and so to *save*, as the Apostle here avers of Baptism." Commentary on 1 Pet. iii. 21.

SERMON VIII.

JUSTIFICATION IN CONTINUANCE.

"Albeit that Good Works, which are the fruits of Faith, and follow after Justification, cannot put away our sins, and endure the severity of God's judgment; yet are they pleasing and acceptable to God in Christ, and do spring out necessarily of a true and lively Faith; insomuch that by them a lively faith may be as evidently known, as a tree discerned by the fruit." Art. xii.

"Caveamus ergo diligenter, in adjutorio Domini Dei nostri, non facere homines male securos, dicentes eis, quod si fuerint in Christo baptizati, quomodolibet in ea fide vixerint, eos ad salutem æternam esse venturos. Sed potius sanam doctrinam Dei Magistri in utroque teneamus; ut sancto baptismo consona sit vita Christiana, nec cuiquam homini, si utrumlibet defuerit, vita promittatur æterna. Qui enim dixit, 'Nisi quis renatus fuerit ex aqua et Spiritu, non intrabit in regnum cœlorum,' ipse etiam dixit, ' Nisi abundaverit justitia vestra super Scribarum et Pharisæorum, non intrabitis in regnum cœlorum.'" Augustin. De Fide et Oper. §. xxvi.

Rev. iii. 11.

Behold, I come quickly; hold that fast which thou hast, that no man take thy crown.

It has greatly tended to perplex and confuse men's views on the subject of Justification, and to throw difficulties in the way of the right understanding of it, that sufficient attention has not been paid to the distinction between the *first entrance* on a state of justification, and *continuance* in it; between *continuance* in that state, and *restoration* to it, if, in any instance, it has been forfeited or suspended. Very much of the difficulty which is felt with regard to justification as connected with baptism, in the case of infants, arises from this very source. If justification is God's gracious gift bestowed on those who believe, how can infants be justified in baptism, who have no faith? If infants are justified in baptism, does not this, in a Christian country, where almost all are baptized in infancy, virtually annul the doctrine that we are justified by faith; rendering it a mere theory, a speculation which may indeed be realized where adult converts are being brought into the Church, but which has no actual place among ourselves? This is practically, if I mistake not, the feeling of numbers; and the effect is, that on the one hand, the blessed boon conveyed in baptism to infants is disbelieved; and, on the other, the great and precious doctrine of Justification by Faith is set aside, as though men might leave it out of their system with impunity, and live themselves, and teach others to live, otherwise than as St. Paul lived, by the faith of the Son of God, who loved them, and gave Himself for them[a].

The truth is, the divine life needs not only to be *begun*, but to be *continued;* and if unhappily in any case it should be impaired and almost extinguished, to be *restored*. Baptism is the *birth-day* of that life, both in adults and infants, and so far it is proper only to the first of these three states; but faith is the very *breath* of that life, and belongs therefore to them all. And though infants are admitted into a state of justification before they are capable of faith, yet, if they would *maintain* their blessed privilege, and *abide* in God's favour, they must begin to exercise faith from the moment they are capable of it; and thenceforward to the end of their course, the life which they live in the flesh, they must live by faith. And thus, though in the first entrance upon a justified state, there is this difference between adults and infants, that, in the one, faith precedes baptism and makes it effectual, in the other justification is given without faith; yet from the moment

[a] Gal. ii. 20.

the infant is capable of faith, thenceforward both are circumstanced alike. And though they have, neither of them, to seek justification, as for the first time, yet they have both to labour to preserve it, and, should they be so unhappy as to forfeit it, to labour to recover it. And thus, whatever has been said, on a previous occasion, of the necessity of faith to justification, and which might have seemed, for a moment, by what was said of baptism, to be reduced to a mere theory in the case of those who, like ourselves, have been baptized in infancy, still holds in full force. And it is as needful to insist upon the doctrine of Justification by Faith, in a Christian country and to a Christian people, as it can possibly be in addressing those who have not yet been baptized.

But I shall proceed to consider more particularly these two questions. I. How a state of justification is *continued*. II. How (if forfeited or suspended) it is to be *restored*. My object hitherto has been to enquire how a state of justification is *begun:* these are necessary to complete the view of the subject.

I. How then is our justification continued?

i. I answer, first, that *faith* is as essential to the continuance of a justified state as it was to its beginning. If, in the first instance, it was the *hand*, to use Hooker's illustration, by which we *took hold* on Christ, thenceforward, it is the *hand* by which we *hold fast* by Him.

This will be evident, if we consider the manner in which Scripture speaks on this subject.

"I am crucified with Christ;" writes St. Paul to the Galatians, "nevertheless I live; yet not I, but Christ liveth in me; and the life which I now live in the flesh, *I live by the faith of the Son of God,* who loved me, and gave Himself for me[b]." The Apostle is here speaking, not of *the first entrance* upon that divine life of which justification is one of the fruits, but of its *continuance;* and that continuance he expressly ascribes to the instrumentality of faith.

To the same purpose he prays for the Ephesians, "that Christ *may dwell in their hearts by faith*[c];" not, take up His abode for the first time, for that He had done already, but, continue His abode, and continue it, so far as its continuance depends on us, by faith.

"Blessed be the God and Father of our Lord Jesus Christ," says St. Peter, in a passage very full of important doctrine on this subject, "which, according to his abundant mercy, hath begotten us again unto a lively hope by the resurrection of Jesus Christ from the dead:" Thus far he speaks of our first entrance into the Christian life—our birth into that life; and he speaks of it as of an event which has already taken place: "who hath begotten us again," he proceeds, "to an inheritance incorruptible, and undefiled, and that fadeth not away, reserved in

[b] Gal. ii. 20.   [c] Eph. iii. 17.

heaven for you, *who are kept by the power of God, through faith,* unto salvation ready to be revealed at the last time[d]." Here is distinctly the continuance of that heavenly life which we have from God. And as we have it from God in the first instance, so its continuance and preservation also are from Him: "*we are kept by the power* of God." And the instrumental cause is *faith*: " kept by the power of God, *through faith*, unto salvation." It is God who keeps us, and He keeps us by faith, for in giving us faith, He takes us off from dependence upon ourselves, and leads us to rest only upon Him, in whom alone we are strong. The Apostle is speaking throughout this passage of our renewed state generally, from our first entrance upon it at our regeneration, to its completion in our final salvation; but justification is an inseparable part of this; and therefore whatsoever is instrumental to the one, is instrumental to the other. If it is by faith that our living union with Christ is maintained; it is by faith that our justification, which is one of the fruits of that union, is maintained also.

Again; we have another class of passages, which make the continuance of our faith the condition of our continuance in a state of justification, or in that state which necessarily involves justification. As, for example, " You that were sometime alienated and enemies in your mind by wicked works, yet now hath He reconciled in the body of His flesh through death:" thus far we have the first entrance into a

[d] 1 Pet. i. 3—5.

state of justification—"he *hath* reconciled"—a state begun, as at some definite time, and still in progress: "to present you holy and unblameable and unreprovable in His sight,"—here is the same state perfected, "*if ye continue in the faith grounded and settled, and be not moved away from the hope of the Gospel*." And to this is parallel that exhortation of the Apostle, in the third chapter of the Epistle to the Hebrews, which, in the compass of a few sentences, expresses the drift of the whole Epistle. "Take heed, brethren, lest there be in any of you an evil heart of unbelief in departing from the living God: but exhort one another daily, while it is called to-day, lest any of you be hardened through the deceitfulness of sin; for we are made partakers of Christ, *if we hold the beginning of our confidence stedfast unto the end*." It was by faith we were incorporated into Christ in the first instance, and by faith our union must be continued; nor can our need of faith ever cease till it is swallowed up in sight.

In these passages then, the necessity of faith to the maintenance and continuance of the divine life, and consequently of our justification, as well as to its beginning, is pointedly and directly set forth. And it is to be added, that the whole tenor of St. Paul's argument, in his Epistle to the Galatians, tends to the same point. In his Epistle to the Romans, he is concerned chiefly with justification in its commencement, and he shews that faith is the only hand which *puts on* Christ to justification. No works that we

* Col. i. 21—23.   ᶠ Heb. iii. 12—14.

can bring, before baptism, are sufficient to stand the severity of God's righteous judgment. Christ's righteousness, made ours by faith, must be our only plea. In his Epistle to the Galatians, the great point which he keeps in view throughout is to shew, that our justification is continued as it was begun. We were justified by faith in the first instance, we are justified by faith to the end. The Galatians had *begun* well, they had built upon the sure foundation, Christ Jesus; but false teachers had sprung up among them, and had undermined their faith. And they who had once leaned only upon the merits of their crucified Lord, were now being drawn aside to a dependence upon circumcision and the other observances of the Jewish law. It is true these were chiefly of a ceremonial kind; but the point to be observed is, that the *principle* of St. Paul's argument applies equally to all works, moral or ceremonial, Jewish or Christian. "As many," he says, "as are of the works of the Law are under the curse; for it is written, Cursed is every one that continueth not in all things which are written in the book of the Law to do them. But that no man is justified by the Law in the sight of God, it is evident; for, The just shall live by faith. And the Law is not of faith, but, The man that doeth them shall live in them[g]." And presently afterwards, after expounding the allegorical reference of the history of Sarah and Hagar, he proceeds, "Stand fast therefore in the liberty where-

[g] Gal. iii. 10—12.

with Christ hath made us free, and be not entangled again with the yoke of bondage. Behold, I Paul say unto you, that if ye be circumcised, Christ shall profit you nothing. For I testify again to every man that is circumcised, that he is a debtor to do the whole law. Christ is become of no effect unto you, whosoever of you are justified by the Law; ye are fallen from grace. For we through the Spirit wait for the hope of righteousness by faith. For in Christ Jesus, neither circumcision availeth any thing nor uncircumcision, but faith which worketh by love[b]." The whole tenor of this reasoning, while it implies distinctly the indispensable necessity of Christian holiness, concludes against all works of whatsoever kind, so far forth as they are made the ground of our acceptance with God. If we *will* stand before Him on the plea of an inherent righteousness, we must have a *perfect* inherent righteousness;—we must fulfil the whole law. But forasmuch as no man is in a condition to urge this plea, not even the regenerate, great and wonderful as are the achievements of divine grace in those who have faithfully followed the motions of God's good Spirit, which they have in Christ, even the best and holiest of them all must be content to make mention of God's righteousness only, from the first beginning of his Christian course even to the end. And that righteousness, as it is appropriated by faith in the first instance, so it is retained by faith throughout.

[b] Gal. v. 1—6.

Thus then, faith is as essential to the continuance of our justification as it was to its beginning, and it justifies us, from first to last, in that it leads us simply and at once to Christ, that we may be found in Him, not having our own righteousness which is of the Law, but that which is through the faith of Christ, the righteousness which is of God by faith[i].

And, as it was remarked of faith *in its first formation*, that it is God's gift, wrought in us ordinarily by the ministry of the word; so, in like manner, are its *preservation* and *increase* to be ascribed to the same agency. God, who was its Author, is its Finisher also; and the word, by the ministry of which it was formed in the first instance, is now the food, so to speak, by which it is nourished and supported. And accordingly St. Peter exhorts those, as new-born babes, *to desire the sincere milk of the word, that they may grow thereby*, whom he had just before described as " *born again by the word of God*, which liveth and abideth for ever[k]."

ii. But while Faith was the instrumental cause, on our parts, in procuring our justification, Baptism was the sacrament, in which God formally conveyed and made over to us the grant. And the efficacy of baptism continues in such sort, that faith is thenceforward directly and at once available. Before baptism, though a man had faith, yet his faith lacked its full efficacy. The covenant, though

[i] Phil. iii. 9.   [k] 1 Pet. ii. 2. and i. 23.

agreed to, was not formally signed and sealed; and the blessings of the covenant therefore were not made over. But now, faith attains its end at once. The Christian is within the covenant, and faith has only to put forth its hand and take the gracious gifts which God has provided for it in Christ Jesus.

And though baptism is not repeated, God has instituted another Sacrament, for the nourishment and support of that divine life, which had its first beginning in baptism[1]. And this Sacrament as essential as the former. For He who said of the one,

---

[1] "There have grown in the doctrine concerning Sacraments many difficulties, for want of distinct explication what kind or degree of grace doth belong unto each Sacrament. For by this it hath come to pass, that the true immediate cause why Baptism, and why the Supper of our Lord is necessary, few do rightly and distinctly consider. It cannot be denied, but sundry the same effects and benefits, which grow unto men by the one Sacrament, may rightly be attributed to the other. Yet then doth Baptism challenge to itself but the inchoation of those graces, the consummation whereof dependeth on mysteries ensuing. We receive Christ Jesus in Baptism, once, as the first beginner, in the Eucharist, often, as being by continual degrees the finisher of our life." Hooker, E. P. v. §. 57. "Life being proposed unto all men as their end, they which by Baptism have laid the foundation and attained the first beginning of a new life, have here (in the holy Eucharist) their nourishment and food prescribed *for continuance of life* in them. Such as will live the life of God, must eat the flesh and drink the blood of the Son of man, because this is a part of that diet, which if we want, we cannot live." Hooker, E. P. v. §. 67.

"Except a man be born of water and of the Spirit, he cannot enter into the kingdom of God[m]," said also of the other, "Except ye eat the flesh of the Son of man, and drink His blood, ye have no life in you[n];" and if no life, then no righteousness,

---

[m] John iii. 5.

[n] John vi. 53. St. Cyprian explains the petition in the Lord's Prayer, "Give us this day our daily bread," of a request, that, through the daily participation of the Eucharist, our union with Christ may be continued and preserved day by day. "Hunc panem dari nobis quotidie postulamus, ne qui in Christo sumus, et Eucharistiam quotidie ad cibum salutis accipimus, intercedente aliquo graviore delicto, dum abstenti et non communicantes a cœlesti pane prohibemur, a Christi corpore separemur; ipso prædicante et monente, 'Ego sum panis vitæ qui de cœlo descendi. Si quis ederit de meo pane vivet in æternum. Panis autem quem ego dedero, caro mea est pro seculi vita.' Quando ergo dicit, In æternum vivere si quis ederit de ejus pane; ut manifestum est, eos vivere, qui corpus ejus attingunt, et Eucharistiam jure communicationis accipiunt; ita contra timendum est et orandum, ne dum quis abstentus separatur a Christi corpore, procul remaneat a salute, comminante ipso et dicente: 'Nisi ederitis carnem filii hominis et biberitis sanguinem ejus, non habebitis vitam in vobis.' Et ideo panem nostrum, id est, Christum, dari nobis quotidie petimus, ut qui in Christo manemus et vivimus, a sanctificatione ejus et corpore non recedamus." Cypr. de Orat. Dom. St. Cyprian's commentary on this petition is but an expansion of Tertullian's, "Christus panis noster est, quia vita Christus, et vita panis. 'Ego sum,' inquit, 'panis vitæ:' et paulo supra, 'Panis est sermo Dei vivi qui descendit de cœlis.' Tum quod et corpus ejus in pane censetur: 'Hoc est corpus meum.' Itaque petendo panem quotidianum, perpetuitatem postulamus in Christo, et individuitatem a corpore ejus." De orat. c. vi. p. 131, 132.

neither that imputed righteousness of Christ, which is our justification, nor that inherent righteousness infused by His Spirit, which is our sanctification.

The manner in which the Eucharist is effectual to the maintenance of our union with Christ, so far as we may venture to speak of the way in which God accomplishes His works, corresponds to that in which Baptism is effectual to its formation. Baptism is the first solemn ratification of the great Christian covenant; the other Sacrament is the solemn renewal of that covenant[o]. And as Baptism serves the threefold purpose, first, of formally incorporating us into Christ; secondly, of assuring us that we are incorporated; and thirdly, of standing as our solemn pledge and *sacrament* to God, that we cheerfully and unreservedly devote ourselves and all we have to His blessed service; so, in like manner, in the holy Eucharist, God, first, confirms and strengthens our union with His Son, and gives us a larger measure of His Spirit; secondly, He assures us thereby that we are " very members incorporate" in Christ's mystical body; and thirdly, we give to Him and He receives from us a renewed pledge and assurance of fidelity and devotedness to His service. But yet, here also, as in Baptism, it is faith which gives life and efficacy to the Sacrament, or, in other words, which enables us to touch Christ, so to speak, in the

---

[o] On the Eucharist considered as a covenanting rite, see Waterland, vol. vii. c. 11.

sacrament, and draw virtue from the touch[p]; as he who came with a true and lively faith to baptism, was washed, as St. Jerome says of the Ethiopian Eunuch[q], not merely in water, but in the Blood of Christ, so he who comes with a true and lively faith to the other Sacrament, feeds, not merely on bread and wine, but on the Body and Blood of his Lord[r].

[p] " Utquid paras dentes et ventrem ? Crede et manducasti." August. in Joan. Tract. xxv. §. 12. " Panis iste interioris hominis quærit esuriem......Daturus ergo Dominus Spiritum Sanctum, dixit se panem qui de cœlo descendit, hortans ut credamus in eum. Credere enim in eum, hoc est manducare panem vivum. Qui credit manducat: invisibiliter saginatur, quia invisibiliter renascitur. Infans intus est, novus intus est : ubi novellatur, ibi satiatur." Ibid. Tract. xxvi. §. 1. One cannot read the Homilies in which these passages occur, (those on John vi.) without remarking, not only the absence of any such doctrine as Transubstantiation, but the inconsistency between the teaching therein contained and any such doctrine. What St. Augustine says of the gross and carnal sense which the Jews put upon our Lord's words, is equally applicable to that which the Church of Rome has put upon them since : " Isti cito defecerunt talia loquente Domino Jesu: non crediderunt aliquid magnum dicentem et verbis illis aliquam gratiam cooperientem ; sed prout voluerunt ita intellexerunt, et more hominum, quia poterat Jesus, aut hoc disponebat Jesus, *carnem, qua indutum erat Verbum, veluti concisam distribuere credentibus in se.*" Ibid. Tract. xxvii. §. 2.

[q] Hieron. in Esai. lviii. 7.

[r] Our Church holds, that Christ is really present in the Sacrament of the Lord's Supper, but spiritually and mystically, not corporally and substantially ; and that His Body and Blood are verily and indeed taken and received, but only *by the faithful*. " The wicked, and such as be void of a lively faith, although they

But, if faith be wanting, the fountain, which should have been opened for sin and for uncleanness in the

do carnally and visibly press with their teeth" (as St. Augustine saith) " the *Sacrament* of the Body and Blood of Christ, yet in no wise are they partakers of *Christ;* but rather, to their condemnation, do eat and drink (not *the thing* itself—but) *the sign* or *sacrament* of so great a thing." Art. xxix. Those excellent men who suffered martyrdom in Queen Mary's reign, constantly held and taught that Christ is really and truly present in the Sacrament; that which cost them their lives was, that they would not affirm Him to be corporally and substantially present. " To believe," says one of them, (Bradford, Letters of the Martyrs, p. 193.) " that in the Supper of Christ, which ' the Sacrament of the altar,' as the Papists call it and use it, doth utterly overthrow, is a *true* and *very presence* of whole Christ, God and man, to the faith of the receiver, but not to the stander by and looker on, as it is a true and very presence of bread and wine to the senses of men; to believe this, I say, will not serve; and therefore as a heretic I am condemned and shall be burned." " In speaking thus of the Sacrament of the Lord's Supper," says Bp. Jewel, " and denying the strange and new learning of transubstantiation, and making it known that the bread and wine continue still that they were before, we do not conceive basely or irreverently of the Sacrament, we do not make it a bare or naked token. Let no man be deceived. We do both think and speak soberly and with reverence of the holy mysteries. As we cannot call them more than they are, so may we not esteem them less than they are, by the ordinance and institution of Christ. We say they are changed, that they have a dignity and preeminence which they had not before; that they are not now common bread or common wine, but the Sacrament of the Body and Blood of Christ; a holy mystery; a covenant between Christ and us; a testimony unto our conscience, that Christ is the Lamb of God; a perfect seal and sufficient warrant of God's promises, whereby God bindeth Himself to us,

one Sacrament, dries up at his approach, and the heavenly food, which should have strengthened and

and we stand likewise bounden unto God, so as God is our God, and we are His people. In Baptism, the nature and substance of water doth remain still: and yet is not it bare water. It is changed and made the Sacrament of our regeneration. It is water consecrated and made holy by the Blood of Christ. They which are washed therein, are not washed with water, but in the Blood of the unspotted Lamb. One thing is seen and another understood. We see the water, but we understand the Blood of Christ. Even so we see the bread and wine, but with the eyes of our understanding we look beyond these creatures, we reach our spiritual senses into heaven, and behold the ransom and price of our salvation. We do behold in the Sacrament not what it is, but what it doth signify." Bp. Jewel, Treatise of the Sacraments. " It seemeth much amiss, that against them, whom they term Sacramentaries, so many invective discourses are made, all running upon two points, that the Eucharist is not a bare sign or figure only, and that the efficacy of His Body and Blood is not all we receive in this Sacrament. For no man having read their books and writings which are thus traduced, can be ignorant that both these assertions they confess to be most true. They do not so interpret the words of Christ, as if the name of His Body did import but the figure of His Body, and to be, were only to signify His Blood. They grant that these holy mysteries, received in due manner, do instrumentally both make us partakers of the grace of that Body and Blood, which were given for the life of the world, and besides also impart unto us even in true and real, though mystical, manner, the very Person of our Lord Himself, whole, perfect, and entire, as hath been shewed. Now whereas all three opinions do thus far accord in one, that strong conceit, which two of the three have embraced as touching a literal, corporal, and oral manducation of the very substance of His Flesh and Blood, is surely an opinion no where delivered in holy Scripture, whereby they should think

refreshed his soul, in the other, turns to gall and wormwood in his mouth.

iii. But the faith of which such mighty things are spoken has this inseparable property belonging to it, that, whenever it brings a man to Christ for justification, it brings him with the full purpose of unreserved obedience. Faith incorporates us into Christ, and, by incorporating, justifies us, in that it leads us to close sincerely and cordially with the terms of the Gospel covenant. So that though obedience is not, and cannot be, the ground of our acceptance with God, it is yet the unfailing fruit and inseparable accompaniment of that faith through which we obtain acceptance. Faith which comes to Christ for forgiveness, and does not come at the same time with the sincere purpose of unreserved obedience, and the earnest desire for grace in order to such obedience, a purpose and desire evidenced, from the first, as time and opportunity are given, by acts of obedience, is not the faith which obtains justification. And though faith were such in the first instance, yet if it should afterwards cease to be such, and become what St. James calls a *dead* faith, and no longer " work

---

themselves bound to believe it, and (to speak with the softest terms we can use) greatly prejudiced, in that when some others did so conceive of eating His flesh, our Saviour, to abate that error in them, gave them directly to understand, how His flesh, so eaten, could profit them nothing, because the words which He spake were spirit, that is to say, they had a reference to a mystical participation, which mystical participation giveth life." Hooker, Eccles. Pol. book v. §. 67.

by love," and, through love, produce obedience, from that moment it relinquishes its hold on Christ and Christ's righteousness.

And thus we are brought to the consideration of the place which *works* hold in respect of our justification.

We have seen, that in no stage whatever of our course can they be rested on *as the ground of our acceptance*. We need a better righteousness than the holiest of God's servants ever reached, in which to stand before Him, in whose sight the very heavens are not clean[s], and who chargeth even His angels with folly[t]. No obedience, whether of our unregenerate or of our regenerate state, can endure the severity of His righteous judgment.

But though we cannot plead works as the ground of our acceptance with God, they are yet intimately connected with our justification. How they are so connected will best be understood, if we consider, in the first place, the relation which they bear to that Union which we have with Christ, from which our justification springs.

1. And first, they are the genuine *fruits* of that union, and the great end for which we have been admitted into it. Mark how distinctly this truth is set forth in the following passages. " By grace are ye saved through faith, (and that not of yourselves, it is the gift of God;) not of works, lest any man should boast. For we are His workmanship, created in Christ

---

[s] Job xv. 15.   [t] Job iv. 18.

Jesus unto good works, which God hath before ordained that we should walk in them[u]." Here is God's grace the moving cause of our salvation, faith, and this too of God, the instrumental cause, works excluded from being a cause in any sense, but declared expressly to be the fruit of our union with Christ, and the end for which we have been incorporated into Him. Elsewhere we find the Apostle representing the Christian as married to Christ, and works as the offspring of his union. " Ye are dead," he says, " to the law, by the Body of Christ, that ye should be married to another, even to Him who is raised from the dead, that we should bring forth fruit unto God[x]." Here is still the same great truth, though under another image. Works of righteousness the fruit of our union with Christ, and the end for which we have been incorporated into Him. To the same effect is our Lord's parable of the vine and its branches. " Abide in Me, and I in you; as the branch cannot bear fruit of itself, except it abide in the vine, no more can ye, except ye abide in Me........Herein is my Father glorified, that ye bear much fruit[y]." In all these and a multitude of other passages, holiness is harmoniously represented under the same twofold aspect; first, as the fruit of our union with Christ; and, secondly, as the great end for which we have been incorporated into Him. It is not the cause of our union, but its effect. It does not precede our union, but follows

[u] Eph. ii. 8—10.   [x] Rom. vii. 4.   [y] John xv. 4—8.

it; at least, it follows our first entrance into it, and thenceforward accompanies it, as vital action the union of soul and body, while it subsists. So that, in truth, wherever there is a real and living union with Christ, works of righteousness will infallibly manifest themselves, though not always in the same measure in different persons, or in the same measure in the same person at different times.

2. And such works, though they are not able to endure the severity of God's judgment, seeing they are, even at the best, defiled by manifold imperfections, and need His merciful indulgence, are yet well-pleasing unto God in Christ, both for that they are done by those, whose persons are, to use the Apostle's expression, " accepted in the beloved[z];" and also, because, so far as they are good, they are the fruits of His Spirit; and yet further, because they are, so far, the accomplishment of the end which God had in view in incorporating us into Christ. The Apostle's words can bear no meaning short of this, when he tells the Philippians, that their affection for Him and their ministration to his wants were " an odour of a sweet smell, a sacrifice, acceptable, well-pleasing to God[a]." And that passage in the Epistle to the Hebrews is to the same effect: " God is not unrighteous to forget your work and labour of love, which ye have shewed toward His name, in that ye have ministered to the saints and do minister[b]." Men would not have scrupled to acknowledge fully, and to

[z] Ephes. i. 8.   [a] Phil. iv. 18.   [b] Heb. vi. 10.

assign to it its due prominence, a doctrine so plainly set forth in Scripture, if the unscriptural teaching of the Church of Rome, respecting merits, had not led them to look with a suspicious eye upon whatever even seemed to lie in that direction. But it is one thing to imagine works, whether our own or any other man's, of such worth as to merit heaven, another thing to regard them, as Scripture plainly teaches us they are to be regarded, as well-pleasing to God in Christ, in that they proceed from those whom He hath already pardoned and accepted, are wrought by His Spirit dwelling within them, and are the accomplishment in them, so far, of the great object which He had in view in incorporating them into His Son.

3. Further, as works of righteousness are the fruits of our union with Christ and the end for which we have been incorporated into Him, so are they intimately connected with the maintenance of our union. Christ dwells in us by His Spirit, and works of righteousness are the fruits of our union with Christ, because they are the fruits of the Spirit by whom He dwells in us. And that Christian will have the largest measure of such works, and will bring forth the most abundant fruit of holiness, who is most under the influence of the Spirit. And as cause and effect act reciprocally upon each other in the natural world, so, in the spiritual also, the more a man is under the influence of the Spirit, the more abundantly will he bring forth the fruits of holi-

ness; and the more he brings forth the fruits of holiness, the larger will be the measure of the Spirit's influence vouchsafed to him. And thus, unto him that hath shall be given, and he shall have more abundance: while, on the other hand, from him that hath not shall be taken away even that he hath[e]. A man may, whether by indolence in cultivating the divine life, by negligence in keeping his heart, or by positive acts of sin, grieve the Holy Spirit, and tempt Him to withdraw His influence; the effect of which will be to produce still greater remissness, and more entire abandonment of himself to the power of evil: and this will be followed by a yet further withdrawal of the presence of that blessed Being, who had vouchsafed to take up His abode within him; till, it may be, he is at length given up altogether to his own devices, and the unclean spirit, who had been driven out, returns, and with him seven other spirits more wicked than himself, and they enter in and dwell there, and the last state of that man is worse than the first[d].

At what precise point, however, matters reach this fearful crisis, when God's good Spirit takes His final departure, and abandons a man utterly, God has not given us the means of ascertaining. When we see instances of those, once under the influence of the Holy Spirit, in whom yet for a time there have been no signs visible of the divine life, perhaps, on the contrary, signs which seemed almost certainly to

[e] Matt. xiii. 12.   [d] Luke xi. 26.

indicate a state of death, who yet, by God's wondrous mercy, have been reclaimed, and their feet led back into the paths of righteousness, we are constrained to believe, that the Holy Spirit, grieved as He had been, and almost driven to desert His desecrated temple, had yet not quite deserted it; but had still lingered near it, that He might again purify it from its idols, and once more fill it with His presence. So that, in such a case, it would seem, the union with Christ, which is maintained by the indwelling of the Holy Spirit, and which Scripture would lead us to think, if once severed, can never be renewed, was not, though suspended for the time, wholly destroyed[e].

4. And in this view, good works, how much soever some have objected to the expression, who yet have held the thing itself, may truly be said to be a *condition* on which our union with Christ is maintained, inasmuch as they are the proper energizings of that blessed Spirit, whose presence within us is the life and stay of our union; and we cannot refuse to follow His holy motions, without grieving Him and provoking Him, first, to diminish His influence, and, if we persist in our course, eventually to withdraw from us altogether.

5. Further, it is the express teaching of Scripture, that we shall be judged by our works, and by no other test, at the last day. They that have *done good* shall go into life everlasting, and they that have

---

[e] See this subject considered in the Union between Christ and His people, Sermon III.

done evil into everlasting fire. But then the ground of this is, not that our works have any thing in them, from first to last, which can merit eternal life, but that they are the only proofs, which God will accept, of our being true and living members of that Saviour, in whose righteousness alone we can stand before the judgment seat. For what part has he in Christ, who has not brought forth the fruits of Christ's Spirit, and has not answered the end for which he has been, or should have been, incorporated into Him? Our works then are the test by which God will judge us. These will declare, beyond all controversy, how far we have maintained that blessed fellowship into which we were once admitted: how far we have improved the talents intrusted to us: how far we are qualified and prepared for that kingdom, into which " there shall in no wise enter any thing that defileth[f];" where " the people shall be all righteous[g];" where the merciful " shall receive mercy[h]," where the pure in heart " shall see God[i];" where the servant, who has so improved the pound entrusted to him as to have gained five pounds, shall be appointed to reign over five cities; and he who has gained ten pounds, shall have authority over ten cities[k].

In the view which has been taken, works of righteousness have been regarded under this single aspect, as the *fruit* of our union with Christ, and

[f] Rev. xxi. 27.   [g] Isaiah lx. 21.   [h] Matt. v. 7.
[i] Matt. v. 8.   [k] Luke xix. 11—27.

consequently as *following after*, not preceding, that union. The truth is, that a state of union with Christ is the only state in which holiness, in the strict sense of that word, can be produced. The branch must be in the vine, in order that it may bring forth good fruit. It is true, that in the case of those who are first brought to Christ as *adults*, some *earnests* and *foretastes* of holiness must *ordinarily* precede their union with Him, inasmuch as these are the inseparable accompaniments, where time and opportunity are given, of that preventing grace of Christ, and preparatory assistance of His Spirit, by which God has already begun to draw them to Himself, though He has not as yet *formally* incorporated them into the body of His Son. And so far, they may be spoken of as conditions, ordinarily, even of the formation of that union in the first instance. And doubtless, as in the case of Cornelius, they ascend up as a memorial before God, and are accepted of Him, as proofs that His grace has not been received in vain. Still they stand upon a different footing from works done after we are incorporated into Christ, inasmuch as the persons, from whom they proceed, stand upon a different footing. And there may be cases, as in the instance of the penitent thief, besides the case of those baptized in infancy, where incorporation into Christ's body is granted without such works, though not without the purpose and intention of bringing forth such works; that is, in other words, without such works *in act*, though not without *the habit*, which, if time and opportunity were given, would produce such works[1].

Such then is the relation which works bear to our *Union with Christ :* their relation to our Justification may be deduced in few words.

1. And first, seeing that there is so intimate a connection between the benefits which God graciously bestows upon us in Christ, that whosoever is invested with His righteousness for justification, is endued at the same time with His Spirit for sanctification, it follows, that good works, which are the fruits of the Spirit, are inseparable from justification. *The habit* from which they spring accompanies it when first given, for it is itself the unfailing produce of the faith, by which we are justified; and *the works them-*

---

[1] " From hence we may easily understand what St. Austin meant by his famed maxim, which many have often perverted to a very wrong sense, namely, *that good works follow after justification, and do not precede it.* In reality, he meant no more than that men must be *incorporated into Christ*, must be Christians, and good Christians, (for such only are justified,) before they could practise Christian works, or righteousness strictly so called : for such works only have an eminent right and title to the name of good works, as they only are salutary, within the covenant, and have a claim upon promise. Works before justification, that is, before salutary baptism, are not, in his account, within the promise, but are excluded rather according to the ordinary rule laid down in John iii. 5. and divers other texts before cited." Waterland on Justification, Works, vol. ix. p. 449, 450. See also p. 457—461. and Davenant de Justitia Actuali, cap. xxxi.

selves follow after, as time and opportunity are afforded.

And truly, the very circumstance of our being justified, so far as we have the comfortable assurance of it, is itself among the most powerful motives to holiness. For, first, the peace of mind, which arises from the sense of God's favour and of sin forgiven, is like oil poured upon the troubled waters of our natural lusts and passions: and the soul, being delivered from the hand of her enemies, is free to serve God without fear, in holiness and righteousness before Him[m]; or, in the Psalmist's words, to run the way of God's commandments, because He hath set her heart at liberty[n]. A conscience ill at ease is the secret cause of no small portion of the sin and misery, which every day brings to light, in the unruly lusts, the ungoverned tempers, the unrestrained passions, of ungodly men. And then, further, the sense of God's abounding mercy towards us in Christ Jesus, exceedingly sinful and unworthy as we are, how should it not stir us up to present our bodies a living sacrifice, holy and acceptable unto God, which is our reasonable service[o]? Thus it was most eminently in St. Paul. A deep and devout thankfulness for redemption, as a blessing in which he felt that he was personally interested, pervades his whole writings. He is never weary of recurring to the subject; and his thoughts seem ready to turn to it, as their natural resting-place, at every opportunity.

[m] Luke i. 74, 75.   [n] Ps. cxix. 32.   [o] Rom. xii. 1.

And how could that, which had so powerful an influence upon his heart and affections, fail to have a corresponding influence upon his life and conversation?

2. But to return: As good works follow after justification, as regards our first entrance into that state, so they accompany it thenceforward, the surest evidences of its continuance. For they spring out necessarily of that faith, by which we are both justified in the first instance, and our justification is maintained afterwards. And they are unequivocal manifestations of the lively presence of that Spirit, by whom we were incorporated into Christ, that in Him we might have justification, at the first, and by whom our union with Christ, for the continuance of our justification, is still preserved.

3. And as good works are the evidences of a state of justification, so also are they conditions of its continuance. For they are conditions of the continuance of that union with Christ, on which our justification depends. A state of justification cannot consist with a state of wilful sin, or, what amounts to the same thing, of wilful barrenness in respect of good works. "Know ye not," says the Apostle, "that so many of us as were baptized into Jesus Christ, were baptized into His death? Therefore we are buried with Him by baptism into death, that like as Christ was raised up from the dead by the glory of the Father, even so we also should walk in newness

of life ᵖ." To go back to sin, to live in the neglect of holiness, is so far to cast off God's covenant, and to defeat the very end for which we have been incorporated into Christ. And if this state should be persisted in, and either death should overtake us, or Christ, on His second coming, find us still without fruit of holiness, we cannot doubt the sentence, which we shall receive at the hands of that righteous Judge, who without respect of persons judgeth according to every man's work.

II. But the question arises, What is the present condition of such persons? and how are they to be restored, if they may be restored, to a state of favour and acceptance with God? There is no portion of our whole subject which has a more deeply practical bearing upon the actually existing circumstances of a country, such as our own, in which Christianity has been long established. And it is of the utmost consequence to us, both as private persons, and, much more, as God's ministers, that we should be able rightly to divide the word of truth respecting it.

With regard to the present condition of those who are living in a state of allowed unfruitfulness, or of wilful sin, one thing is certain, that while they continue thus, they are exposed to God's wrath and damnation, and that, should they die in this state, they could not possibly be saved. But it is not

ᵖ Rom. vi. 3, 4.

certain, while God still spares them, that that blessed Spirit who is the bond of union between Christ and His people, and on whose presence within us our spiritual life depends, has wholly ceased to strive with them, and therefore has wholly forsaken them. The Church of Sardis, which, in one verse, is described as *dead*, is yet bidden, in the next, to " strengthen the things which remain, that are *ready* to die^q," as though some sparks of life were still left. Every wilful sin, while unrepented of, puts a man out of a state of pardon; but not every such sin, even though committed after Baptism, is sin against the Holy Ghost and unpardonable^r. We may not therefore give up hope of such persons; neither may they, if once they are awakened to a sense of their misery, and to a sincere longing for restoration to God's favour, give up hope of themselves. While they continue impenitent, no one's case can be more full of peril; but let them return with all their hearts to Him, who once vouchsafed to own them as His children, earnestly bewailing and renouncing their past sins, and seeking forgiveness, with full purpose of renewed obedience, in Christ's name, and we may not doubt of their acceptance.

The teaching of Scripture is so express on this point, that, it should seem, no room could be left for question in so plain a matter. They were baptized persons, and not such as had never been admitted into the Christian covenant, to whom St. John wrote,

^q Rev. iii. 1, 2.   ^r Art. xvi.

"My little children, these things write I unto you, that ye sin not. And if any man sin, we have an Advocate with the Father, Jesus Christ the righteous, and He is the propitiation for our sins; and not for ours only"—for the sins of Christians,—"but also for the sins of the whole world *." They were baptized persons to whom St. Paul wrote, " Now then we are ambassadors for Christ, as though God did beseech you by us: we pray you in Christ's stead, be ye reconciled to God. For He hath made Him to be sin for us who knew no sin, that we might be made the righteousness of God in Him. We then, as workers together with Him, beseech you also, that ye receive not the grace of God in vain t." Simon Magus had been baptized, and yet St. Peter, though he speaks of him, at the moment, as in the gall of bitterness and bond of iniquity, does not hesitate to urge him to repentance and calling upon God, which it would have been a mockery to do, if these would not have availed to his recovery u. The Galatians had been baptized, and had afterwards so grievously fallen from the true faith, that St. Paul stood in doubt of them, as though all the labour he had bestowed upon them had been in vain: and yet he tells them, that he travails in birth again until Christ be formed in them x. The incestuous Corinthian had been baptized, and had afterwards been guilty of such fearful wickedness, that St. Paul bade his brethren cast him out of the Church, and

* 1 John ii. 1, 2. t 2 Cor. v. 20, 21. vi. 1. u Acts viii. 22. x Gal. iv. 19.

deliver him over to Satan for the destruction of the flesh, but yet it was in the hope, that the Spirit might be saved in the day of the Lord Jesus [y]. And when, afterwards, he had reason to believe that the discipline had had its desired effect, and had brought him to sincere and earnest repentance, he wrote to the Corinthians, exhorting them to forgive him, and to confirm their love to him, lest peradventure he should be swallowed up with overmuch sorrow, and the medicine which was meant to heal, should prove the cause of death [z]. Though David had not been baptized, yet he had certainly been made partaker of those blessings which are the inheritance of Christians—pardon of sin, and the gift of the Holy Ghost—and no man ever sinned under more aggravated circumstances than he did afterwards; yet we find him, on coming to himself, praying God to restore unto him the joy of His salvation, to receive him once more into a state of favour and acceptance, yea and to give him some measure of assurance that he had been restored, (for this at least is implied in "the joy of His salvation,") and that He would not take His Holy Spirit from him—as though he trusted that that blessed Being, fearfully as He had been sinned against, and deeply as He had been grieved, had not wholly abandoned him. And we know that David's prayer was heard and answered [a].

[y] 1 Cor. v. 1—5.   [z] 2 Cor. ii. 6—11.

[a] Ps. li. 12, &c. " Iste Psalmus, sicut cautos facit eos qui non

We may not doubt then, but that God's arms of mercy are still open to receive those who truly and earnestly turn to Him, even though they have forsaken the guide of their youth and forgotten the covenant of their God[b]. The repenting Prodigal,

---

ceciderunt, sic desperatos esse non vult qui ceciderunt. Quisquis peccasti, et dubitas agere pœnitentiam pro peccato tuo, desperando salutem tuam, audi David gementem. Ad te Nathan propheta non est missus; ipse David ad te missus est. Audi eum clamantem, et simul clama; audi gementem, et congemisce; audi flentem, et lachrymas junge; audi correctum, et condelectare. Si tibi non potuit intercludi peccatum, spes veniæ non intercludatur." August. in Psalm. l. §. 5.

[b] Κἂν γὰρ μυρία ὦμεν ἡμαρτηκότες, καὶ μετὰ τὸ βάπτισμα, ἂν ἐθέλωμεν, δυνησόμεθα ἅπαντα ταῦτα ἀποθέσθαι τῶν ἁμαρτημάτων τὰ φορτία. Chrysost. Homil. in Pentecost. i. "Although we do, after we be once come to God, and grafted in His Son Jesus Christ, fall into great sins, (for there is no righteous man upon the earth that sinneth not, and, if we say we have no sin, we deceive ourselves, and the truth is not in us;) yet, if we rise again by repentance, and with a full purpose of amendment of life, do flee unto the mercy of God, taking sure hold thereof, through faith in His Son Jesus Christ, there is an assured and infallible hope of pardon and remission of the same, and that we shall be received again into the favour of our Heavenly Father." Homily on Repentance, part i. "While we are in this life, encompassed with flesh, while the allurements of the world, while the stratagems of Satan, while the infirmities and corruptions of our nature, betray us to the transgression of the law of God, we are always subject to offend, (from whence whosoever saith that he hath no sin is a liar, contradicting himself, and contracting iniquity by pretending innocency;) and so long as we can offend, so long we may apply ourselves unto God by repentance, and be renewed by His grace, and pardoned by His mercy. And therefore the Church of God,

for whom the fatted calf was killed, was no stranger to the hall in which he was received with such lively demonstrations of joy; the kiss with which he was welcomed, was the well-known kiss with which his childhood had been familiar; and when, in his deep shame and unfeigned humiliation, he would have asked a *servant's* place, it was his Father's voice which sounded in his ear, " This *my son* was dead and is alive again, he was lost and is found[c]."

How then are they to be restored, who, after having once dedicated themselves to God, and having been received by Him into His family, have wandered from their Father's home into the forbidden paths of sin; or, though they have not brought shame upon themselves by open wickedness, have yet lived in cold and wilful neglect of His laws, forgetful of

in which remission of sin is preached, doth not only promise it at first by the laver of regeneration, but afterwards also upon the virtue of repentance; and to deny the Church this power of absolution is the heresy of Novatian." Bp. Pearson on the Creed, Art. ix. See to the same purpose Barrow's Exposition of the Creed, Works, vol. vi. p. 425—428.

[c] Luke xv. 24. " Καὶ ὁ ὀφείλων, ὑπὲρ τῆς ἀκαίρου δαπάνης καὶ τῆς οὕτω μακρᾶς φυγῆς, τὸν παῖδα ἀπαιτῆσαι δίκην, οὐδὲν τούτων ἐποίησεν, ἀλλ' ὡς εὐδοκιμηκότα εἶδε, καὶ οὐδὲ μέχρι ῥημάτων ὀνειδίσαι τῷ παιδὶ, μᾶλλον δὲ οὐδὲ ἁπλῶς αὐτὸν ἀναμνῆσαι τῶν προτέρων ἠνέσχετο, ἀλλὰ καὶ περιεχύθη, καὶ κατεφίλησε, καὶ μόσχον ἔθυσε, καὶ στολὴν ἐνέδυσε, καὶ ἐν πολλῷ τῷ κόσμῳ κατέστησε. Ταῦτα οὖν ἔχοντες καὶ ἡμεῖς τὰ ὑποδείγματα, θαρρῶμεν καὶ μὴ ἀπογινώσκωμεν. Οὐ γὰρ οὕτω χαίρει καλούμενος Δεσπότης ὡς Πατὴρ, οὐδὲ δοῦλον ἔχων ὡς υἱόν· καὶ μᾶλλον τοῦτο βούλεται ἢ ἐκεῖνο." Chrysost. in Rom. Hom. x. §. 5.

His love, unmindful of His covenant? Does God prescribe other terms to them, than those on which He received them at the first? Are His ministers charged with another Gospel? Is the exhortation, which must be used towards them, no longer summed up under the two heads, of repentance towards God, and faith towards our Lord Jesus Christ?

Scripture gives us no intimation of any other mode of restoration, than that by which we were brought nigh to God at first. Baptism indeed is not repeated, for the covenant, once ratified, holds in its full obligation to the end, and no man disannulleth or addeth thereto. But the faith which wrought effectually in baptism, or which it behoved to follow baptism if administered in infancy, must be revived and strengthened. And that faith, as it implied deep and earnest repentance in the one instance, so does it in the other, only the more deep and the more earnest in the latter, in proportion as the sins which have been committed are greatly more aggravated. "Remember how thou hast received and heard," is the Saviour's message to the fallen Church of Sardis; "Remember how thou hast received and heard, (which implies a return to her first faith,) and hold fast, and repent[d]."

[d] Rev. iii. 3. "Οὐδεὶς κατεκρίθη, εἰ μὴ μετανοίας κατεφρόνησε, καὶ οὐδεὶς ἐδικαιώθη, εἰ μὴ ταύτης ἐπεμελήσατο." Marc. Erem. de Pœn. in Hooker Eccles. Pol. book vi. c. 3. "As particular acts of repentance upon the commission of any particular sins, do not so much differ in nature, as in measure or degree, from that general

But besides the inward turning of the heart to God, and the outward conversion of the life, the Church of Rome teaches her children, that Christ has instituted the sacrament of *Penance*, for the express purpose of restoring those who have fallen into mortal sin after baptism; and that this sacrament is ordinarily as indispensable for the *recovery* of a state of grace, as Baptism is for its commencement, and the Eucharist for its continuance[e]. Nor is it antecedently so unlikely, that a sacrament should have been instituted for this purpose, that we should have had cause for surprise, had it been so. Yet as we dare not reject those sacraments which Christ hath appointed, so neither may we venture to accept for sacraments any ordinances which He hath not appointed. As we may not *take from* His covenant, so neither may we *add to* it.

---

conversion practised in embracing the Gospel; so the grace vouchsafed upon these penitential acts is only in largeness of extent, and solemnity of administration, diversified from that; especially considering that repentance, after baptism, is but a reviving of that first great resolution and engagement we made in baptism; that remission of sin upon it is only the renovation of the grace then exhibited; that the whole transaction in this case is but a reinstating the covenant then made (and afterward by transgression infringed) upon the same terms, which were then agreed upon; that consequently, by congruous analogy, this remission of sins and restoring to favour, granted to a penitent, are only the former justification reinforced." Barrow, Of Justification by Faith, Sermons on the Creed, Works, vol. iv. p. 389, 390.

[e] Concil. Trid. Sess. xiv. cap. 1.

Their chief warrant, in proof that Penance is a sacrament ordained by Christ, rests, as the Trent decree asserts, on our Lord's commission to His Apostles recorded in John xx. 23: "Whosesoever sins ye remit, they are remitted unto them; and whosesoever sins ye retain, they are retained[f]." From which they gather, first, that sins cannot be remitted, unless by the priest's absolution; and secondly, since absolution cannot be given but upon a knowledge of the offence committed, the necessity of auricular confession[g]; and these, together with

---

[f] "Dominus autem sacramentum Pœnitentiæ tunc præcipue instituit, cum, a mortuis excitatus, insufflavit in discipulos suos, dicens: Accipite Spiritum Sanctum: quorum remiseritis peccata, remittuntur eis; et quorum retinueritis, retenta sunt. Quo tam insigni facto, et verbis tam perspicuis, potestatem remittendi et retinendi peccata ad reconciliandos fideles post baptismum lapsos, Apostolis et eorum legitimis successoribus fuisse communicatam, universorum Patrum consensus semper intellexit." Concil. Trid. Sess. xiv. cap. 1.

[g] "Universa Ecclesia semper intellexit, institutam etiam esse a Domino integram peccatorum Confessionem, et omnibus post baptismum lapsis jure divino necessariam existere: quia Dominus noster Jesus Christus, e terris ascensurus ad cœlos, Sacerdotes sui ipsius Vicarios reliquit, tanquam præsides et judices, ad quos omnia mortalia crimina deferantur, in quæ Christi fideles ceciderint: quo, pro potestate clavium, remissionis aut retentionis peccatorum sententiam pronuntient. Constat enim, Sacerdotes judicium hoc, incognita causa, exercere non potuisse, neque æquitatem quidem illos in pœnis injungendis servare potuisse, si in genere duntaxat, et non potius in specie ac sigillatim, sua ipsi peccata declarassent." Concil. Trid. Sess. xiv. cap. 5.

contrition, or at least attrition, and the penitential satisfaction which is to follow, constitute, as they teach, the essential parts of Penance [g].

Yet it is surely not a little remarkable, on the supposition that our Lord intended to enjoin Penance as a sacrament, that He should have left us to gather its obligation from a passage, which certainly does not, of itself, yield the conclusions they would draw from it, however it might be thought to harmonize with them, if they were clearly taught elsewhere. For how does it follow from the words, " Whosesoever sins ye remit, they are remitted unto them, and whosesoever sins ye retain, they are retained," that therefore no sins are remitted but by the Priest's absolution [h]? Certainly on the same principle it ought to follow, that no sins are retained, but such as the Priest *formally retains.* And it is the more remarkable, that our Lord should have left us to gather the obligation of a sacrament—if Penance be a sacrament ordained by Him—from a passage so inconclusive as to the point alleged, when it is considered, how very prominent a place such a sacrament must needs hold, in the practical working of the Church's system. The power of binding and loosing, which our Lord gave to His Apostles in these words, applies to the two Sacraments which we all acknowledge, at least as strictly as to any other mode of retaining or remitting sin; and so

[g] Concil. Trid. Sess. xiv. cap. 3.
[h] See Hooker, Eccles. Pol. book vi. c. 6. §. 3.

the words were always understood by the ancients[1]; yet He has not left us thus to gather the obligation of Baptism and of the Lord's Supper. We have, in both instances, first, an intimation of their necessity[k], and then, at a subsequent time, their solemn institution[l]. Might not we reasonably have looked for as unequivocal a declaration of His will, in the case of another sacrament, which, if it were a sacrament, would be no less necessary to the generality of Christians? That *doctrines* should be in some instances obscurely taught, is not perhaps to be thought matter of surprise; but it certainly is contrary to what we should have looked for, contrary to God's usual mode of dealing with us, for *duties*— duties so necessary that our salvation depends upon their performance,—to be only vaguely and indistinctly hinted at.

But, it may be, the universal practice of the early Church was so plainly in accordance with what is now the practice of the Church of Rome, as to warrant the conclusion which she draws from our Saviour's words. But neither will antiquity, any more than the direct teaching of Scripture, support the Romish doctrine of Penance. "I dare boldly affirm," says Hooker, "that, for many hundred years after

---

[i] See Bingham's Antiquities, book xix. c. i. §. 2. and his first Sermon On the Nature and Necessity of the several sorts of Absolution.

[k] John iii. 3—5. and vi. 53. [l] Matt. xxviii. 19. and xxvi. 26—28.

Christ, the Fathers held no such opinion: they did not gather from our Saviour's words any such necessity of seeking the Priest's absolution from sin by secret, and, as they term it, sacramental confession: public confession they thought necessary by way of discipline, not private confession as in the nature of a sacrament necessary[m]."

---

[m] Eccles. Pol. book vi. c. 4. §. 6. The following is Hooker's account of the progress of Penance, from the Discipline of Repentance instituted by Christ, and practised by the Fathers, to its present state in the Church of Rome:

"The course of discipline, in former ages, reformed open transgressors, by putting them unto offices of open penitence, especially confession; whereby they declared their own crimes in the hearing of the whole Church, and were not, from the time of their first convention, capable of the holy mysteries of Christ, till they had solemnly discharged this duty.

"Offenders in secret, knowing themselves altogether as unworthy to be admitted to the Lord's Table, as the others which were withheld; being also persuaded, that if the Church did direct them in the offices of their penitency, and assist them with public prayer, they should more easily obtain that they sought, than by trusting wholly to their own endeavours; finally, having no impediment to stay them from it but bashfulness, which countervailed not the former inducements, and besides was greatly eased by the good construction, which the charity of those times gave to such actions, wherein men's piety and voluntary care to be reconciled to God did purchase them much more love, than their faults (the testimonies of common frailty) were able to procure disgrace; they made it not nice to use some one of the ministers of God, by whom the rest might take notice of their faults, prescribe them convenient remedies, and, in the end, after public confession, all join in prayer unto God for them.

Of public penance, in the way of *discipline* indeed, we have both abundant examples in antiquity, and

"The first beginner of this custom had the more followers, by means of the special favour, which always was with good consideration shewed towards voluntary penitents above the rest. But as professors of Christian belief grew more in number, so they waxed worse, when kings and princes had submitted their dominions unto the sceptre of Jesus Christ, by means whereof persecution ceasing, the Church immediately became subject to those evils which peace and security bringeth forth; there was not now that love, which before kept all things in tune, but every where schisms, discords, dissensions among men, conventicles of heretics bent more vehemently against the sounder and better sort, than very infidels and heathens themselves; faults not corrected in charity, but noted with delight, and kept for malice to use, when deadliest opportunities should be offered. Whereupon, forasmuch as public confessions became dangerous and prejudicial to the safety of well-minded men, and in divers respects advantageous to the enemies of God's Church, it seemed first unto some, and afterwards generally requisite, that voluntary penitents should surcease from open confession.

"Instead whereof, when once private and secret confession had taken place with the Latins, it continued as a profitable ordinance, till the Lateran Council (A.D. 1215.) had decreed, that all men, once in a year at the least, should confess themselves to the Priest. So that being thus made a thing both general and also necessary, the next degree of estimation whereunto it grew, was to be honoured and lifted up to the nature of a sacrament; that as Christ did institute Baptism to give life, and the Eucharist to nourish life, so Penitency might be thought a sacrament ordained to recover life, and Confession a part of the sacrament." Eccles. Pol. book vi. c. 4. §. 2.

The doctrine of Scripture and the practice of the ancient Church, as regards Confession, is discussed at considerable length in the following sections, §. 4—13. See also for the most plain warrant in Scripture, " such persons as stood convicted of notorious sins being put to open penance and punished in this world, that their souls might be saved in the day of the Lord, and that others, admonished by their example, might be the more afraid to offend ⁿ." Thus St. Paul dealt by the incestuous Corinthian, partly with a view to his being brought, through penance, to repentance; partly to prevent the evil leaven of his sin from spreading throughout the Church °.

And, doubtless, it is deeply to be lamented, that this godly discipline of primitive and apostolic times has fallen so wholly into desuetude. God only knows, in how many instances, individual Christians, who have fallen, have fallen to rise no more, who yet might have been raised, had a wholesome discipline schooled them to repentance and faith unfeigned.

practice of the ancient Church, Bingham Antiq. book xviii. c. 3. Bingham shews that " no necessity was laid upon any man to make private confession of all or any of his secret sins to a Priest, as a matter of indispensable obligation, either to qualify him for the reception of the Eucharist, or to give him a title to the Communion of the Church and eternal life." The Exomologesis, so often mentioned in the ancient writers, signifies the whole exercise of public penance, of which *public* confession was a noted part; but it is altogether distinct from *private auricular* confession, with which many Romish writers would confound it.

ⁿ Commination Service. See Barrow on The Power of the Keys, Works, vol. vi. p. 401—419. On the Discipline of the Ancient Church, see Bingham's Antiq. books xvi. xvii. xviii. xix.

° 1 Cor. v. 3—7.

God only knows, in how many instances, false doctrine and corrupt practice have been suffered to diffuse themselves to a fearful extent, which yet might have been checked, had a wholesome discipline purged out the evil leaven, when it first began to spread. Yet while we must not forget, that our own sins have too justly deserved the continuance of this state of things, it is not to be overlooked, that one of its main causes, in the first instance, was the shameless abuse of penance in that Church, which first turned a salutary ordinance into a sacrament, and then made merchandise of the pardons and indulgences which she hung upon it.

But it is time to draw the subject, which has occupied our attention throughout these Lectures, to a close. In doing so, I would throw together briefly into one view, the principal heads of doctrine, which it has been my endeavour to set forth. And it is the more necessary, because they cannot properly be understood or rightly judged of, except in connection with the whole and with each other.

1. Man, as he comes into the world, is suffering under two fearful evils, inherited as his birthright from his first father, an entailed condemnation and a corrupt nature; and the actual transgressions, proceeding from the second of these, are continually adding to the weight of the former. He is, in the

strong and expressive language of Scripture, " a child of wrath," " dead in trespasses and sins." Had he been left to himself, nothing could have been more miserable than his condition[p].

2. But God, in His abounding mercy, has not left us to ourselves. In the fulness of time, the eternal Son took man's nature upon Him, in the womb of the blessed Virgin, that He might become a second Adam, the federal Head of a second race, the Fountain and Source of life to all, who, by a second birth, should be born of Him. These great truths, the incarnation of the eternal Son, and the union between Christ and His Church, of which it is the basis, lie at the foundation of what the Scriptures teach us respecting our salvation, and their doing so is a proof, by the way, of the deeply practical importance of a right belief both in the Trinity and in our Lord's incarnation. Whatsoever we either have or hope for, in reference to eternal life, is given us *in Christ*, and by virtue of our union with Him. And it is therefore available to us, because He in Whom it is given, and with Whom we are united, is one also with the Father and the Holy Ghost[q].

3. Justification is one of the precious gifts thus bestowed upon us, and it consists, not in an *imperfect* righteousness of our own *inherent* in us, but in *Christ's perfect* righteousness *imputed* to us—ours because we are one with Christ, and Christ with us. In Hooker's forcible enunciation of this doctrine[r],

[p] Sermon I.   [q] Sermon II.   [r] Hooker on Justification, sect. 6.

"Christ hath merited righteousness for as many as are found in Him. In Him God findeth us, if we be faithful, for by faith we are incorporated into Christ. Then, although in ourselves we be altogether sinful and unrighteous, yet even the man which is impious in himself, full of iniquity, full of sin, him, being found in Christ, through faith, and having his sin remitted through repentance, him God beholdeth with a gracious eye, putteth away his sin, by not imputing, taketh quite away the punishment due thereunto by pardoning it, and accepteth him in Jesus Christ, as perfectly righteous, as if he had fulfilled all that was commanded him in the law[s]."

4. It is true, whomsoever God justifies them He also glorifies, adorning them with the graces of His Spirit here, as earnests and pledges of that perfect righteousness with which He shall array them hereafter, when He shall make His Church, inherently, as well as by imputation, a glorious Church, not having spot or wrinkle or any such thing. Being one with Christ and Christ with them, they not only have His righteousness imputed unto them for their justification, but they have also His Spirit infused into them for their sanctification. The one gift can no more be severed from the other, than the Spirit of Christ from Christ. So that the surest evidence, and indeed the only sure evidence, of our justification is the sanctifying work of the Spirit in our hearts and lives. Still, the ground of our acceptance with God is not our sanctification, which His Spirit hath

[s] Sermon III.

wrought within us—as yet, by reason of the remaining corruption of our nature, marred by manifold scars and imperfections—but the righteousness of Christ imputed to us, a righteousness so perfect and free from all blemish, that whosoever hath it may plead it even before the righteous King, when He shall sit upon His throne of judgment[t].

5. And who is he that is endowed with this inestimable gift? How may we be made partakers of this most blessed righteousness? God gives it to those who believe. None else indeed will value it, none else seek for it[u].

6. And faith is effectual, whether to our incorporation into Christ, or to our justification, which flows from our union with Him, in that it leads us straight to Him, with full purpose of heart to renounce, by His grace, all other lords who have had dominion over us, and to consecrate ourselves, our time, our talents, our substance, our health, our strength, whatsoever we have, unreservedly to His service; it leads us straight to Him, that we may receive, in and from Him, that perfect and all-sufficient righteousness, which we have not, and cannot have, in ourselves[x].

7. If it be asked, At what precise time, faith first produces its effect, in incorporating us into Christ, and, consequently, justifying us—whether the instant it is formed in the heart, or at some subsequent period? The answer is virtually contained in what

[t] Serm. IV.   [u] Serm. V.   [x] Serm. VI.

St. Paul says to the Galatians, " Ye are all the children of God by faith in Christ Jesus; for as many of you as have been baptized into Christ have put on Christ[y]." It is by faith that we are incorporated into Christ; but, for the first time, in Baptism. And for this reason—so far as we may venture to assign reasons, in matters respecting which we can at best know so little—because Baptism is the solemn and formal ratification of that covenant with God in Christ, to which faith has already led us to assent with our whole hearts. And thus, if Faith is the hand, by which we appropriate to ourselves Christ's righteousness, Baptism is the instrument, by which God formally makes over and conveys it to us. And seeing that whosoever is truly incorporated into Christ, is, at the same time, made a partaker of the Spirit of Christ, by which Spirit Christ dwells in us, therefore in Baptism we receive not only the first grant of justification, but also the first developement of sanctification; the one, perfect and complete the moment it is given, the other, small, it may be, in its beginning, but designed, if duly cherished, to diffuse and spread itself, while the soul is renewed more and more, day by day, in righteousness and true holiness, till it shall at length bring every thought, and word, and work, into captivity to the obedience of Christ, and that divine Image, in which man was originally created, but which Adam forfeited for himself and his whole race, shall be again perfectly restored. Not

[y] Gal. iii. 26, 27.

indeed that this full measure of holiness will be reached on earth, but it is that, which, if the Christian cherishes the divine gift within him, he is constantly tending to, and approaching nearer and nearer day by day[z].

8. And this divine life is to be continued as it was begun. By faith we were incorporated into Christ, and so justified, in the first instance, and by faith we retain these precious gifts. Baptism is not repeated, for the covenant, once signed and sealed, remains in its full obligation. As there is no second birth in the natural world, so there is no second regeneration in the spiritual. But faith, by which the soul at first *took hold* on Christ, is still as requisite that she may *retain her hold*.

From this point, we are able, with the best advantage, to approach the case of those, who, having been baptized in infancy, were, at their baptism, incapable of faith, and yet, as we must believe, were truly incorporated into Christ in that Sacrament, and truly justified. Though faith was not necessary for their justification in the first instance, yet it is necessary for the *continuance* of their justification; and from the moment they are capable of faith, they must begin to exercise it; and thenceforward to the end of their course, the life which they live in the flesh, they must live by the faith of the Son of God, who loved them, and gave Himself for them.

And though Baptism, as we have seen, is not re-

[z] Serm. VII.

peated, God hath instituted another Sacrament, that in it we may, from time to time, renew our covenant with Him; and that, as in Baptism He first gave us life, so in the Eucharist He might sustain the life given, by supplying us with the bread of life—even the Body and Blood of Christ, which, taken and received by faith, are meat indeed and drink indeed, and which He gave for the life of the world.

Good works—by which we are to understand, be it remembered, not isolated and occasional actions, but a consistent course of holy obedience, and a uniform endeavour after entire conformity to the mind of Christ and the will of God, not merely outwardly, but in the heart and its affections—good works are inseparable from a state of justification. They are the fruits of that union with Christ into which we have been admitted, and the grand end for which we have been admitted into it. Hence they are the proper *evidences* of our justification; nay they are more than evidences, they are *conditions* of our retaining a state of justification, inasmuch as wilful sin, and even allowed unfruitfulness, are inconsistent with such a state now, and they will be found to be inconsistent with salvation, which is justification perfected, hereafter, when God shall judge every man according to his works, when they that have done good, shall go into life everlasting, and they that have done evil, into everlasting fire.

With regard to those, who, whether by wilful sin, or indulged sloth, have fallen from that blessed state of justification, into which they were once admitted, fearful as their case is, and far more fearful, while they continue such, than that of those who have never yet been brought nigh to God,—it is not, blessed be His name, a hopeless case. But then, the only reason why it is not hopeless, is because the sentence, " Cut it down, why cumbereth it the ground," is not yet executed. While they continue as they are, there is not one bright spot in the wide heavens to cheer them; and instances, such as the past week has brought before us, of the immediate summoning into God's presence of those, who but a moment before were in the full enjoyment of health and strength, exulting in the anticipation of long years of earthly happiness, may well fill them with sad and anxious apprehensions, lest, if their call should be as sudden, they should be found, like the unready virgins in the parable, with no oil in their vessels, and their lamps gone out.

But the Lord is long suffering to usward, not willing that any should perish, but that all should come to repentance, and there is yet mercy for them if they will return. But their return must be no *feigned* return. They must come back as they came at the first, humbly confessing, and earnestly bewailing and renouncing their past sins, and sincerely purposing and desiring, henceforth, to yield themselves unreservedly to God's service, in all holy obedience; and yet, with all this, trusting neither to their confessions, nor their humiliation, nor their renunciation of the past, nor their purposes and desires for the future, as the meritorious ground of their acceptance, but resting all their hope singly on God's mercy in Christ Jesus. Then shall Christ's righteousness again be theirs for justification, and His Spirit theirs for sanctification; then shall they again have communion with their Lord, and in Him with their brethren, in the Eucharist, and find that His flesh, eaten in faith, is meat indeed, and His Blood, drunk in faith, is drink indeed. Then shall their hearts again be purified with holy affections, and their lives again adorned with works of righteousness, well-pleasing unto God forasmuch as they are sprinkled with the Blood of Christ, and edifying unto men. And they shall have in these, increasing, and, as they increase, unquestionable evidences, that God has dealt with them according to the tenour of the Psalmist's prayer[a]: that He hath hid His face from their sins, and blotted out all their iniquities; that He hath created in them a clean heart, and renewed a right spirit within them; that He hath not cast them away from His presence, nor taken His Holy Spirit from them; that He hath restored unto them the joy of His salvation, and upheld them with His free Spirit. Yea, and God may yet put such high honour upon them, that they shall go forth and teach transgressors His ways, and sinners shall be converted unto Him[b].

Now unto Him that is able to keep us from falling,

[a] Ps. li. 9—13.   [b] Serm. VIII.

and to present us faultless before the presence of His glory with exceeding joy—to the only wise God our Saviour, be glory and majesty, dominion and power, both now and ever. Amen.[e]

[e] Jude 24, 25.

THE END.

By the same Author.

SERMONS

PREACHED BEFORE THE UNIVERSITY OF OXFORD

IN THE YEARS 1836 AND 1837.

THE UNION BETWEEN CHRIST AND HIS PEOPLE

FOUR SERMONS

PREACHED BEFORE THE UNIVERSITY OF OXFORD.